# Lecture Notes in Economics and Mathematical Systems

493

Founding Editors:

M. Beckmann
H. P. Künzi

Co-Editors:

C. D. Aliprantis, Dan Kovenock

Editorial Board:

P. Bardsley, A. Basile, M.R. Baye, T. Cason, R. Deneckere, A. Drexl,
G. Feichtinger, M. Florenzano, W. Güth, M. Kaneko, P. Korhonen, M. Li Calzi,
P. K. Monteiro, Ch. Noussair, G. Philips, U. Schittko, P. Schönfeld, R. Selten,
G. Sorger, F. Vega-Redondo, A. P. Villamil, M. Wooders

Managing Editors:

Prof. Dr. G. Fandel
Fachbereich Wirtschaftswissenschaften
Fernuniversität Hagen
Feithstr. 140/AVZ II, 58084 Hagen, Germany

Prof. Dr. W. Trockel
Institut für Mathematische Wirtschaftsforschung (IMW)
Universität Bielefeld
Universitätsstr. 25, 33615 Bielefeld, Germany

Springer
*Berlin*
*Heidelberg*
*New York*
*Barcelona*
*Hong Kong*
*London*
*Milan*
*Paris*
*Singapore*
*Tokyo*

Jianwei Zhu

# Modular Pricing of Options

## An Application of Fourier Analysis

 Springer

332.645
Z63m

Author

Dr. Jianwei Zhu
Eberhard-Karls-Universität Tübingen
Wirtschaftswissenschaftliche Fakultät
Mohlstrasse 36
72074 Tübingen, Germany

Cataloging-in-Publication data applied for

Die Deutsche Bibliothek - CIP-Einheitsaufnahme

Zhu, Jianwei:
Modular pricing of options : an application of Fourier analysis /
Jianwei Zhu. - Berlin ; Heidelberg ; New York ; Barcelona ; Hong Kong
; London ; Milan ; Paris ; Singapore ; Tokyo : Springer, 2000
 (Lecture notes in economics and mathematical systems ; 493)
 ISBN 3-540-67916-2

ISSN 0075-8442
ISBN 3-540-67916-2 Springer-Verlag Berlin Heidelberg New York

This work is subject to copyright. All rights are reserved, whether the whole or part
of the material is concerned, specifically the rights of translation, reprinting, re-use
of illustrations, recitation, broadcasting, reproduction on microfilms or in any other
way, and storage in data banks. Duplication of this publication or parts thereof is
permitted only under the provisions of the German Copyright Law of September 9,
1965, in its current version, and permission for use must always be obtained from
Springer-Verlag. Violations are liable for prosecution under the German Copyright
Law.

Springer-Verlag Berlin Heidelberg New York
a member of BertelsmannSpringer Science+Business Media GmbH

© Springer-Verlag Berlin Heidelberg 2000
Printed in Germany

The use of general descriptive names, registered names, trademarks, etc. in this
publication does not imply, even in the absence of a specific statement, that such
names are exempt from the relevant protective laws and regulations and therefore
free for general use.

Typesetting: Camera ready by author
Printed on acid-free paper     SPIN: 10779782     42/3142/du     543210

# To My Family

# 献给我的家人

University Libraries
Carnegie Mellon University
Pittsburgh, PA 15213-3890

# Foreword

From a technical point of view, the celebrated Black and Scholes option pricing formula was originally developed using a separation of variables technique. However, already Merton mentioned in his seminal 1973 paper, that it could have been developed by using Fourier transforms as well. Indeed, as is well known nowadays, Fourier transforms are a rather convenient solution technique for many models involving the fundamental partial differential equation of financial economics.

It took the community nearly another twenty years to recognize that Fourier transform is even more useful, if one applies it to problems in financial economics without seeking an explicit analytical inverse transform. Heston (1993) probably was the first to demonstrate how to solve a stochastic volatility option pricing model quasi analytically using the characteristic function of the problem, which is nothing else than the Fourier transform of the underlying Arrow/Debreu-prices, and doing the inverse transformation numerically. This opened the door for a whole bunch of new closed form solutions in the transformed Fourier space and still is one of the most active research areas in financial economics.

Dr. Jianwei Zhu contributes to this literature with his concept of modularization. He develops an integrated approach to search systematically for new solutions in the Fourier space. The modularization of the characteristic functions makes the implementation and development of computer code much more efficient. In Schöbel and Zhu (1999), a stochastic volatility model for an Ornstein-Uhlenbeck process in the presence of arbitrary correlation with stock prices is developed. However, as Dr. Zhu shows in detail in his dissertation, the modular pricing approach has much more potential and is certainly not restricted to the stochastic volatility problem.

I hope, that Dr. Zhu's results will stimulate applications and further research in this fascinating new area of contingent claims analysis.

Tübingen, June 2000                                Rainer Schöbel

# Acknowledgements

This book is a revised version of my doctoral dissertation submitted to the University of Tübingen. I would like to thank two referees of my thesis, Professor Rainer Schöbel and Professor Gerd Ronning, for their helpful comments and encouragement. During my research activities at the University of Tübingen, my mentor Professor Schöbel provided me with rich freedom in researching the interesting and exciting topics that are discussed in this book. The past four years have been a highly spiritual experience for me to enjoy the beauty and rigor of financial economics.

In addition, I am grateful to Dr. Juri Hinz for some discussions and, to Professor Herbert Heyer for the lectures on stochastic calculus, both from the mathematical institute at the University of Tübingen. As a further result, Professor Heyer and Professor Schöbel launched seminars on mathematical finance, in which I was also actively participated.

Furthermore, I would like to thank my colleagues, Philipp Kellerhals and Stephan Heilig, and secretary Vera Klöckner for the wonderful work atmosphere. My research project was funded by the Deutsche Forschungsgemeinschaft (DFG) (German Science Foundation). Its financial support is gratefully acknowledged.

Finally, but by no means least, I would like to express my gratitude to my parents and brothers for their unbroken and warm support during my entire study. Without their help and support, I would have never been so far in my life.

Tübingen, June 2000                                    Jianwei Zhu

# Contents

# 1 Introduction

## 1.1 Purposes of this Book

Since more than twenty-five years the markets for financial derivatives have developed exponentially. The Black-Scholes (1973) model provides us with a basic tool for the valuation of financial instruments traded in the markets. Pricing formulae for almost all options, both plain vanilla and exotic style, have been derived in the Black-Scholes framework and form a valuation formula class with identical assumptions and a standardized structure: constant interest rate, constant volatility and no discontinuous component in the asset price process. Obviously, in many circumstances, this framework is too restrictive to meet the new emerging challenges and empirical findings in more involved financial markets. Nowadays, option pricing theory is undergoing a significant technical innovation: Fourier analysis and characteristic functions, which are successfully applied to stochastic volatility models. This class of models is suggested to capture the leptokurtic property of empirical distributions of stock returns, a property that is not consistent with the normal distribution in the Black-Scholes model. Wiggins (1987), Hull and White (1987), Scott (1987) as well as Stein and Stein (S&S) (1991) undertook their pioneer works in modelling stochastic volatility. The first closed-form solution for stochastic volatility whose square is specified as a mean-reverting square root process was given by Heston (1993). His influential paper introduces characteristic functions to express a tractable closed-form solution for options. As long as the characteristic functions (CFs) underlying the involved probabilities are known analytically, these probabilities can be expressed via Fourier inversion and a closed-form solution for options can then be given. Following Heston's technique, Bates (1994), Scott (1997), Bakshi, Cao and Chen (BCC) (1997) developed some more complicated option models partially associated with stochastic interest rate, stochastic volatility and jumps in the framework of a square-root process. Using Fourier analysis, Schöbel and Zhu (1999) derived a closed-form pricing formula for options where volatilities follow a mean-reverting Ornstein-Uhlenbeck (O-U) process and are correlated with stock returns. In this book, I will give another closed-form solution formula for options with squared variance following a double square root process. This process was initially applied by Longstaff (1989) to specify the dynamics of interest rates. With these two additional stochastic volatility models, the modelling spectrum for the dynamics of stock prices becomes essentially richer, and we have three different volatility models with closed-form solutions: square-root process, O-U process and double square-root process.

At the same time, research on the dynamics of interest rates, the term structure of interest rates and the valuation of bonds has given rise to a comprehensive theoretical field in finance. An obvious thing to do would be to enhance the options pricing models by incorporating the dynamics of interest rates such as in Merton (1973), BCC (1997) and others. In fact, the above mentioned three processes also play a central role in modelling interest rate dynamics. As shown later, the pricing formulae both for stochastic volatility models and for stochastic interest rate models share a common pricing kernel as long as they are specified to follow the same process. This point becomes especially obvious by using Fourier analysis and was discussed in Madan and Bakshi (1999), Goldstein (1997). Consequently, we could incorporate the dynamics of interest rates into an option pricing model more flexibly and efficiently in the framework of Fourier analysis.

What are the advantages of Fourier analysis by using characteristic functions when compared to the traditional method? The answer to this question is at least fourfold: The first gain is the tractability and easy manipulation of CFs which allow us to arrive at closed-form solutions in terms of CFs. In contrast, by applying the traditional partial differential equation (PDE) approach it is difficult to make variable transformations to get closed-form solutions. Therefore, one can sometimes only solve a PDE numerically although a closed-form solution using CFs does exist, for example, in the stochastic volatility model with an O-U process. Secondly, this approach can be extended to exotic options and enables us to value them with stochastic volatilities and stochastic interest rates as well as with random jumps. Thirdly, CFs are always continuous in their domain even for a discontinuous distribution. This property is of great advantage when we consider to model jumps in an asset price process. Finally, Fourier analysis allows us to build a flexible option pricing framework wherein each stochastic factor can be considered as a module. I call this idea "modular pricing of options" (MPO), and this concept is the main purpose of this book.

I will discuss an extended valuation framework for European options including the Black-Scholes world, stochastic interest rates, stochastic volatilities and even random jumps by applying characteristic functions. The common property of the pricing formulae *à la* Black-Scholes is the (log-) normal distribution. Obviously, in the extended framework the probabilities in the pricing formulae are no longer strictly (log-) normally distributed. However, they can be expressed by Fourier inversion of the associated characteristic functions which have closed-form solutions under different specifications of the stochastic factors. Consequently, valuation formulae in this new framework also have closed-form solutions. Furthermore, characteristic functions in a comprehensive option pricing model are simply composed of the characteristic functions of the independent stochastic factors. This enables us to develop a number of option pricing models by simply combining different stochastic factors. In this sense, stochastic volatilities, stochastic interest rates and random jumps work as modules which can be withdrawn from or inserted into a pricing formula by assembling the corresponding characteristic functions. However, all pricing formulae for options have a common shell: the Fourier inversion. The immediate gain of this modular concept is its applicability and its convenient implementation which implies essentially a modular programming approach: every characteristic function corresponds to a module.

Modular pricing concept differs from affine pricing concept in various ways. While affine asset pricing models in Duffie, Pan and Singleton's (1999) term are essentially multi-factor models with exponential affine solutions, modular pricing of options focuses more on how to efficiently derive and implement an option pricing model with different stochastic factors by applying Fourier analysis, and is not restricted to exponential affine solutions. For example, the stochastic volatilities models with an

O-U process or a double-square root process that will be embedded in our modular concept do not possess affine solutions and instead have nonlinear terms of factors in exponential level. By using modular programming implied in our modular pricing, practitioners can master much more better the computational problem encountered in implementing and testing comprehensive option pricing models. I will give some numerical examples to show this concept. In addition, modular pricing concept gains also expositional value and provides us with more intuition and understanding how different factors influence option prices.

This book is organized as follows: Chapter 1 deals with the general financial and mathematical background of Fourier analysis. This includes constructing characteristic functions in an option pricing environment (Section 1.2), interpreting characteristic functions from the point of view of completing security markets via options (Section 1.3), and connecting Fourier analysis with the traditional valuation method (PDE) (sections 1.4 and 1.5). In Chapter 2, the valuation framework of MPO will be discussed in detail. Both stochastic (squared) volatilities and stochastic interest rates are specified either as square root processes, O-U processes or double square root processes. Random jumps are classified as pure jumps, lognormal jumps or Pareto jumps. Sections 2.2, 2.3 and 2.4 handle these three different stochastic factors respectively. In Section 2.5, we show how to integrate these factors using our modular concept for option pricing.

Chapter 3 focuses on how to extend our MPO approach for exotic options. In Section 3.2, we deal with barrier options and obtain valuation formulae in two special cases: for barrier options on futures, and for barrier options on assets which follow a particular process. A general result for barrier options in our extended framework can not be given. Following in Section 3.3, we derive valuation formulae for lookback options in an analogous way with Section 3.2. In Section 3.4, we handle Asian options and obtain closed-form solutions for geometric average Asian options with stochastic volatilities, stochastic interest rates and random jumps. Next, we address correlation options including exchange options, quotient options as well as product options in Section 3.5. Since these options involve two underlying assets, two processes with two joint standard Brownian motions are introduced in order to deal with these particular options, and we can arrive at some closed-form solutions for correlation options by MPO. Finally, Chapter 4 reviews and concludes this book.

## 1.2 Constructing Characteristic Functions

We start with a rather general setting, where the processes of two important financial factors: the stock price process (risky asset process) and the default-free short rate process, are given as follows:

$$\frac{dS(t)}{S(t)} = a(u(t), t)dt + b(v(t), t)dw_1(t), \tag{1.1}$$

where $a(\cdot, t) \in \mathfrak{L} : \mathbb{R}^k \times [0, T] \to \mathbb{R}$, $b(\cdot, t) \in \mathfrak{L}^2 : \mathbb{R}^m \times [0, T] \to \mathbb{R}^n$ and $dw_1$ is a n-dimensional standard Brownian motion. $\mathfrak{L}$ and $\mathfrak{L}^2$ denote the set of functions $y(t)$ such that $\int_0^T |y(t)| \, dt < \infty$ almost surely and $\int_0^T y^2(t)dt < \infty$ almost surely, respectively. $u(t) \in \mathbb{R}^k$ and $v(t) \in \mathbb{R}^m$ could also follow Ito processes and are subordinated to the process $S(t)$. Defining $x(t) \equiv \ln S(t)$ and applying Ito's lemma gives

$$dx(t) = \left( a(u(t), t) - \frac{1}{2}b^2(v(t), t) \right) dt + b(v(t), t)dw_1(t). \tag{1.2}$$

In fact, $a(\cdot, t)$ is irrelevant for the risk-neutral processes of $dS(t)$ and $dx(t)$. For simplicity, we consider only a one-factor version of the short rate process which is defined by

$$dr(t) = c(r, t)dt + e(r, t)dw_2(t), \tag{1.3}$$

where $c(\cdot, t) \in \mathfrak{L} : \mathbb{R} \times [0, T] \to \mathbb{R}$, $e(\cdot, t) \in \mathfrak{L}^2 : \mathbb{R} \times [0, T] \to \mathbb{R}$ and $dw_2(t)$ is a one-dimensional Brownian motion and might be correlated with $dw_1(t)$. At the moment, we do not need to specify the volatility process $v(t)$ concretely. However, all of the functions $a(\cdot, t), b(\cdot, t), c(\cdot, t)$ and $e(\cdot, t)$ shall satisfy the technical conditions that guarantee the existence of a solution for the above two stochastic differential equations.[1] In coherence with most of the existing literature, we apply risk-neutral

---

[1] The technical conditions sufficient for the existence of unique solution of stochastic differential equation are Lipschitz and growth conditions. For their detailed definitions see, for example, Duffie (1996), Malliaris and Brock (1991).

pricing technique, and assume that a European-style option of the underlying stock $S$ with strike price $K$ is a discounted contingent cash flow and can be valued by

$$
\begin{aligned}
C(S_0, T; K) &= \mathbb{E}^Q \left[ \exp\left( -\int_0^T r(t)dt \right) (S(T) - K) \cdot \mathbf{1}_{(S(T)>K)} \right] \\
&= \mathbb{E}^Q \left[ \exp\left( -\int_0^T r(t)dt \right) S(T) \cdot \mathbf{1}_{(S(T)>K)} \right] \\
&\quad - \mathbb{E}^Q \left[ \exp\left( -\int_0^T r(t)dt \right) K \cdot \mathbf{1}_{(S(T)>K)} \right].
\end{aligned}
$$

$$(1.4)$$

where $Q$ denotes the risk-neutral (equivalent martingale) measure at the time $T$. According to Geman, El Karoui and Rochet (1995), Björk (1996) and others, in order to simplify the calculations in the above equation, we change numeraire. For the first term in the second equality, we choose the stock price $S_0$ as numeraire and switch from measure $Q$ to $Q_1$, and for the second term we use the so-called $T$-forward measure to switch from $Q$ to $Q_2$. According to Girsanov's theorem, the relationship between $Q$ and $Q_j$ is given by two Radon-Nikodym derivatives, respectively:

$$
\frac{dQ_1}{dQ} = g_1(T) = \exp\left( -\int_0^T r(t)dt \right) \frac{S(T)}{S_0}
$$

$$(1.5)$$

and

$$
\frac{dQ_2}{dQ} = g_2(T) = \exp\left( -\int_0^T r(t)dt \right) \frac{1}{B(0, T; r_0)}.
$$

$$(1.6)$$

where $Q_1$ and $Q_2$ are again two equivalent martingale measures. $B(0, T; r_0)$ is the price of a zero-bond maturing at time $T$. Dependently on the specification of the short-rate process, one can derive a pricing formula for $B(0, T; r_0)$.[2] Consequently, $g_j(t), j = 1, 2.$, also define two processes with the martingale property, which is demonstrated by the fact that the expected values of $g_j(t)$ are always equal to one:

$$
\mathbb{E}^Q \left[ g_j(t) \right] = 1, \quad \text{for} \quad t \geqslant 0.
$$

$$(1.7)$$

Hence, $g_j(t)$ imply a density function at $t$. We can also call $\{g_1(t)\}_{t \geqslant 0}$ the unit discounted stock process and $\{g_2(t)\}_{t \geqslant 0}$ the unit discounted bond

---

[2]The detailed derivation of $B(0, T; r_0)$ will be studied in Section 3.3.

process due to their martingale property.[3] With these two particular processes, the original equivalent measure $Q$ is switched to the new equivalent measures $Q_j$, respectively. Under these new measures, the option pricing representation (1.4) can be restated as

$$
\begin{aligned}
C &= S_0 \mathbb{E}^{Q_1}\left[\mathbf{1}_{(x(T)>\ln K)}\right] - B(0,T;r_0)K\mathbb{E}^{Q_2}\left[\mathbf{1}_{(x(T)>\ln K)}\right] \\
&= S_0 F_1^{Q_1}(x(T) > \ln K) - B(0,T;r_0)K F_2^{Q_2}(x(T) > \ln K).
\end{aligned}
\tag{1.8}
$$

This representation for an option pricing formula is similar to the Black-Scholes formula where the probabilities $F^{Q_j}, j = 1, 2$, in the latter case are given by two standard normal distributions. Here we express these probabilities by Fourier transform. The characteristic functions of $F_j^{Q_j}$ are defined by

$$
f_j(\phi) \equiv \mathbb{E}^{Q_j}\left[\exp(i\phi x(T))\right] \quad \text{for} \quad j = 1, 2.
\tag{1.9}
$$

By using the above two Radon-Nikodym derivatives again, we obtain new expressions for the CFs $f_j(\phi)$ under the original equivalent martingale measure $Q$:

$$
\begin{aligned}
f_1(\phi) &\equiv \mathbb{E}^{Q_1}\left[\exp(i\phi x(T))\right] = \int_{\mathbb{R}} \exp(i\phi x(T))dQ_1 \\
&= \int_{\mathbb{R}} \exp(i\phi x(T))g_1(T)dQ = \mathbb{E}^Q\left[g_1(T)\exp(i\phi x(T))\right]
\end{aligned}
\tag{1.10}
$$

and

$$
\begin{aligned}
f_2(\phi) &\equiv \mathbb{E}^{Q_2}\left[\exp(i\phi x(T))\right] = \int_{\mathbb{R}} \exp(i\phi x(T))dQ_2 \\
&= \int_{\mathbb{R}} \exp(i\phi x(T))g_2(T)dQ = \mathbb{E}^Q\left[g_2(T)\exp(i\phi x(T))\right].
\end{aligned}
\tag{1.11}
$$

---

[3]These two processes are also termed as likelihood processes because they imply a probability (see Björk, 1996).

If the analytical forms of the CFs $f_1(\phi)$ and $f_2(\phi)$ are known, we can apply the Fourier inversion theorem and then write $F_1$ and $F_2$ as the following form

$$F_j = \frac{1}{2} + \frac{1}{\pi} \int_0^\infty \mathrm{Re}\left( f_j(\phi) \frac{\exp(-i\phi \ln K)}{i\phi} \right) d\phi, \quad j = 1, 2. \qquad (1.12)$$

This new expression for the probabilities $F_j$ has some advantages: Firstly, we can later show that in most existing and new option pricing models the CFs $f_j(\phi)$ can be expressed by elementary functions. Secondly, $F_j$ contains only a single integral which can be calculated in a relatively easy way. Finally, these expressions are independent of the specifications of the processes of the individual stochastic factors. Therefore, the above procedure offers us a comprehensive framework to derive European-style option pricing formulae with a minimal dependence upon process specifications. Summarizing the above results, we have the following principle for constructing characteristic functions for option pricing using the unique risk-neutral measure $Q$.

**Principle for Constructing Characteristic Functions (1)**: *If the stock price process and the short-rate process are of form (2.1) and (2.2), respectively, and the drift and diffusion components of these processes satisfy all technical conditions so that the solutions to (2.1) and (2.2) exist, then the characteristic functions of $F_1$ and $F_2$ in a European-style call option*

$$C(S_0, T; K) = S_0 F_1 - KB(0, T) F_2$$

*have the expression of (1.10) and (1.11) respectively. This is independent of the specifications of the stock price process and the short-rate process.*

An enhanced principle for constructing CFs will be given in the following section. In fact, one can extend the one-factor version of the short-rate process to a multi-factor version without having any effect on the above procedure. This principle provides us with the ability to construct much more complicated and interesting variants of option pricing formulae. Note that there are no particular constraints on the processes of $S(t)$, $v(t)$ and $r(t)$. Therefore, they can be specified rather arbitrarily.

The following chapters show the effectiveness of this method in developing closed-form solutions.

For European-style currency options, one needs a well-known modification for $g_1(T)$, since the arbitrage procedure for currency options involves two currencies.[4] This is

$$\frac{dQ_1}{dQ} = g_1(T) = \exp\left(-\int_0^T r(t)dt\right)\frac{S(T)}{S_0 B^*(0,T)}, \qquad (1.13)$$

where $B^*(0,T)$ denotes the price of a foreign zero-bond maturing at time $T$. In this book, if not explicitly noted, expectations are always taken under the measure $Q$. Obviously, the principle of constructing CFs is also valid for European-style put options whose valuation formula is given by

$$P(S_0, T; K) = KB(0,T)F_2 - S_0 F_1. \qquad (1.14)$$

with

$$F_j = \frac{1}{2} - \frac{1}{\pi}\int_0^\infty \text{Re}\left(f_j(\phi)\frac{\exp(-i\phi\ln K)}{i\phi}\right)d\phi, \quad j = 1, 2. \qquad (1.15)$$

Expressing a probability via its characteristic function is equivalent to expressing a probability via a density function from many points of view. Firstly, both alternatives involve a single integral (for the one-dimensional case), and hence need a similar procedure to calculate the integral. Secondly, the one-to-one correspondence between a characteristic function and its distribution guarantees a unique form of the option pricing formula. Finally, the moments of a distribution can be derived from its characteristic function. Thus, some important statistical parameters such as variance, skewness and kurtosis are automatically available if the characteristic function is known.[5] Let $m_n^*(x(T))$ denote the $n$-th

---

[4] The pricing formula for currency (exchange rate) options can be generally expressed as

$$C(S_0, T; K) = S_0 B^*(0, T; r_0^*)F_1 - KB(0, T; r_0)F_2,$$

where $S$ denotes exchange rate. Garman and Kohlhagen (1983) haven given the pricing formula for currency options in the Black-Scholes framework.

[5] See Stuard and Ord (1994) for more details on this topic.

order non-central moment of $x(T)$, we have the following relationship between $m_n^*(x(T))$ and CF $f(\phi; x(T))$:

$$m_n^*(x(T)) = (-i)^n \left[ \frac{\partial^n f(\phi; x(T))}{\partial \phi^n} \right]_{\phi=0}. \tag{1.16}$$

It must be emphasized that the CF $f(\phi; x(T))$ for calculating the moments should be derived from the original measure $Q$ since we need the moments under actual measure,[6] that is

$$f(\phi; x(T)) \equiv \mathbb{E}^Q \left[ \exp(i\phi x(T)) \right]. \tag{1.17}$$

Thus, $f(\phi; x(T))$ is generally not identical to $f_j(\phi)$ as given above. To get skewness and kurtosis, the first four central moments $m_n(x(T))$ should be known and can be given by a recursive scheme (Stuard and Ord, 1994):

$$
\begin{aligned}
m_2 &= m_2^* - (m_1^*)^2 \\
m_3 &= m_3^* - 3m_2^* m_1^* + 2(m_1^*)^2 \\
m_4 &= m_4^* - 4m_3^* m_1^* + 6m_2^*(m_1^*)^2 - 3(m_1^*)^4.
\end{aligned} \tag{1.18}
$$

Skewness and kurtosis are then given by

$$skewness \equiv \frac{m_3}{(m_2)^{3/2}}, \qquad kurtosis \equiv \frac{m_4}{m_2^2}. \tag{1.19}$$

respectively. It is empirically evident that the actual distribution of stock returns displays a negative skewness and excess kurtosis. To capture a leptokurtic distribution, a reasonable stock price process should display this property. This can be checked in advance by employing (1.16) to (1.19).

## 1.3 Economic Interpretation of CFs

At first glance, expressing the probabilities $F_1$ and $F_2$ by Fourier inversion of CFs is more technical than economic. In fact, an economic

---

[6]Strictly speaking, the moments are calculated under the risk-neutralized measure $Q$. To obtain the actual probability measure of stock returns, we must change the risk-neutralized parameters to their empirical counterparts.

interpretation of CFs could be exploited by its implicit spanning of the state space. This aspect gains significance especially with respect to market completeness and Arrow-Debreu securities in a state-space approach. Ross (1976) has proved that contingent claims (options) enhances market efficiency in a state-space framework since creating options can complete (span) markets in an uncertain world. A recent paper by Bakshi and Madan (1999) demonstrates that spanning via options and spanning via CFs are completely interchangeable. To see this, we note that the CF $f(\phi; x(T)) \equiv \mathbb{E}^Q [\exp(i\phi x(T))]$ under the risk-neutral measure $Q$ can be rewritten as follows:

$$
\begin{aligned}
f(\phi; x(T)) &\equiv \mathbb{E}^Q [\exp(i\phi x(T))] \\
&= \mathbb{E}^Q [\cos(\phi x(T)) + i \sin(\phi x(T))].
\end{aligned}
\tag{1.20}
$$

Let us imagine two "contingent claims" of $x(T)$ with time-$T$ payoff $\cos(\phi x(T))$ and $\sin(\phi x(T))$.[7] Thus, from the point of view of valuation, $f(x(T); \phi)$ is a "security" consisting of two trigonometric assets of $x(T)$ while the stock price is only an exponential asset of $x(T)$. For the spanning equivalence via options and via CFs, the following two equations hold:

$$
\cos(\phi x(T)) = 1 - \int_0^\infty \phi^2 \cos(\phi \ln K) \max(0, x(T) - \ln K) d \ln K
\tag{1.21}
$$

$$
\sin(\phi x(T)) = x(T) - \int_0^\infty \phi^2 \sin(\phi \ln K) \max(0, x(T) - \ln K) d \ln K.
$$

These two equations state that trigonometric functions can be expressed by payoffs of options. Hence, it follows that the spanned security space of options and their underlying is the same one spanned by $\cos(\phi x(T))$ and $\sin(\phi x(T))$. We can regard two exercise probabilities $F_1$ and $F_2$ as Arrow-Debreu prices in the space spanned by options and the underlying primitive assets; analogously, the CFs $f_1(\phi)$ and $f_2(\phi)$ in the previous section can be interpreted as the Arrow-Debreu prices in the

---

[7]The contingent claim with payoff $\cos(\phi x_T)$ or $\sin(\phi x_T)$ is an "asset" with unlimited liability since $\cos(\phi x_T)$ and $\sin(\phi x_T)$ can become negative.

Fourier-transformed space.[8]

Starting from this equivalence, we can price more general contingent claims on $x(T)$ by using CFs. As a useful feature of CFs, differentiation and translation of CFs can simplify considerably the construction of primitive and derivative assets on $x(T)$. To expound this interesting feature of CF in the context of option pricing, we define a discounted CF (also called the CF of the remaining uncertainty):[9]

$$f^*(\phi; x(T)) = \mathbb{E}^Q\left[\exp\left(-\int_0^T r(t)dt\right)\exp(i\phi x(T))\right].\qquad(1.22)$$

Setting $\phi = 0$, we have

$$f^*(0; x(T)) = \mathbb{E}^Q\left[\exp\left(-\int_0^T r(t)dt\right)\right] = B(0,T;r_0).\qquad(1.23)$$

Thus the CF $f_2(\phi)$ in (1.11) can be expressed by

$$f_2(\phi) = \frac{f^*(\phi; x(T))}{f^*(0; x(T))} = \frac{1}{B(0,T;r_0)}f^*(\phi; x(T)).\qquad(1.24)$$

Note that with

$$f^*(\phi - i; x(T)) = \mathbb{E}^Q\left[\exp\left(-\int_0^T r(t)dt\right)\exp((1+i\phi)x(T))\right],$$

$$f^*(-i; x(T)) = \mathbb{E}^Q\left[\exp\left(-\int_0^T r(t)dt\right)\exp(x(T))\right] = S_0,$$

we immediately obtain an alternative expression for $f_1(\phi)$ :

$$f_1(\phi) = \frac{f^*(\phi - i; x(T))}{f^*(-i; x(T))} = \frac{f^*(\phi - i; x(T))}{S_0},\qquad(1.25)$$

where $x(T) = \ln S(T)$. As indicated in (1.16), we can construct the moments of the random variable $x(T)$ by partially differentiating the CF

---

[8]It is well-known that normal Arrow-Debreu prices should (must) be positive and smaller than one. Since the transformed spanned space is the complex plane, we can impose the usual $\mathcal{L}_1$-norm on $f_1$ and $f_2$. It follows immediately that $|f_1| \leq 1$ and $|f_2| \leq 1$. Thus, $f_1$ and $f_2$ are well-defined.

[9]See Bakshi and Madan (1999).

with respect to $\phi$. In the same manner, partially differentiating the discounted CF with respect to $\phi$ yields the "futures price" of the moments of $x(T)$. Generally, we have the following result on the relationship between the $n$-th order polynomial of $x(T)$ and the $n$-th order partial differential of $f^*(\phi; x(T))$:

$$(-i)^n \left[ \frac{\partial^n f(\phi; x(T))}{\partial \phi^n} \right]_{\phi=0}$$

$$= \mathbb{E}^Q \left[ \exp\left( -\int_0^T r(t)dt \right) x^n(T) \exp(i\phi x(T)) \right]_{\phi=0}$$

$$= \mathbb{E}^Q \left[ \exp\left( -\int_0^T r(t)dt \right) x^n(T) \right]$$

$$= (-i)^n f_{\phi n}^*(0; x(T)). \tag{1.26}$$

It follows

$$H_{x(T)} = \mathbb{E}^Q \left[ \exp\left( -\int_0^T r(t)dt \right) x(T) \right] = \frac{1}{i} f_\phi^*(0; x(T)). \tag{1.27}$$

where $H_{x(T)}$ is the futures price of $x(T)$. Note that a real payoff function $L(x(T)) \in \mathbf{C}^\infty$ can be sufficiently approximated by a (Taylor-) polynomial series, and hence the futures price of $L(x(T))$ can be approximated by a series of $f_{\phi n}^*(0; x(T))$. This approach states that $f_{\phi n}^*(0; x(T))$ forms a polynomial basis for the market of contingent claims on $x(T)$. Without loss of generality, we denote the spot price or the forward price of the contingent claim $L(x(T))$ by $L_0$ and expand $L(x(T))$ around zero:

$$G(T, \phi) = \mathbb{E}^Q \left[ \exp\left( -\int_0^T r(t)dt \right) L(x(T)) \exp(i\phi x(T)) \right]$$

$$= f^*(\phi; x(T))L(0) + \sum_{k=1}^\infty \frac{f_{\phi k}^*(\phi; x(T))}{(i)^k k!} \frac{\partial^k L}{\partial x^k}(0) \tag{1.28}$$

and

$$G(T, 0) = L_0 = \mathbb{E}^Q \left[ \exp\left( -\int_0^T r(t)dt \right) L(x(T)) \right]$$

$$= f^*(0; x(T))L(0) + \sum_{k=1}^\infty \frac{f_{\phi k}^*(0; x(T))}{(i)^k k!} \frac{\partial^k L}{\partial x^k}(0). \tag{1.29}$$

In many cases, for example, in the case of stock options, the spot price $L_0$, i.e., $G(T, 0)$ is directly observable and does not have to be derived from the CFs. $G(T, 0)$ plays an important role in valuation only for the case where no spot prices or forward prices of the contingent claim $L(x(T))$ are quoted in the markets. Using $L_0$ as numeraire, we can construct the first CF:

$$
\begin{aligned}
f_1(\phi) &= \mathbb{E}^Q\left[\exp\left(-\int_0^T r(t)dt\right)\frac{L(x(T))}{L_0}\exp(i\phi x(T))\right] \\
&= \frac{G(T, \phi)}{G(T, 0)}.
\end{aligned}
\tag{1.30}
$$

To guarantee $f_1(\phi)$ to be a well-defined CF, a sufficient and necessary condition must be satisfied:

$$
\mathbb{E}^Q\left[\exp\left(-\int_0^T r(t)dt\right)\frac{L(x(T))}{L_0}\right] = 1.
\tag{1.31}
$$

Equation (1.31) implies that $L(x)$ is an arbitrage-free process and admits no free-lunch. The construction of $f_2(\phi)$ for pricing general contingent claims follows a similar pattern. Therefore, we are able to derive closed-form valuation formulae for a call on particular contingent claims in an unified framework. A simple example can be an option on interest rates if we specify $x(t)$ as $r(t)$. Summing up, we have a more general principle for constructing CFs:[10]

**Principle for Constructing Characteristic Functions (2)**: *Assume a (primitive) asset return process $x(t)$, with $x(0) = 0$, follows an Ito process and satisfies the usual necessary technical conditions. In the market there is a basic security $L(x) \in \mathbf{C}^\infty$ on this return, which is strictly positive and invertible. Furthermore, the arbitrage-free condition (1.31) is satisfied. Then a European-style call option $C$ on $L(x)$ with a strike price $K$ and a maturity time of $T$ can be valued by*

$$
C(x_0, T; K) = L_0 F_1 - KB(0, T)F_2,
$$

*with*

$$
F_j = \frac{1}{2} - \frac{1}{\pi}\int_0^\infty \mathrm{Re}\left(f_j(\phi)\frac{\exp(-i\phi L^{-1}(K))}{i\phi}\right)d\phi, \quad j = 1, 2,
$$

---

[10]This principle is essentially identical to the case 3 in Bakshi and Madan (1999).

*where*

$$L_0 = G(T,0), \qquad B(0,T) = f^*(0; x(T)),$$

$$f_1(\phi) = \frac{G(T,\phi)}{G(T,0)}, \qquad f_2(\phi) = \frac{f^*(\phi; x(T))}{f^*(0; x(T))},$$

$$G(T,\phi) = f^*(\phi; x(T))L(0) + \sum_{k=1}^{\infty} \frac{f^*_{\phi k}(\phi; x(T))}{(i)^k k!} \frac{\partial^k L}{\partial x^k}(0).$$

This generalized principle for constructing CFs is useful in deriving a tractable valuation formula for options on securities with an unconventional payoff function $L(x)$ and provides us with a structural and amenable tool to analyze quantitative effects of uncertainty in economics and finance.

## 1.4 Examination of Existing Option Models

Since Black and Scholes (1973) derived their celebrated option pricing formula, an enormous number of variants of option pricing models have been developed. Merton (1973) examined an option valuation problem with stochastic interest rates using the assumption that the zero-bond price is lognormally distributed. Geske (1979) gave a pricing formula for compound options. Merton (1976), Cox and Ross (1976) studied issues of option valuation where the underlying asset price follows a jump process and introduced for the first time a discontinuous price process in option pricing theory. Since the middle of 1980s, the valuation of options with stochastic volatilities has drawn more and more the attention of financial economists. The models of S&S (1990), Heston (1993), BCC (1997) are the most influential works on modelling stochastic volatility. Here, we give a brief overview of some important closed-form pricing solutions for options under the risk-neutral measure using Fourier transformation techniques, but without detailed derivations. As shown later, all of these models are special cases of our framework presented in this book.

(1). The Black-Scholes Model (1973). It includes only one stochastic process:

$$dS(t) = rS(t)dt + \sigma S(t)dw(t).$$

Let $x(t) = \ln S(t)$,

$$dx(t) = \left[r - \frac{1}{2}\sigma^2\right]dt + \sigma dw(t). \qquad (1.32)$$

Hence,

$$g_1(T) = \exp(-rT + x(T) - x_0), \qquad g_2(T) = 1.$$

The two CFs can be calculated as follows:

$$
\begin{aligned}
f_1(\phi) &= \mathbb{E}\left[g_1(T)e^{i\phi x(T)}\right] = \mathbb{E}\left[\exp((1+i\phi)x(T) - rT - x_0\right] \\
&= \exp\left[i\phi(rT + x_0) - \frac{1+i\phi}{2}\sigma^2 T + \frac{(1+i\phi)^2}{2}\sigma^2 T\right] \\
&= \exp\left[i\phi\left(rT + x_0 + \frac{1}{2}\sigma^2 T\right) - \frac{\phi^2}{2}\sigma^2 T\right] \qquad (1.33)
\end{aligned}
$$

and

$$
\begin{aligned}
f_2(\phi) &= \mathbb{E}\left[g_2(T)e^{i\phi x(T)}\right] = \mathbb{E}\left[\exp i\phi x(T)\right] \\
&= \exp\left[i\phi\left(rT + x_0 - \frac{1}{2}\sigma^2 T\right) - \frac{\phi^2}{2}\sigma^2 T\right]. \qquad (1.34)
\end{aligned}
$$

It is not hard to verify that

$$N(d_j) = \frac{1}{2} + \frac{1}{\pi}\int_0^\infty \mathrm{Re}\left(f_j(\phi)\frac{\exp(-i\phi\ln K)}{i\phi}\right)d\phi, \quad j = 1, 2.$$

$N(d_j)$ are the usual probability terms in the Black-Scholes formula.[11] Thus, we have shown that the Black-Scholes formula can be easily derived by using Fourier inversion.

---

[11]Since the CF of a normal density function $n(\mu, \sigma)$ is $f(\phi) = \exp\left(i\phi\mu - \frac{1}{2}\sigma^2\phi^2\right)$, two probabilities $N(d_j), j = 1, 2$, in the Black-Scholes formula are distributed according to $n(rT + x_0 \pm \frac{1}{2}\sigma^2 T, \frac{1}{2}\sigma^2 T)$ respectively.

(2). **The Heston Model (1993).** This model is characterized by the following processes:

$$\frac{dS(t)}{S(t)} = r(t)dt + \sqrt{v(t)}dw_1(t)$$
$$\text{or} \tag{1.35}$$
$$dx(t) = \left[r(t) - \frac{1}{2}v(t)\right]dt + \sqrt{v(t)}dw_1(t),$$
$$dv(t) = [\kappa\theta - (\kappa + \lambda)v(t)]dt + \sigma\sqrt{v(t)}dw_2(t);$$

with

$$dw_1(t)dw_2(t) = \rho dt.$$

Here, the squared volatilities follow a mean-reverting square-root process which was used in finance for the first time by CIR (1985b) to specify stochastic interest rates. Hence, we have

$$g_1(T) = \exp(-rT + x(T) - x_0), \qquad g_2(T) = 1.$$

The detailed derivation of this pricing formula for options is given in Section 2.2.2.

(3). **The Model of Bakshi, Cao and Chen (1997).** Their model includes stochastic volatility, stochastic interest rates and random jumps where the first two factors are specified by a mean-reverting square-root process. Random jumps follow a Poisson process with a lognormally distributed jump size.

$$\frac{dS(t)}{S(t)} = [r(t) - \lambda\mu_J]dt + \sqrt{v(t)}dw_1(t) + J(t)dY(t)$$
$$\text{or}$$
$$dx(t) = \left[r(t) - \lambda\mu_J - \frac{1}{2}v(t)\right]dt + \sqrt{v(t)}dw_1(t) + \ln[1 + J(t)]dY(t),$$
$$\tag{1.36}$$
$$dv(t) = [\theta_v - \kappa_v v(t)]dt + \sigma_v\sqrt{v(t)}dw_2(t),$$
$$dr(t) = [\theta_r - \kappa_r r(t)]dt + \sigma_r\sqrt{r(t)}dw_3(t),$$

with

$$dw_1(t)dw_2(t) = \rho dt,$$
$$\ln[1 + J(t)] \sim N(\ln[1 + \mu_J] - \frac{1}{2}\sigma_J^2, \sigma_J^2),$$
$$dY(t) \sim \delta_1 \lambda dt + \delta_0(1 - \lambda)dt,$$

where $\delta_n$ is an indicator function for the value $n$. Here the stock price process includes a jump component $J(t)dq(t)$. Since the jump has no impact on the Ito process, after taking the market price of the jump risk $\lambda \mu_J$ into account, we can use our scheme again. So we have

$$g_1(T) = \exp\left(-\int_0^T r(t)dt + x(T) - x_0\right),$$
$$g_2(T) = \exp\left(-\int_0^T r(t)dt\right)/B(0, T; r_0).$$

The detailed derivation of this option valuation formula is available in Section 2.5.1. Scott (1997) developed a similar model incorporating stochastic interest rates and jumps.

(4). The Bates (1996) model for currency option. This model differs only slightly from the above one due to a different process for the underlying asset. Let $S(t)$ denote the exchange rate,

$$\frac{dS(t)}{S(t)} = [r - r^* - \lambda \mu_J]dt + \sqrt{v(t)}dw_1(t) + J(t)dY(t)$$
$$\text{or}$$
$$dx(t) = [r - r^* - \lambda \mu_J - \frac{1}{2}v(t)]dt + \sqrt{v(t)}dw_1(t) + \ln[1 + J(t)]dY(t),$$
$$\tag{1.37}$$
$$dv(t) = [\theta_v - \kappa_v v(t)]dt + \sigma_v \sqrt{v(t)}dw_2(t),$$

with

$$dw_1(t)dw_2(t) = \rho dt,$$
$$\ln[1 + J(t)] \sim N(\ln[1 + \mu_J] - \frac{1}{2}\sigma_J^2, \sigma_J^2),$$
$$dY(t) \sim \delta_1 \lambda dt + \delta_0(1 - \lambda)dt.$$

Thus it follows

$$g_1(T) = \exp(-(r - r^*)T + x(T) - x_0), \qquad g_2(T) = 1.$$

The above models represent the recent state of the art of the option pricing theory. All of these models (except for the BS model) have some common properties: First of all, stock prices (underlying assets) are characterized only by a Brownian motion with a subordinated process for variance. Squared volatility (variance) follows a square-root process. Secondly, the short rates process is one-dimensional and also follows a square root process. As shown in Section 2.2.2, a square root process allows for a nice derivation of characteristic functions, but, obviously, it is not the only way to describe volatilities and interest rates. The Ornstein-Uhlenbeck process, for example, may be an appealing alternative (S&S, 1991; Schöbel and Zhu, 1999). Furthermore, we can extend the one-dimensional stock price process to a multi-dimensional case. We will face such multi-dimensional problems in pricing basket options and correlation options.[12]

## 1.5 Equivalence of CFs to PDEs

In this section, we attempt to establish an equivalent relation between the Fourier inversion approach and the traditional partial differential equation (PDE) approach. In fact, the original works of Heston (1993), Bates (1996), BCC (1997) are based on the PDE-approach. We take the stochastic volatility model as an example for demonstrating this equivalence. If the processes of stock prices and squared volatilities are specified as in (1.35), a European-style call option $C(S_0, v_0, T)$ must satisfy a PDE as follows

$$\frac{1}{2} v S^2 \frac{\partial^2 C}{\partial S^2} + \rho \sigma v S \frac{\partial^2 C}{\partial S \partial v} + \frac{1}{2} \sigma^2 v \frac{\partial^2 C}{\partial v^2} +$$

$$rS\frac{\partial C}{\partial S} + \kappa(\theta - v)\frac{\partial C}{\partial v} - rC - \frac{\partial C}{\partial T} = 0 \qquad (1.38)$$

where $T$ denotes the maturity of option. This is a three-dimensional PDE that has no trivial solution. The idea of the Heston model is that

---

[12]In Section 3.5, we will develop a complex two dimensional pricing model for correlation options.

if the option pricing formula has a structure à la Black-Scholes, then the probabilities $F_j$ must also satisfy the corresponding PDEs. Suppose that the option pricing formula has the following form

$$C(S_0, v_0, T) = S_0 F_1 - e^{-rT} K F_2.$$

Differentiating $C$ with respect to $x = \ln S_0, v_0$ and $T$ and setting these partial derivatives into (1.38) gives us two new PDEs which are respectively given by

$$\frac{1}{2}v\frac{\partial^2 F_1}{\partial x^2} + \rho\sigma v\frac{\partial^2 F_1}{\partial x\partial v} + \frac{1}{2}\sigma^2 v\frac{\partial^2 F_1}{\partial v^2} +$$

$$(r + \frac{1}{2}v)\frac{\partial F_1}{\partial x} + (\kappa(\theta - v) - \rho\sigma)\frac{\partial F_1}{\partial v} - \frac{\partial F_1}{\partial T} = 0 \qquad (1.39)$$

subject to the boundary condition at the expiration date $T = 0$

$$F_1(x_0, v_0, 0) = \mathbf{1}_{(x \geqslant \ln K)},$$

and

$$\frac{1}{2}v\frac{\partial^2 F_2}{\partial x^2} + \rho\sigma v\frac{\partial^2 F_2}{\partial x\partial v} + \frac{1}{2}\sigma^2 v\frac{\partial^2 F_2}{\partial v^2} +$$

$$(r - \frac{1}{2}v)\frac{\partial F_2}{\partial x} + \kappa(\theta - v)\frac{\partial F_2}{\partial v} - \frac{\partial F_2}{\partial T} = 0, \qquad (1.40)$$

subject to the boundary condition at the expiration date $T = 0$

$$F_2(x_0, v_0, 0) = \mathbf{1}_{(x \geqslant \ln K)}.$$

Equations (1.39) and (1.40) are two-dimensional Kolmogorov's backward equations which have an interesting property, that is, all the moments generated by the probabilities $F_j$ also fulfill the same PDEs. Consequently, the CFs $f_j(\phi)$ as moment-generating function fullfil the above PDEs:

$$\frac{1}{2}v\frac{\partial^2 f_j}{\partial x^2} + \rho\sigma v\frac{\partial^2 f_j}{\partial x\partial v} + \frac{1}{2}\sigma^2 v\frac{\partial^2 f_j}{\partial v^2} +$$

$$(r \pm \frac{1}{2}v)\frac{\partial f_j}{\partial x} + (\kappa(\theta - v(t) + a_j)\frac{\partial f_j}{\partial v} - \frac{\partial f_j}{\partial T} = 0 \qquad (1.41)$$

with the changed boundary conditions

$$f_j(x_0, v_0, 0) = \exp(i\phi x_0), \qquad j = 1, 2,$$

where $a_1 = \rho\sigma$ and $a_2 = 0$. Using an exponential affine solution "guess",

$$f_j(\phi; x_0, v_0, T) = \exp[A_j(T) + B_j(T)v_0 + i\phi x_0], \qquad (1.42)$$

we arrive at a closed-form solution for the CFs $f_j(\phi)$ and obtain a closed-form pricing formula for options using Fourier inversion.[13] Looking at equation (1.39) again, we see that $x(t)$ no longer follows the process given originally since the drift term of $x(t)$ in (1.39) is now $(r + \frac{1}{2}v)$ instead of $(r - \frac{1}{2}v)$. The change of drifts is caused by the change of measures from $Q$ to $Q_1$.

On the other hand, we know that $f_1(\phi) = \mathbb{E}\left[g_1(T)\exp(i\phi x(T))\right]$ and $f_2(\phi) = \mathbb{E}\left[g_2(T)\exp(i\phi x(T))\right]$ are the CFs associated with the probabilities $F_1$ and $F_2$, respectively, then the Kolmogorov's backward equation can be applied, which states

$$\frac{\partial u}{\partial t} = \mathcal{K}u \quad for \quad u = \mathbb{E}\left[f(t, \mathbf{y})\right], \quad t \geqslant 0, \quad \mathbf{y} \in \mathbb{R}^n$$

with $\mathbf{y}$ as a n-dimensional Ito process and the boundary condition

$$u(0, \mathbf{a}) = f(0, \mathbf{a}), \quad \mathbf{y}(0) = \mathbf{a} \in \mathbb{R}^n,$$

and the operator $\mathcal{K}$ is given by

$$\mathcal{K} = \sum_j \mathrm{drift}_j \frac{\partial}{\partial y_j} + \frac{1}{2} \sum_{i,j} \mathrm{covariance}_{ij} \frac{\partial^2}{\partial y_i y_j}.$$

A direct application of the operator $\mathcal{K}$ will confirm that the CFs $f_1(\phi)$ and $f_2(\phi)$ satisfy the PDEs (1.39) and (1.40). For $f_2(\phi) = \mathbb{E}[g_2(T) \times \exp(i\phi x(T))] = \mathbb{E}\left[\exp(i\phi x(T))\right]$, we have

$$\mathcal{K}f_2 = \frac{1}{2}v\frac{\partial^2 f_2}{\partial x^2} + \rho\sigma v\frac{\partial^2 f_2}{\partial x\partial v} + \frac{1}{2}\sigma^2 v\frac{\partial^2 f_2}{\partial v^2} + \\ (r - \frac{1}{2}v)\frac{\partial f_2}{\partial x} + \kappa(\theta - v)\frac{\partial f_2}{\partial v},$$

$$(1.43)$$

---

[13]See Heston (1993) for details.

with which an identical PDE as (1.40) is obtained immediately. For $f_1(\phi) = \mathbb{E}\left[g_1(T)\exp(i\phi x(T))\right]$, we make a manipulation as follows:

$$
\begin{aligned}
f_1(\phi) &= \mathbb{E}\left[g_1(T)\exp(i\phi x(T))\right] = \mathbb{E}\left[\frac{e^{-rT}}{S_0}\exp((1+i\phi)x(t))\right] \\
&= \mathbb{E}\left[\exp\left(i\phi[x_0 + rT - \frac{1}{2}\int_0^T v(t)dt + \int_0^T \sqrt{v(t)}dw_1]\right.\right. \\
&\qquad \left.\left. -\frac{1}{2}\int_0^T v(t)dt + \int_0^T \sqrt{v(t)}dw_1\right)\right].
\end{aligned}
\tag{1.44}
$$

Using the above introduced Radon-Nikodym derivative

$$
\begin{aligned}
\frac{dQ}{dQ_1} &= \exp\left(\frac{1}{2}\int_0^T v(t)dt - \int_0^T \sqrt{v(t)}dw_1\right) \\
&= g_1^{-1}(T) = \frac{S_0}{e^{-rT}S(T)},
\end{aligned}
$$

and applying Girsanov's theorem yields

$$
\begin{aligned}
f_1(\phi) &= \mathbb{E}^{Q_1}\left[\exp\left(i\phi(x_0 + rT - \frac{1}{2}\int_0^T v(t)dt + \int_0^T \sqrt{v(t)}dw_1)\right)\right] \\
&= \mathbb{E}^{Q_1}\left[\exp\left(i\phi\widehat{x}(T)\right)\right].
\end{aligned}
\tag{1.45}
$$

This equation justifies why we can consider $f_1(\phi)$ as a CF under the measure $Q_1$, and at the same time implies that $\widehat{x}(t)$ under the measure $Q_1$ follows a process

$$
d\widehat{x}(t) = \left(r - \frac{1}{2}v(t)\right)dt + \sqrt{v(t)}dw_1^{Q_1}.
\tag{1.46}
$$

The random variable $\widehat{x}(t)$ follows the same process under the measure $Q_1$ as the random variable $x(t)$ under the measure $Q$. However, we can see that $\widehat{x}(t)$ under the original measure $Q$ follows the process

$$
d\widehat{x}(t) = \left(r + \frac{1}{2}v(t)\right)dt + \sqrt{v(t)}dw_1^{Q},
\tag{1.47}
$$

since according to Girsanov's theorem a change from the measure $Q_1$ to the measure $Q$ only causes a shift of the drift from $r - \frac{1}{2}v(t)$ to

$r + \frac{1}{2}v(t)$. Therefore, by applying Kolmogorov's operator $\mathcal{K}$ to the above process again, we obtain an identical PDE as (1.39):

$$\mathcal{K}f_1 = \frac{1}{2}v\frac{\partial^2 f_1}{\partial \widehat{x}^2} + \rho\sigma v\frac{\partial^2 f_1}{\partial \widehat{x}\partial v} + \frac{1}{2}\sigma^2 v\frac{\partial^2 f_1}{\partial v^2} + (r + \frac{1}{2}v)\frac{\partial f_1}{\partial \widehat{x}} + \kappa(\theta - v)\frac{\partial f_1}{\partial v}. \tag{1.48}$$

Thus, an equivalent relation between the Fourier transformation approach and PDE-approach is established. If interest rates are taken as stochastic, the above proof remains valid. However, in many cases, it is not easy to get a "right" guess for a suitable solution form for the CFs if we carry out the above procedure. For example, with volatility specified as a mean-reverting O-U process, the above procedure can not help us any more. In contrast, if we first calculate CFs and then apply PDEs as done in Scott (1997), Schöbel and Zhu (1999), we can indeed arrive at closed-form solutions for the CFs.

# 2 Modular Pricing of Options (MPO)

## 2.1 Stochastic Factors as Modules

If we want to value a European-style option without dividend payment, several parameters have to be specified, some of which are simply given in the option contract, such as strike price $K$ and time to maturity $T$. The other variables such as the stock price $S(t)$, the interest rate $r(t)$ and the volatility $v(t)$, are strongly dependent on the market situation and change from day to day. The objective of an option pricing model is to specify these variables and then to value options. Obviously, the process of stock price $S(t)$ plays a crucial and fundamental role since the interest rate and the volatility are merely two parameters of the process $S(t)$ in a risk-neutral pricing framework. Additionally, we can extend the usual Brownian motion for $S(t)$ by adding a discontinuous jump component, hoping that jump phenomena in the stock price movement, for instance, during the crash of 1987, could be described better and more realistically.

In a comprehensive option pricing model, we have at least three stochastic factors beside the stock price. Since each stochastic factor can be specified in many alternative ways, the number of possible option pricing models is theoretically equal to the product of the number of possible specifications of each factor. Up to now, most option pricing models are separately developed and implemented. It is certainly tedious to develop every possible model and to derive every possible option pricing formula. On the other hand, each possible option pricing model could be a good candidate to match a changing market situation and to meet the needs of financial practitioners. In fact, instead of dealing with a single model, we only need to establish a flexible framework as illustrated in Table 2.1. We call this "Modular Pricing of Options", abbreviated by "MPO". To make MPO work efficiently, we use Fourier analysis and characteristic functions.

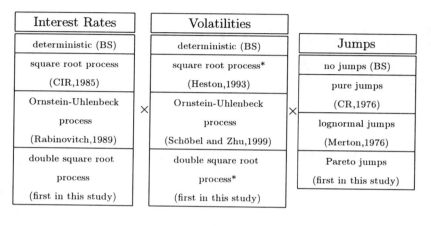

| Interest Rates | | Volatilities | | Jumps |
|---|---|---|---|---|
| deterministic (BS) | | deterministic (BS) | | no jumps (BS) |
| square root process (CIR,1985) | | square root process* (Heston,1993) | | pure jumps (CR,1976) |
| Ornstein-Uhlenbeck process (Rabinovitch,1989) | × | Ornstein-Uhlenbeck process (Schöbel and Zhu,1999) | × | lognormal jumps (Merton,1976) |
| double square root process (first in this study) | | double square root process* (first in this study) | | Pareto jumps (first in this study) |

*: Squared volatilities (variances) are specified

Table 2.1 Stochastic Factors as Modules

In Table 2.1, for stochastic interest rates, we adopt four alternatives: deterministic, mean-reverting square-root process and mean-reverting Ornstein-Uhlenbeck (O-U) process as well as double square root process. The deterministic case is from Black-Scholes world. Specifying interest rates as a mean-reverting square-root process is the CIR model (1985b) whereas the interest rate model with a mean-reverting O-U process developed by Vasicek (1977) is the first dynamic pricing model for bonds and term structure of interest rates. These two cases form the fundament of interest rate modelling. Rabinovitch (1989) incorporated the Vasicek model into an option pricing formula. Longstaff (1989) modified the CIR model and developed a so-called mean-reverting double square root process. Similarly, the specification of volatility follows the same alternatives: deterministic, mean-reverting square-root process, mean-reverting O-U process and double square root process. Again, the deterministic case corresponds to the Black-Scholes model. In Heston's model, as briefly outlined in Section 1.2, instead of volatility, the variance follows a square-root process and a closed-form solution is available. Scott (1987), S&S (1991) studied the case where the volatility is modelled by

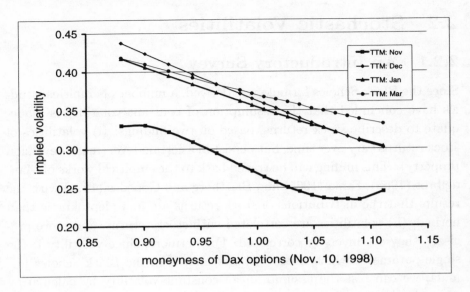

Figure 2.1: Empirical implied volatility patterns of Dax call options

a mean-reverting O-U process. Scott arrived at no closed-form solution and, S&S could only give a quasi closed-form solution for options in the absence of correlation between stock prices and volatilities. To fill this gap, Schöbel and Zhu (1999) derived a closed-form pricing formula for options in the presence of non-zero correlation. Specifying volatility as a double square root process is studied here for the first time and offers us an alternative way to value options with stochastic volatility. Finally, we distinguish random jumps in four categories, too: no jump, such as in the Black-Scholes formula; pure jumps, such as in Cox and Ross (1977); lognormal jumps, such as in Bates (1996) and BCC (1997), and Pareto jumps. Duffie, Pan and Singleton (1999) applied Pareto jumps to model the abnormalities in volatility. Here, Pareto jumps are suggested for the first time to capture the abnormalities in the stock return process. The following sections will deal with MPO in detail.

## 2.2   Stochastic Volatilities

### 2.2.1   An Introductory Survey

Since the Black-Scholes formula was derived, a number of empirical studies have concluded that the assumption of constant volatility is inadequate to describe stock returns, based on two findings: (i) volatilities of stock returns vary over time, but persist in a certain level (mean-reversion property). This finding can be traced back to the empirical works of Mandelbrot (1963), Fama (1965) and Blattberg and Gonedes (1974) with the results that the distributions of stock returns are more leptokurtic than normal; (ii) volatilities are correlated with stock returns, and more precisely, they are inversely correlated. Furthermore, since volatility is the single parameter which needs to be estimated in the Black-Scholes formula, we can test the assumption of constant volatility by calculating implied volatilities from a series of option market prices. If this assumption holds, implied volatilities should keep constant. Unfortunately, such tests are almost rejected and present us a so-called "volatility smile", which means that implied volatilities in the Black-Scholes formula display an inconsistent pattern with moneyness. In fact, volatilities "smile" in different ways: they could be down-sloping or down and up-sloping.[14] Figure 2.1 illustrates several patterns in the implied volatilities of DAX calls. Black (1976a), Schmalensee and Trippi (1978), Beckers (1980) investigated the time-series property between stock returns and volatilities, and found an imperfect negative correlation. Recently, BCC (1997) and Nandi (1998) also reported a negative correlation between the implied volatilities and stock returns. Moreover, Beckers (1983), Pozerba and Summers (1984) gave evidence that shocks to volatility persist and have a great impact on option prices, but tend to decay over time. These uncovered properties associated with volatility such as leptokurtic distribution, correlation, mean-reversion and persistence of shocks, should be considered in a suitable option pricing model.

In order to model variability of volatility and to capture the "volatility smile", several methods have been suggested. The first one was so-called constant elasticity of variance diffusion model developed by Cox (1975). He assumed that volatility is a function of the stock price with the fol-

---

[14]Down-sloping smile pattern, meaning that implied volatility increases with moneyness, is often referred to as a smirk.

lowing form:

$$v(S(t)) = aS(t)^{\delta-1}, \quad \text{with} \quad a > 0, \quad 0 \leqslant \delta \leqslant 1. \qquad (2.49)$$

Since $v(S(t))$ is a decreasing function of $S(t)$, volatilities are inversely correlated with stock returns. However, this deterministic function can not describe other features of volatility. Derman and Kani (1994), Dupire (1994) and Rubinstein (1994) hypothesized that volatility is a deterministic function of the stock price and time, and developed a deterministic volatility function (DVF), with which they attempt to fit the observed cross-section of option prices exactly. This approach, as reported by Dumas, Fleming and Whaley (1998), does not perform better than an *ad hoc* procedure that merely smooths implied volatilities across strike prices and times to maturity.

A more general approach is to model volatility by a diffusion process and has been examined Johnson and Shanno (1987), Wiggins (1987), Scott (1987), Hull and White (1987), S&S (1991), and Heston (1993). Of course, this list is not complete. Table 2.2 gives an overview of several representatives of this approach.

| | | |
|---|---|---|
| 1: | $dv(t) = \kappa v dt + \sigma v dw(t)$ | Johnson/Shanno (1987) |
| 2: | $d\ln v(t) = \kappa(\theta - \ln v)dt + \sigma dw(t)$ | Wiggins (1987) |
| 3: | $dv(t)^2 = \kappa v^2 dt + \sigma v^2 dw(t)$ | Hull/White (1987) |
| 4: | $dv(t)^2 = \kappa v^2(\theta - v)dt + \sigma v^2 dw(t)$ | Hull/White (1987) |
| 5: | $dv(t) = \kappa(\theta - v)dt + \sigma dw(t)$ | S&S (1991), Schöbel/Zhu (1999) |
| 6: | $dv(t)^2 = \kappa(\theta - v^2)dt + \sigma v dw(t)$ | Heston (1993) |
| 7: | $dv(t)^2 = \kappa(\theta - v - \lambda v^2)dt + \sigma v dw(t)$ | suggested in this book |

Table 2.2: Overview of Stochastic Volatility Models

There are no known closed-form option pricing formulae in the case of non-zero correlation between volatilities and stock returns for all models listed in Table 2.2 except model (5) [Schöbel and Zhu, 1999], model (6) [Heston, 1993] as well as model (7). Models (1) and (3) perform no mean-reversion property and therefore can not capture the effects of shocks to volatility in the valuation of options. Models (1), (2), (3) and (4) are not stationary processes and violate the feature of the volatility's stationarity. Consequently, only models (5) and (6) are reasonable and worthwhile to study in detail. As shown in Hull and White (1987),

Ball and Roma (1994), if stock returns are uncorrelated with volatilities, the option price can be approximated very accurately by replacing the variance in the Black-Scholes formula by the expected average variance which is defined by

$$AV = \mathbb{E}\left(\frac{1}{T}\int_0^T v(t)^2 dt\right).$$ (2.50)

The mathematical background for this replacement is that the conditional distribution of the terminal stock price, given the expected average variance, is still lognormal. However, this argument fails in the presence of correlation between stock returns and volatilities. Heston (1993) showed that the correlation between volatility and spot returns is necessary to create negative skewness and excess kurtosis in a leptokurtic distribution of spot returns. BCC (1997), Heston and Nandi (1997) and Nandi (1998) demonstrated that non-zero correlation is important in eliminating the "smile" or "sneer" of implied volatilities and leads to significant improvements both in pricing and in hedging options.

Some econometric models also attract attention when studying stochastic volatility. In fact, each model from (1) to (7) in Table 2.2 corresponds to an econometric counterpart by discretization of time scale, and are referred to as the so-called autoregressive random variance models (ARV). Nelson and Foster (1994), Duan (1996) showed that some existing stochastic volatility models can be considered as the week limits of some generalized autoregressive conditional heteroskedasticity (GARCH) models.[15] The discrete-time versions of stochastic models play an important role in empirical tests. More recently, Heston and Nandi (1997) suggested a GARCH option pricing model and derived a closed-form solution which allows for correlation between stock returns and variance and even admits multiple lags in the GARCH process.

## 2.2.2  Square Root Process

This subsection reexamines the Heston (1993) model by directly constructing the CFs and deriving the option pricing formula in an alterna-

---

[15] The crucial difference between ARV models and GRACH models is that ARV models include two innovations to generate data while GRACH models have only one innovation with conditional variances dependent upon the past information.

tive way. The stock prices and their logarithms are derived by the usual dynamics as follows:

$$dS(t) = rS(t)dt + \sqrt{v(t)}S(t)dw_1(t),$$

$$dx(t) = \left[r - \frac{1}{2}v(t)\right]dt + \sqrt{v(t)}dw_1(t).$$

(2.51)

The volatility $\eta(t)$ in the Heston model initially follows an Ornstein-Uhlenbeck process with a mean-reverting level as zero [Equation (2) in Heston (1993)], that is

$$d\eta(t) = -\beta\eta(t)dt + \delta dw_2(t).$$

(2.52)

So from Ito's lemma, the square of volatility $v(t) = \eta(t)^2$, namely the variance of the instantaneous stock return, follows a square-root process which is given by

$$dv(t) = \kappa[\theta - v(t)]dt + \sigma\sqrt{v(t)}dw_2(t),$$

(2.53)

with

$$\beta = \frac{\kappa}{2}, \quad \delta = \frac{\sigma}{2}, \quad \theta = \frac{\delta^2}{\kappa}.$$

(2.54)

where $dw_1(t)dw_2(t) = \rho dt$. For notational convenience, we denote here instantaneous variance, not volatility by $v(t)$. The stochastic volatility models are generally not complete and the parameter $\lambda$ is dependent on risk-preferences. Based on the models of Breeden (1979), Cox, Ingersoll and Ross (1985a), Heston proposes a risk premium proportional to the variance $v(t)$, i.e., $\lambda v(t)$.[16] After adjusting the volatility process

---

[16]The market price of volatility risk $\lambda$ depends on the assumption about the risk aversion. A common way to determine $\lambda$ is to assume $\lambda dt = \gamma Cov[dv, dC/C]$ where $\gamma$ and $C$ is the relative-risk aversion and consumption respectively. From the well-known Cox, Ingersoll and Ross (1985a) equilibrium model, one can get a consumption process [also see Equ. (8) in Heston]:

$$dC = \mu_c v(t)^2 Cdt + \sigma_c v(t)Cdw_c(t).$$

Consequently, the risk premium is proportional to $v$, $\lambda(v) = \lambda v$ with $\lambda$ a constant.

(2.53) by the market price of risk, we restate the volatility process as follows:

$$dv(t) = [k\theta - (k+\lambda)v(t)]dt + \sigma\sqrt{v(t)}dw_2(t). \qquad (2.55)$$

To simplify the notations, we express the volatility process by

$$dv(t) = \kappa[\theta - v(t)]dt + \sigma\sqrt{v(t)}dw_2(t). \qquad (2.56)$$

Although the processes (2.53) and (2.56) are identical in form, we have to bear in mind that $\kappa$ in (2.56) is a risk-neutralized parameter. We now calculate the first CF:[17]

$$
\begin{aligned}
f_1(\phi) &= \mathbb{E}\left[\frac{S(T)}{S_0 e^{rT}}\exp\left(i\phi\ln S(T)\right)\right] \\
&= \exp[-rT - \ln S_0]\mathbb{E}\left[\exp((1+i\phi)x(T))\right] \\
&= \exp[-rT - \ln S_0]\exp[(1+i\phi)\ln S_0 + (1+i\phi)rT] \times \\
&\quad \mathbb{E}\left[\exp\left((1+i\phi)\left(-\int_0^T \frac{1}{2}v(t)dt + \int_0^T \sqrt{v(t)}dw_1(t)\right)\right)\right]
\end{aligned}
$$

Since $v(t)$ and $dw_1(t)$ are correlated in general, we make a decomposition of the Brownian motion $w_1(t)$, that is, we split $dw_1(t)$ into two independent components: $dw_1(t) = \rho dw_2(t) + \sqrt{1-\rho^2}dw(t)$, where Brownian motions $dw(t)$ and $dw_2(t)$ are mutually independent. Through this decomposition we can express $dw_1(t)$ by $dw_2(t)$ and another independent Brownian motion $w(t)$. Thus,

$$
\begin{aligned}
f_1(\phi) &= \exp[i\phi(\ln S_0 + rT)] \times \\
&\quad \mathbb{E}\left[\exp\left((1+i\phi)\left(-\int_0^T \frac{1}{2}v(t)dt + \rho\int_0^T \sqrt{v(t)}dw_2(t)\right.\right.\right. \\
&\quad \left.\left.\left. +\sqrt{1-\rho^2}\int_0^T \sqrt{v(t)}dw(t)\right)\right)\right]
\end{aligned}
$$

---

[17]In the following calculations, two techniques are employed. The first is the decomposition of a standard Brownian motion. If two standard Brownian motions $dw_1$ and $dw_2$ are correlated with $dw_1 dw_2 = \rho dt$, so $dw_1$ can be expressed as $dw_1 = \rho dw_2 + \sqrt{1-\rho^2}dw$ where $dw$ is correlated neither with $dw_1$ nor with $dw_2$. The second is the so-called Ito's isometry which says $Var[\int_0^T v(t)dw(t)] = \mathbb{E}[\int_0^T v^2(t)dt]$ with $v(t)$ as any Ito process.

$$= \exp[i\phi(\ln S_0 + rT)] \times \mathbb{E}\Big[\exp((1 + i\phi)$$

$$\times \left(-\frac{1}{2}\int_0^T v(t)dt + \frac{\rho}{\sigma}[v(T) - v_0 - \kappa\theta T + \kappa\int_0^T v(t)dt]\right)$$

$$\times \exp\left(\frac{1}{2}(1 + i\phi)^2(1 - \rho^2)\int_0^T v(t)dt\right)\Big].$$

In the last step, we took the conditional expectation value of the term $\exp\left((1 + i\phi)\sqrt{1 - \rho^2}\int_0^T \sqrt{v(t)}dw(t)\right)$, that is, the expectation operator works only under the probability law of $dw(t)$. A straightforward calculation using Ito's isometry leads to the above result. Additionally, we replace the term $\int_0^T \sqrt{v(t)}dw_2(t)$ by $[v(T) - v_0 - \kappa\theta T + \kappa\int_0^T v(t)dt]/\sigma$ because of the following equality:[18]

$$v(T) - v_0 = \kappa\theta T - \kappa\int_0^T v(t)dt + \sigma\int_0^T \sqrt{v(t)}dw_2(t). \qquad (2.57)$$

Therefore,

$$f_1(\phi)$$
$$= \exp[i\phi(\ln S_0 + rT) - \frac{\rho}{\sigma}(1 + i\phi)(v_0 + k\theta T)] \times$$
$$\mathbb{E}\left[\exp\left((1 + i\phi)\left(-\frac{1}{2} + \frac{\rho\kappa}{\sigma} + \frac{1}{2}(1 + i\phi)(1 - \rho^2)\right)\int_0^T v(t)dt\right)\right.$$
$$\left. + (1 + i\phi)\frac{\rho}{\sigma}v(T)\right)\Big]$$
$$= \exp\left(i\phi(\ln S_0 + rT) - s_2(v_0 + \kappa\theta T)\right) \times$$
$$\mathbb{E}\left[\exp\left(-s_1\int_0^T v(t)dt + s_2v(T)\right)\right]$$

$$(2.58)$$

with

$$s_1 = -(1 + i\phi)\left(-\frac{1}{2} + \frac{\rho\kappa}{\sigma} + \frac{1}{2}(1 + i\phi)(1 - \rho^2)\right),$$

$$s_2 = \frac{(1 + i\phi)\rho}{\sigma}.$$

---

[18] This equality is derived from a direct stochastic integration of process (2.5).

So far the calculation of $f_1(\phi)$ is reduced to the calculation of the expectation $y = \mathbb{E}\left[\exp\left(-s_1 \int_0^T v(t)dt + s_2 v(T)\right)\right]$, which is solvable by applying the Feynman-Kac formula. Let $\tau$ denote time to maturity, if $v(\tau)$ follows the mean-reverting square-root process, we obtain the following PDE:

$$\frac{\partial y}{\partial \tau} = -s_1 v y + \kappa(\theta - v)\frac{\partial y}{\partial v} + \frac{1}{2}\sigma^2 v \frac{\partial^2 y}{\partial v^2} \qquad (2.59)$$

with the boundary condition

$$y(v_0, 0) = \exp(s_2 v_0).$$

This one-dimensional PDE is easy to resolve and has the following solution:[19]

$$y(v, \tau) = \exp(A(\tau)v_0 + C(\tau)) \qquad (2.60)$$

with

$$A(\tau) = \frac{-(1 - e^{-\gamma_1 \tau})(2s_1 + \kappa s_2) + \gamma_1 s_2(1 + e^{-\gamma_1 \tau})}{\gamma_2},$$

$$C(\tau) = \frac{2\kappa\theta}{\sigma^2} \ln\left[\frac{2\gamma_1 \exp[\frac{1}{2}(\kappa - \gamma_1)\tau]}{\gamma_2}\right],$$

$$\gamma_1 = \sqrt{\kappa^2 + 2\sigma^2 s_1},$$

$$\gamma_2 = 2\gamma_1 e^{-\gamma_1 \tau} + (\kappa + \gamma_1 - \sigma^2 s_2)(1 - e^{-\gamma_1 \tau}).$$

Setting $s_1$ and $s_2$ into the functions $A(\tau)$ and $C(\tau)$, we get a closed-form expression for the CF $f_1(\phi)$. The second CF $f_2(\phi)$ is derived in the same fashion:

$$\begin{aligned}
f_2(\phi) &= \exp\left(i\phi(\ln S_0 + rT) - s_2^*(v_0 + \kappa\theta T)\right) \times \\
&\quad \mathbb{E}\left[\exp(-s_1^* \int_0^T v(t)dt + s_2^* v(T))\right] \\
&= \exp\left(i\phi(\ln S_0 + rT) - s_2^*(v_0 + \kappa\theta T)\right) \times \\
&\quad \exp\left(A(T; s_1^*, s_2^*)v_0 + C(T; s_1^*, s_2^*)\right) \qquad (2.61)
\end{aligned}$$

---

[19]Because the solution to this PDE is only a slight extension of the CIR zero-bond pricing formula, we do not discuss it in detail.

with

$$s_1^* = -i\phi \left( -\frac{1}{2} + \frac{\rho\kappa}{\sigma} + \frac{1}{2}i\phi(1-\rho^2) \right), \qquad s_2^* = \frac{i\phi\rho}{\sigma}.$$

The pricing formula for call options is then given by

$$C = S_0 F_1 - e^{-rT} K F_2$$

with

$$F_j = \frac{1}{2} + \frac{1}{\pi} \int_0^\infty \mathrm{Re} \left( f_j(\phi) \frac{\exp(-i\phi \ln K)}{i\phi} \right) d\phi, \quad j = 1, 2. \qquad (2.62)$$

Readers can verify that the above solution is identical to the one derived by Heston. By using put-call parity, we can obtain the pricing formula for put options:

$$P = e^{-rT} K F_2 - S_0 F_1$$

with

$$F_j = \frac{1}{2} - \frac{1}{\pi} \int_0^\infty \mathrm{Re} \left( f_j(\phi) \frac{\exp(-i\phi \ln K)}{i\phi} \right) d\phi, \quad j = 1, 2. \qquad (2.63)$$

Our method, inspired by Scott (1997), differs from Heston's method in that we reduce a two-dimensional PDE into a one-dimensional PDE by manipulation of the CFs. A manipulated CF provides us with a hint whether the CF possesses a closed-form solution. The Feynman-Kac formula is crucial in deriving the final form of the CFs. In the following sections, it will be used repeatedly to help us arrive at closed-form solutions.

The Heston model is reasonable because some necessary properties of stochastic volatility, for instance, mean-reversion, negative correlation and persistence of shocks to volatility, can be fulfilled in this model in spite of the fact that the modelling is not directly connected with volatility, but with squared volatility (variance). Therefore, it is sometimes difficult to discuss the properties of volatility, for instance, how great is the mean-level and reverting velocity of volatility itself. The following section attempts to fill this gap. The hedge ratios in the Heston model can be given analytically and it is convenient to use these results in risk management. Some popular hedge ratios are:

$$\Delta_S = \frac{\partial C}{\partial S_0} = F_1, \tag{2.64}$$

$$\Delta_v = \frac{\partial C}{\partial v_0} = S_0 \frac{\partial F_1}{\partial v_0} - e^{-rT} K \frac{\partial F_2}{\partial v_0}, \tag{2.65}$$

$$\Gamma_S = \frac{\partial^2 C}{\partial S_0^2} = \frac{\partial F_1}{\partial S_0}, \tag{2.66}$$

$$\Gamma_v = \frac{\partial^2 C}{\partial v_0^2} = S_0 \frac{\partial^2 F_1}{\partial v_0^2} - e^{-rT} K \frac{\partial^2 F_2}{\partial v_0^2}, \tag{2.67}$$

where for $h = S_0, v_0$ and $j = 1, 2$

$$\frac{\partial F_j}{\partial h} = \frac{1}{\pi} \int_0^\infty \text{Re}\left( \frac{\partial f_j(\phi)}{\partial h} \frac{\exp(-i\phi \ln K)}{i\phi} \right) d\phi, \quad j = 1, 2.$$

and

$$\frac{\partial^2 F_j}{\partial h_0^2} = \frac{1}{\pi} \int_0^\infty \text{Re}\left( \frac{\partial^2 f_j(\phi)}{\partial h^2} \frac{\exp(-i\phi \ln K)}{i\phi} \right) d\phi, \quad j = 1, 2.$$

Because the pricing formula (2.62) has already been discussed in detail in Heston (1993), BCC (1997), we do not present numerical examples here. Nandi (1998) examines the importance of correlation between stock returns and volatility in this model by testing the pricing and hedging in the S&P 500 index options market. It is found that non-zero correlation leads to significant improvements both in pricing options and in hedging by options, especially for out-of-the money options.

## 2.2.3   Ornstein-Uhlenbeck Process

In this subsection,[20] we consider a case where volatilities follow a mean-reverting Ornstein-Uhlenbeck process and are correlated with the stock returns. S&S (1991) have only given a quasi closed-form solution for options in the case of zero correlation. Suppose that the dynamics of volatility are described by

---

[20]This subsection is based on the joint paper of Schöbel and Zhu, entitled "Stochastic Volatility With an Ornstein-Uhlenbeck Process: An Extension" (1999).

$$dv(t) = \kappa[\theta - v(t)]dt + \sigma dw_2(t), \qquad (2.68)$$

which can be interpreted under the risk-neutral measure by applying the same argument used in the Heston model.[21] Then the risk-neutral process of $\ln S(t) = x(t)$ is

$$dx(t) = \left[r - \frac{1}{2}v^2(t)\right]dt + v(t)dw_1(t). \qquad (2.69)$$

Here we suggest that $dw_2$ and $dw_1$ are possibly correlated, $dw_1dw_2 = \rho dt$, which extends the S&S model and should generate a leptokurtic distributions of stock returns. As in the Vasicek (1977) model for interest rates , modelling stochastic volatility as a mean-reverting O-U process raises a possibility that the volatility could be negative. This feature is certainly of theoretical disadvantage, but from the practical point of view, it should not cause no serious problem. For the empirically consistent parameters in process (2.68), the probability for negative $v(t)$ is negligibly small.[22] Additionally, as shown later, we can always find a positive implied volatility for every positive $S(t)$ by using our option pricing formula. Thus, regarding the favorite features of the process (2.68) such as mean-reversion, persistence to shocks and relatively easy estimation of parameters due to the normal distribution, we consider this model as a good candidate for capturing the dynamics of volatility and for practical application.

According to the principle stated in Section 1.2, the CFs of the European call option have the form of

$$f_j(\phi) = \mathbb{E}^Q\left[g_j(T)\exp(i\phi x(T))\right], \quad j = 1, 2.$$

---

[21] According to the arguments in the Heston model, the risk premium is proportional to $v$, $\lambda(v) = \lambda v$ with $\lambda$ a constant (see footnote 2 in this section). S&S assumed $\lambda$ to be equal to zero. These two different interpretations of $\lambda$ do not change the form of the risk-neutralized process.

[22] Since an O-U process is Gaussian, the distribution of $v(T)$ conditional on $v_0$ is normal with the mean $a = \mathbb{E}[v(T)] = \theta + (v_0 - \theta)e^{-\kappa T}$ and variance $b^2 = \mathbb{V}[v(T)] = \frac{\sigma^2}{2\kappa}(1 - e^{-2\kappa T})$. Thus, the probability that $v(T)$ becomes negative is given by $P = N(-a/b)$. For example, setting $\kappa = 4, \theta = 0.2, \sigma = 0.1, T - t = 0.3$ and $v_0 = 0.2$ gives $P = 1.50 \times 10^{-9}$. Setting $\kappa = 1, \theta = 0.2, \sigma = 0.1, T - t = 0.5$ and $v_0 = 0.2$ gives $P = 1.87 \times 10^{-4}$. These probabilities are so small that it does not raise any serious problem at all.

with

$$g_1(T) = \exp(-rT)\frac{S(T)}{S_0}, \qquad g_2(T) = 1.$$

Despite of the correlation between $dw_1$ and $dw_2$, one can derive an analytical expression of the above expectation. As shown in Appendix A, using the same technique that has been shown in the above subsection, we obtain $f_1(\phi)$ which has the following form:

$$
\begin{aligned}
f_1(\phi) &= \exp\left(i\phi(rT + \ln S_0) - \frac{\rho}{2\sigma}(1+i\phi)v_0^2 - \frac{\sigma T}{2}(1+i\phi)\right) \times \\
&\quad \mathbb{E}\left[\exp -s_1 \int_0^T v^2(t)dt - s_2 \int_0^T v(t)dt + s_3 v^2(T)\right] \\
&= \exp\left(i\phi(rT + \ln S_0) - \frac{\rho}{2\sigma}(1+i\phi)v_0^2 - \frac{\rho\sigma T}{2}(1+i\phi)\right) \times \\
&\quad \exp\left(\frac{1}{2}D(T; s_1, s_3)v_0^2 + E(T; s_1, s_2, s_3)v_0 + F(T; s_1, s_2, s_3)\right)
\end{aligned}
$$

(2.70)

with

$$
\begin{aligned}
s_1 &= -\frac{1}{2}(1+i\phi)\left(i\phi - \rho^2 - i\phi\rho^2 + \frac{2\rho\kappa}{\sigma}\right), \\
s_2 &= \frac{\rho\kappa\theta}{\sigma}(1+i\phi), \qquad s_3 = \frac{\rho}{2\sigma}(1+i\phi).
\end{aligned}
$$

The functions $D(t)$, $E(t)$ and $F(t)$ are also derived in Appendix A. Similarly, $f_2(\phi)$ is given by

$$
\begin{aligned}
f_2(\phi) &= \exp\left(i\phi(rT + \ln S_0) - \frac{\rho}{2\sigma}i\phi v_0^2 - \frac{\sigma T}{2}i\phi\right) \times \\
&\quad \mathbb{E}\left[\exp\left(-s_1^* \int_0^T v^2(t)dt - s_2^* \int_0^T v(t)dt + s_3^* v^2(T)\right)\right] \\
&= \exp\left(i\phi(rT + \ln S_0) - \frac{\rho}{2\sigma}i\phi v_0^2 - \frac{\rho\sigma T}{2}i\phi\right) \times \\
&\quad \exp\left(\frac{1}{2}D(T; s_1^*, s_2^*, s_3^*)v_0^2 + B(T; s_1^*, s_2^*, s_3^*)v_0 + C(T; s_1^*, s_2^*, s_3^*)\right)
\end{aligned}
$$

(2.71)

with

$$s_1^* = -\frac{1}{2}i\phi\left(i\phi - 1 - i\phi\rho^2 + \frac{2\rho\kappa}{\sigma}\right),$$

$$s_2^* = \frac{\rho\kappa\theta}{\sigma}i\phi, \qquad s_3^* = \frac{\rho}{2\sigma}i\phi.$$

After the CFs are computed, the probabilities $F_1$ and $F_2$ can be correspondingly derived via Fourier inversion:

$$F_j = \frac{1}{2} + \frac{1}{\pi}\int_0^\infty \mathrm{Re}\left(f_j(\phi)\frac{\exp(-i\phi\ln K)}{i\phi}\right)d\phi, \quad j = 1, 2. \qquad (2.72)$$

The formula for European-style puts can be derived through the usage of put-call parity. Formula (2.72) is more general than S&S since here the volatilities are correlated with the stock prices. Furthermore, our closed-form solution has a clear structure and gives the two probabilities $F_1$ and $F_2$ directly. Hence, the hedge ratio $\Delta$ and other Greeks can also be given analytically. In contrast, one would have difficulty in deriving these ratios from the formula of S&S. Some popular hedge ratios are:

$$\Delta_S = \frac{\partial C}{\partial S_0} = F_1, \qquad (2.73)$$

$$\Delta_v = \frac{\partial C}{\partial v_0} = S_0\frac{\partial F_1}{\partial v_0} - e^{-rT}K\frac{\partial F_2}{\partial v_0}, \qquad (2.74)$$

$$\Gamma_S = \frac{\partial^2 C}{\partial S_0^2} = \frac{\partial F_1}{\partial S_0}, \qquad (2.75)$$

$$\Gamma_v = \frac{\partial^2 C}{\partial v_0^2} = S_0\frac{\partial^2 F_1}{\partial v_0^2} - e^{-rT}K\frac{\partial^2 F_2}{\partial v_0^2}, \qquad (2.76)$$

where for $h = S_0, v_0$ and $j = 1, 2$

$$\frac{\partial F_j}{\partial h} = \frac{1}{\pi}\int_0^\infty \mathrm{Re}\left(\frac{\partial f_j(\phi)}{\partial h}\frac{\exp(-i\phi\ln K)}{i\phi}\right)d\phi, \quad j = 1, 2.$$

and

$$\frac{\partial^2 F_j}{\partial h^2} = \frac{1}{\pi}\int_0^\infty \mathrm{Re}\left(\frac{\partial^2 f_j(\phi)}{\partial h^2}\frac{\exp(-i\phi\ln K)}{i\phi}\right)d\phi, \quad j = 1, 2.$$

Our results on hedge ratios are similar to those in BCC (1997). While Heston (1993), Bates (1994) and BCC (1997) got $f_j(\phi)$ via two-dimensional partial differential equations, as shown in the Appendix, the key technique is that we separate the volatility shocks in two components by decomposition of the Brownian motion $w_2(t)$: the shocks orthogonal to stock prices, and the shocks perfectly correlated with stock prices. Thanks to this manipulation, we only need to solve a one-dimensional PDE using the Feynman-Kač theorem after reducing the explicit form of $f_j(\phi)$ to a one-dimensional problem. Note that $\ln f_j(\phi)$ are square functions of $v(t)$ in (2.70) and (2.71). If we calculate the implied volatility using the option pricing formula (2.72), we can always find a positive $v(t)$ for any given market data although there also exists a negative $v(t)$. It is logical to choose positive $v(t)$ as implied volatility not only for merely economic reasons, but also because, given empirical consistent $\kappa$, $\theta$ and $\sigma$, the probability for positive volatility is almost one.

Ball and Roma (1994) discussed the difference between the absolute value process of $v(t)$ and the reflected process of $v(t)$, and claimed that S&S used the absolute value process since "the volatility enters option pricing only as $v^2(t)$". Unfortunately, their claim is incorrect. Firstly, in fact, volatility enters the option pricing formula both in the S&S model and in our model explicitly not only as $v^2(t)$, but also as $v(t)$. This is obvious in the equation (B6) for any function $M_1 \neq 0$ in S&S (1991). In our model, setting $\rho = 0$ does not let the function $B(t,T)$ in (2.70) and (2.71) vanish. Secondly, if we are working with an absolute value process, we can expect the same option prices for $|v(t)| = v$. But we do not get the same option prices for this case applying both S&S formula and our pricing formula. Finally, most rigorously, Schöbel and Zhu (1999) show that (i) for arbitrary values of the long-term mean $\theta \neq 0$, the absolute value O-U process, the reflected O-U process and the unrestricted O-U process are substantially different; however, (ii) only for the special (symmetric) case $\theta = 0$ the reflecting barrier process coincides with the absolute value process; (iii) the density function derived by applying the same backward equation in S&S and in our model is identical to the one for the unrestricted O-U process and does not satisfy the boundary condition which is necessary for an absolute value process. All of these arguments contradict Ball and Roma's claim.

We compare now our model with Heston's solution. Looking at the processes (2.68) and (2.52) again, we find that the only difference between them is the mean-reversion parameter $\theta$. While $\theta$ in (2.68) generally differs from zero, $\theta$ in (2.52) is always zero. Since $\theta$ gives a level that a volatility approaches in a long run, process (2.52) does not seem to be very reasonable. Therefore, this restricted Heston model can be considered as a special case of our model in the sense of equations (2.52) and (2.53). Our model is reduced to the Heston model by setting the following parameters:

$$\kappa = \frac{\kappa_h}{2}, \quad \sigma = \frac{\sigma_h}{2}, \quad \theta = 0, \quad \theta_h = \frac{\sigma^2}{\kappa_h}. \tag{2.77}$$

where $\kappa_h, \sigma_h$ and $\theta_h$ stand for the parameters in process (2.52). However, note that the parameters in process (2.53) are overdetermined by (2.77), then for a wide range of the values of $\kappa_h, \sigma_h$ and $\theta_h$, the volatility process (2.53) can not be derived from (2.52). This means that (2.52) and (2.53) are not mutually consistent for many parameter values. Hence, in this sense, the Heston model is not a special case of our model. A favorite property of our model is that both volatility and the square of volatility perform the mean-reversion, but in Heston's model, only the square of volatility follows a mean-reverting process.[23]

Here we calibrate our model based on formula (2.72). For comparison, we shall choose the suitable Black-Scholes (BS) option prices as benchmark. The first possible benchmark is the BS price using the expected average variance $AV$ in equation (2.50) as input. As shown in Ball and Roma (1994), if $v(t)$ follows a mean-reverting O-U process, we have

$$AV = \frac{\sigma^2}{2\kappa} + \theta^2 + \frac{1}{T}\left(\frac{2\theta(v_0 - \theta)}{\kappa}(1 - e^{-\kappa T}) - \frac{\sigma^2 - 2\kappa(v_0 - \theta)^2}{4\kappa^2}(1 - e^{-2\kappa T})\right). \tag{2.78}$$

---

[23] Applying Ito's lemma once again, one can get the process of $v(t) = \sqrt{y(t)}$ :

$$dv(t) = [\frac{1}{2}(\kappa_h\theta_h - \frac{1}{4}\sigma_h^2)v(t)^{-1} - \frac{1}{2}\kappa_h v(t)]dt + \frac{1}{2}\sigma_h dw.$$

Obviously, if (26) is not satisfied, $\kappa_h\theta_h - \frac{1}{4}\sigma_h^2$ will not be zero. Hence the term $v(t)^{-1}$ will appear in the volatility process which seems to be doubtful. Consequently, the specification of $y(t) = v(t)^2$ such as (25) must be also carefully examined.

We denote the BS prices evaluated in this manner by $BS_1$. The second alternative as in S&S is to calculate the BS option prices according to the spot volatility $v(t)$ with $\kappa, \rho$ and $\sigma$ nil. The calculated BS prices called $BS_2$ are identical to these prices by using the BS formula with a constant volatility $v(t)$ being equal to $\theta$. Heston (1993) uses the BS prices with a volatility which equates the square root of variance of the spot stock returns up to maturity. His benchmark is then dependent on the correlation $\rho$ and makes comparisons remarkably complicated.[24] It is difficult to say which benchmark is better. Evaluating $BS_1$ has an implication that volatility follows a stochastic process and is not constant. This is in contradiction with the BS's assumption. In this sense, $BS_1$ is not a logical consistent but only *ad hoc* BS value. In contrast, $BS_2$ implies that the volatility keeps constant and equates the initial value $v(t)$. Perhaps we should take the practical use of the BS formula into account in this issue. That is, how do practitioners apply the BS formula? Use historical average variance or spot variance (volatility)? The answer to this question is obviously ambiguous. Consequently, both $BS_1$ and $BS_2$ might (not) be a right benchmark for comparison with the exact option prices.

In Table 2.3, we choose the parameters suggested by S&S. In order to show the impact of correlation on the option prices, let $\rho$ range from -1.0 to 1.0. Some observations are in order. First of all, options with different moneyness have different sensitivity to the correlation $\rho$. The values of at-the-money (ATM) options do not change remarkably overall. However, the sensitivity of out-of-the-money (OTM) options to $\rho$ is more conspicuous than of in-the-money (ITM) options. For example, in Panel C the relative changes of the OTM option prices due to the correlation $\rho$ for $K = 120$ is about $\pm 14\%$ of the S&S value which is here 2.635.

Secondly, a comparison of Panels A, B and C shows that the mean-reversion level $\theta$ is important for the pricing of options. Keeping other parameters unchanged, the differential $(\theta - v)$ (mean-reversion level minus current volatility) has a great impact on the option values. From Panel A to C, $(\theta - v)$ is 0, -0.1 and 0.1 respectively, and the differences in option prices across these panels are mostly between 0.60\$ and 1.50\$. Since the

---

[24]Since Heston's BS benchmark is a function of the correlation $\rho$, every model option value has a corresponding Heston's benchmark. Thus, we will lose some clarity in comparison if using Heston's benchmark although it is reasonable in some senses.

expectation of the future spot price volatility approaches $\theta$, the prices of options, especially the options with a long-term maturity, should be mainly affected by $\theta$.

Thirdly, as expected, we find the price differences between $BS_1$ and the model values with $\rho = 0$ are smallest for all panels. This confirms Ball and Roma's finding. The good fit of these two values is not surprising since $BS_1$ is by nature an approximation for the exact option value with $\rho = 0$. Panel D in Table 2.3 presents all $BS_1$ values corresponding to Panels E-G. We can see that the $BS_1$ values in Panel D agree very well with the option values in Panel F. However, if $\rho \neq 0$, the price bias between $BS_1$ values and the exact option values are significant. Thus, $BS_1$ is not a suitable approximation for the correlation case. It is also not surprising that the $BS_2$ values match our model values closely for Panel A where $\theta = v$. S&S report an overall overvaluation relative to $BS_2$ due to stochastic volatility. This upward pricing bias should be caused by the zero correlation assumption between volatility and its underlying asset returns in S&S. For $\rho = 0$ the direction of the movement of $S(t)$ is not affected by stochastic volatility, and any stochastic volatility raises only the additional uncertainty of $S(t)$. Consequently, S&S and $BS_1$ values are greater than $BS_2$ values in Panel A.

Finally, ITM options and OTM options react to correlation just oppositely. Whereas ITM options ($K = 90, 95$) decrease in value with increasing correlation $\rho$, OTM option prices ($K = 105, 110, 115, 120$) go up. This finding is consistent with Hull's (1997, pages 492-500) excellent intuitive explanation of how correlation affects option prices. It is also empirically evident that stock returns are inversely correlated with the underlying volatilities. Panels A to C show that a negative correlation $\rho$ leads to ITM (OTM) option prices in our model that are greater (less) than the corresponding BS option prices. This feature caused by negative correlation is useful for explaining volatility "sneers". For example, Figure 2.1 in Subsection 2.2.1 illustrates the pattern in the implied volatility of DAX calls. The "smile" pattern is most of the time not so obvious and appears to be more of a "sneer". The monotonic downward sloping of the implied volatility with moneyness displayed in a "sneer" implies that the market ITM (OTM) options are undervalued (overvalued) by the BS formula. This pattern of pricing biases in the BS formula is reported by a number of empirical studies as in Nandi (1998), Heston and

Nandi (1997), BCC (1997) and MacBeth and Merville (1979). Figure 2.2
shows the calibrated implied volatilities in Panel A where the downward
sloping of implied volatility for $\rho < 0$ is significant. The good fit of our
calibrated examples to the empirical picture supports that incorporating correlation between stock returns and volatilities is a promising way
to improve the performance of option pricing. BCC (1997) and Nandi
(1998) reported that taking stochastic volatility into account is of first-
order importance in eliminating the volatility inconsistence and leads to
significant improvements in hedging performance, but only in the presence of non-zero correlation. Their results should also be valid for our
model.

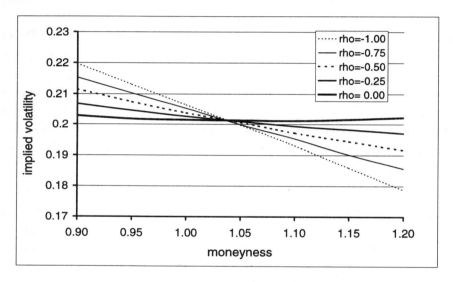

Figure 2.2: Volatility smile (sneer) pattern for the negative and zero
correlations. Calibrated from Panel A in Table 3.3.

In Table 2.4, we examine how the option prices vary with the mean-
reverting level $\theta$. The finding that option prices are very sensible to
$\theta$ is confirmed. Since $\theta$ indicates the long-term level of volatility, this
sensitivity can be considered as the sensitivity of option prices to their
volatilities in the long run. Furthermore, it seems to be that $\theta$ is more
important than the spot volatility $v(t)$ for the pricing of options in the
framework of a mean-reverting process. If the true process of volatility
performs mean-reversion, and option prices are evaluated using the BS

formula regardless of $BS_1$ or $BS_2$, a significant pricing bias will occur although the magnitude of the pricing bias for $BS_1$ is smaller than that for $BS_2$. All prices in Panel F correspond to the case of S&S. The numbers in the first row in panels D, E, F and G are option prices under the restricted Heston model in the sense of equations (2.52) and (2.53). The implied zero level of the mean-reversion leads to an overall undervaluation of options compared with $BS_2$.

Table 2.5 demonstrates the impact of $\rho$ on Delta $\Delta_S$ which is of first-order importance for hedging purposes whenever stochastic volatility models are used. Firstly, for the given parameters almost all of the Deltas are decreasing with correlation $\rho$ except for a few deep-ITM and deep-OTM options across the three Panels H, I and J. Secondly, the changes of values of near-ATM options relative to the correlation $\rho$ are more sensitive than these of deep-ITM and deep-OTM options. The differences between $\Delta_S$ in our model and the BS model ($BS_1$ and $BS_2$) for near-ATM options should not be neglected. For a negative correlation, using $\Delta_S$ of the BS formula and the S&S model seems to cause a severe underhedging for near-ATM options and some OTM options. Furthermore, the long-term level of volatility $\theta$ is also important for hedging. Keeping other parameters unchanged, the greater $\theta$ is, the smaller (greater) $\Delta_S$ will be for ITM (OTM) options. The sensitivity of $\Delta_S$ to $\theta$ is remarkable and can be studied more detailed by the second derivative $\Delta_{S\theta}$. We conclude that an unbiased estimate of $\theta$ is crucial for Delta-hedging.

Stochastic volatility option pricing models provide us with new insights into derivative security markets. In this section, we have derived a closed-form pricing formula for the general case where volatility is allowed to display arbitrary correlation with the underlying stock price. In comparison with the Heston model, this specification for volatility performs additional properties such as a direct link to volatility instead of variance, easy estimation of parameters in a Gaussian framework. Calibrating this model illustrates that it is very promising to eliminate inconsistence of implied volatility in the BS model by incorporating the correlation between stock returns and volatilities. We correct an error in Ball and Roma (1994) and show that S&S (1991) and we here work with an unrestricted mean-reverting O-U process.[25]

---

[25]For the detailed discussion on the Ball and Roma's fallacy see Schöbel and Zhu (1999).

| $\rho$ \ $K$ | 90 | 95 | 100 | 105 | 110 | 115 | 120 |
|---|---|---|---|---|---|---|---|
| BS$_2$ | 15.118 | 11.342 | 8.142 | 5.584 | 3.658 | 2.293 | 1.377 |
| BS$_1$ | 15.152 | 11.391 | 8.203 | 5.650 | 3.722 | 2.349 | 1.422 |
| -1.00 | 15.416 | 11.617 | 8.307 | 5.576 | 3.468 | 1.966 | 0.995 |
| -0.75 | 15.355 | 11.562 | 8.275 | 5.585 | 3.525 | 2.063 | 1.110 |
| -0.50 | 15.292 | 11.503 | 8.243 | 5.595 | 3.582 | 2.156 | 1.218 |
| -0.25 | 15.225 | 11.443 | 8.210 | 5.606 | 3.638 | 2.246 | 1.321 |
| 0.00 | 15.155* | 11.379* | 8.176* | 5.617* | 3.694* | 2.333* | 1.420* |
| 0.25 | 15.081 | 11.313 | 8.141 | 5.628 | 3.749 | 2.416 | 1.514 |
| 0.50 | 15.003 | 11.243 | 8.106 | 5.640 | 3.803 | 2.497 | 1.605 |
| 0.75 | 14.919 | 11.169 | 8.070 | 5.652 | 3.856 | 2.576 | 1.693 |
| 1.00 | 14.828 | 11.092 | 8.034 | 5.665 | 3.909 | 2.653 | 1.777 |

A: $\theta = 0.2, \kappa = 4, \sigma = 0.1, v = 0.2, T = 0.5, S = 100, r = 0.0953$

| $\rho$ \ $K$ | 90 | 95 | 100 | 105 | 110 | 115 | 120 |
|---|---|---|---|---|---|---|---|
| BS$_1$ | 14.501 | 10.348 | 6.829 | 4.132 | 2.282 | 1.150 | 0.530 |
| -1.00 | 14.730 | 10.600 | 6.976 | 4.057 | 1.977 | 0.739 | 0.179 |
| -0.75 | 14.679 | 10.541 | 6.936 | 4.066 | 2.051 | 0.853 | 0.279 |
| -0.50 | 14.626 | 10.480 | 6.894 | 4.075 | 2.121 | 0.957 | 0.371 |
| -0.25 | 14.572 | 10.415 | 6.849 | 4.085 | 2.189 | 1.053 | 0.458 |
| 0.00 | 14.515* | 10.346* | 6.803* | 4.093* | 2.254* | 1.144* | 0.542* |
| 0.25 | 14.456 | 10.271 | 6.753 | 4.102 | 2.316 | 1.230 | 0.621 |
| 0.50 | 14.495 | 10.191 | 6.701 | 4.110 | 2.376 | 1.311 | 0.698 |
| 0.75 | 14.330 | 10.103 | 6.645 | 4.117 | 2.433 | 1.389 | 0.773 |
| 1.00 | 14.261 | 10.005 | 6.587 | 4.125 | 2.489 | 1.463 | 0.845 |

B: $\theta = 0.1, \kappa = 4, \sigma = 0.1, v = 0.2, T = 0.5, S = 100, r = 0.0953$

| $\rho$ \ $K$ | 90 | 95 | 100 | 105 | 110 | 115 | 120 |
|---|---|---|---|---|---|---|---|
| BS$_1$ | 16.111 | 12.666 | 9.711 | 7.264 | 5.305 | 3.786 | 2.646 |
| -1.00 | 16.357 | 12.846 | 9.777 | 7.186 | 5.084 | 3.449 | 2.235 |
| -0.75 | 16.298 | 12.800 | 9.755 | 7.198 | 5.133 | 3.531 | 2.340 |
| -0.50 | 16.236 | 12.751 | 9.732 | 7.210 | 5.182 | 3.611 | 2.441 |
| -0.25 | 16.172 | 12.702 | 9.710 | 7.223 | 5.230 | 3.690 | 2.540 |
| 0.00 | 16.106* | 12.651* | 9.687* | 7.237* | 5.279* | 3.768* | 2.635* |
| 0.25 | 16.037 | 12.598 | 9.665 | 7.251 | 5.328 | 3.844 | 2.728 |
| 0.50 | 15.964 | 12.544 | 9.642 | 7.265 | 5.377 | 3.919 | 2.819 |
| 0.75 | 15.889 | 12.489 | 9.620 | 7.280 | 5.426 | 3.993 | 2.908 |
| 1.00 | 15.810 | 12.432 | 9.598 | 7.296 | 5.475 | 4.065 | 2.994 |

C: $\theta = 0.3, \kappa = 4, \sigma = 0.1, v = 0.2, T = 0.5, S = 100, r = 0.0953$

The numbers with * correspond to the model of S&S.

Table 2.3.   The impact of $\rho$ on option prices.

As discussed earlier, the negligibly small possibilities for negative volatilities in such a process do not raise a serious problem in option pricing. Additionally, since in a diffusion context negative volatilities only mean that upward moves of the driving Brownian motion become downward moves of the stock price and vice versa, we believe that this is not a severe theoretical restriction and suggest this new closed-form pricing formula as an alternative to Heston's solution: Not surprisingly, squared volatilities never become negative here either.

| $\theta$ \\ $K$ | 90 | 95 | 100 | 105 | 110 | 115 | 120 |
|---|---|---|---|---|---|---|---|
| BS$_2$ | 14.515 | 10.374 | 6.867 | 4.175 | 2.322 | 1.180 | 0.550 |
| 0.0 | 14.194* | 9.510* | 5.277* | 2.213* | 0.654* | 0.132* | 0.018* |
| 0.1 | 14.333 | 9.990 | 6.282 | 3.499 | 1.708 | 0.728 | 0.272 |
| 0.2 | 14.864 | 10.962 | 7.662 | 5.060 | 3.155 | 1.859 | 1.037 |
| 0.3 | 15.757 | 12.213 | 9.187 | 6.707 | 4.755 | 3.278 | 2.200 |

D: The BS$_1$ values using the expected average volatility as input
$\kappa = 4, \sigma = 0.1, v = 0.15, T = 0.5, S = 100, r = 0.0953$

| $\theta$ \\ $K$ | 90 | 95 | 100 | 105 | 110 | 115 | 120 |
|---|---|---|---|---|---|---|---|
| 0.0 | 14.189* | 9.459* | 5.141* | 2.173* | 0.763* | 0.244* | 0.075* |
| 0.1 | 14.262 | 9.842 | 6.132 | 3.466 | 1.812 | 0.895 | 0.425 |
| 0.2 | 14.723 | 10.804 | 7.551 | 5.044 | 3.239 | 2.014 | 1.220 |
| 0.3 | 15.608 | 12.082 | 9.109 | 6.703 | 4.828 | 3.414 | 2.376 |

E: $\rho = 0.5, \kappa = 4, \sigma = 0.1, v = 0.15, T = 0.5, S = 100, r = 0.0953$

| $\theta$ \\ $K$ | 90 | 95 | 100 | 105 | 110 | 115 | 120 |
|---|---|---|---|---|---|---|---|
| 0.0 | 14.200* | 9.527* | 5.267* | 2.170* | 0.645* | 0.150* | 0.030* |
| 0.1 | 14.351 | 9,997 | 6.254 | 3.451 | 1.679 | 0.731 | 0.292 |
| 0.2 | 14.871 | 10.952 | 7.632 | 5.022 | 2.124 | 1.845 | 1.040 |
| 0.3 | 15.754 | 12.198 | 9.161 | 6.676 | 4.727 | 3.259 | 2.192 |

F: $\rho = 0.0, \kappa = 4, \sigma = 0.1, v = 0.15, T = 0.5, S = 100, r = 0.0953$

| $\theta$ \\ $K$ | 90 | 95 | 100 | 105 | 110 | 115 | 120 |
|---|---|---|---|---|---|---|---|
| 0.0 | 14.225* | 9.600* | 5.372* | 2.152* | 0.504* | 0.061* | 0.004* |
| 0.1 | 14.441 | 10.130 | 6.361 | 3.435 | 1.529 | 0.545 | 0.155 |
| 0.2 | 15.003 | 11.084 | 7.710 | 5.003 | 3.004 | 1.660 | 0.842 |
| 0.3 | 15.887 | 12.306 | 9.213 | 6.652 | 4.626 | 3.097 | 1.995 |

G: $\rho = -0.5, \kappa = 4, \sigma = 0.1, v = 0.15, T = 0.5, S = 100, r = 0.0953$
The numbers with * correspond to the restricted Heston model.

Table 2.4. The impact of $\theta$ on option prices.

| $\rho$ \ $K$ | 90 | 95 | 100 | 105 | 110 | 115 | 120 |
|---|---|---|---|---|---|---|---|
| BS$_2$ | 0.8755 | 0.7795 | 0.6582 | 0.5249 | 0.3950 | 0.2807 | 0.1890 |
| BS$_1$ | 0.8731 | 0.7773 | 0.6571 | 0.5253 | 0.3968 | 0.2836 | 0.1922 |
| -1.00 | 0.8751 | 0.7949 | 0.6895 | 0.5644 | 0.4299 | 0.3002 | 0.1883 |
| -0.75 | 0.8708 | 0.7916 | 0.6825 | 0.5547 | 0.4204 | 0.2941 | 0.1881 |
| -0.50 | 0.8751 | 0.7881 | 0.6751 | 0.5449 | 0.4113 | 0.2889 | 0.1883 |
| -0.25 | 0.8752 | 0.7844 | 0.6673 | 0.5350 | 0.4027 | 0.2843 | 0.1887 |
| 0.00 | 0.8754* | 0.7802* | 0.6591* | 0.5251* | 0.3945* | 0.2802* | 0.1891* |
| 0.25 | 0.8756 | 0.7757 | 0.6504 | 0.5153 | 0.3868 | 0.2765 | 0.1896 |
| 0.50 | 0.8759 | 0.7707 | 0.6413 | 0.5055 | 0.3795 | 0.2732 | 0.1899 |
| 0.75 | 0.8761 | 0.7649 | 0.6317 | 0.4957 | 0.3725 | 0.2701 | 0.1904 |
| 1.00 | 0.8761 | 0.7584 | 0.6216 | 0.4862 | 0.3659 | 0.2673 | 0.1907 |

H: $\theta = 0.2, \kappa = 4, \sigma = 0.1, v = 0.2, T = 0.5, S = 100, r = 0.0953$

| $\rho$ \ $K$ | 90 | 95 | 100 | 105 | 110 | 115 | 120 |
|---|---|---|---|---|---|---|---|
| BS$_1$ | 0.9344 | 0.8401 | 0.6937 | 0.5166 | 0.3440 | 0.2047 | 0.1093 |
| -1.00 | 0.9246 | 0.8490 | 0.7302 | 0.5684 | 0.3816 | 0.2048 | 0.0763 |
| -0.75 | 0.9267 | 0.8479 | 0.7229 | 0.5554 | 0.3694 | 0.2025 | 0.0867 |
| -0.50 | 0.9293 | 0.8467 | 0.7151 | 0.5424 | 0.3584 | 0.2012 | 0.0947 |
| -0.25 | 0.9323 | 0.8456 | 0.7068 | 0.5293 | 0.3485 | 0.2003 | 0.1012 |
| 0.00 | 0.9359* | 0.8445* | 0.6978* | 0.5163* | 0.3395* | 0.1996* | 0.1065* |
| 0.25 | 0.9403 | 0.8433 | 0.6881 | 0.5033 | 0.3311 | 0.1989 | 0.1111 |
| 0.50 | 0.9458 | 0.8421 | 0.6774 | 0.4903 | 0.3234 | 0.1982 | 0.1149 |
| 0.75 | 0.9530 | 0.8404 | 0.6656 | 0.4773 | 0.3163 | 0.1975 | 0.1182 |
| 1.00 | 0.9629 | 0.8379 | 0.6526 | 0.4645 | 0.3095 | 0.1967 | 0.1211 |

I: $\theta = 0.1, \kappa = 4, \sigma = 0.1, v = 0.2, T = 0.5, S = 100, r = 0.0953$

| $\rho$ \ $K$ | 90 | 95 | 100 | 105 | 110 | 115 | 120 |
|---|---|---|---|---|---|---|---|
| BS$_1$ | 0.8225 | 0.7358 | 0.6373 | 0.5341 | 0.4334 | 0.3410 | 0.2606 |
| -1.00 | 0.8317 | 0.7552 | 0.6646 | 0.5644 | 0.4606 | 0.3599 | 0.2682 |
| -0.75 | 0.8300 | 0.7512 | 0.6584 | 0.5568 | 0.4532 | 0.3541 | 0.2652 |
| -0.50 | 0.8282 | 0.7469 | 0.6519 | 0.5492 | 0.4459 | 0.3487 | 0.2626 |
| -0.25 | 0.8264 | 0.7424 | 0.6452 | 0.5416 | 0.4389 | 0.3437 | 0.2604 |
| 0.00 | 0.8243* | 0.7376* | 0.6383* | 0.5339* | 0.4322* | 0.3390* | 0.2584* |
| 0.25 | 0.8221 | 0.7324 | 0.6311 | 0.5263 | 0.4256 | 0.3347 | 0.2566 |
| 0.50 | 0.8196 | 0.7269 | 0.6237 | 0.5187 | 0.4193 | 0.3306 | 0.2550 |
| 0.75 | 0.8169 | 0.7210 | 0.6162 | 0.5112 | 0.4133 | 0.3267 | 0.2536 |
| 1.00 | 0.8137 | 0.7147 | 0.6084 | 0.5038 | 0.4074 | 0.3231 | 0.2522 |

J: $\theta = 0.3, \kappa = 4, \sigma = 0.1, v = 0.2, T = 0.5, S = 100, r = 0.0953$

The numbers with * correspond to the model of S&S.

Table 2.5.  The impact of $\rho$ on Delta $\Delta_S$.

## 2.2.4 Double Square Root Process

In this subsection, we consider a new variant where the squared volatility is specified as a double square root process. This process was originally introduced by Longstaff (1989) to model stochastic interest rates.[26] Here we use it to model stochastic variance. Heston (1993) considered also the stochastic volatility model with double square root process in his appendix, but did not give an explicit solution for options. Following the method in his paper, we find that it leads to a rather cumbersome procedure and can not decompose the PDEs into several ordinary differential equations which can be solved successively. Here we will give an explicit solution by applying stochastic calculus. In fact, the generator of a double square root process is a Brownian motion or a mean-reverting O-U process.[27] To see this, we assume that volatility $\eta(t)$ (This notation is only for this subsection) is governed by the following process:

$$d\eta(t) = \mu dt + \varepsilon dw_2(t), \tag{2.79}$$

where $\mu$ and $\varepsilon$ are constant, and $dw_1 dw_2 = \rho dt$. Applying Ito's lemma yields the dynamics of the variance:

$$
\begin{aligned}
d\eta^2(t) &= [\varepsilon^2 + 2\mu\eta(t)]dt + 2\varepsilon\eta(t)dw_2(t) \\
&= \kappa[\theta - \eta(t)]dt + \sigma d\eta(t)w_2(t)
\end{aligned}
$$

with

$$\kappa = -2\mu, \qquad \kappa\theta = \varepsilon^2, \qquad \sigma = 2\varepsilon.$$

Let $v(t) = \eta^2(t)$ denote the squared volatility, we then arrive at a process of $v(t)$ as follows:

$$dv(t) = \kappa\left[\theta - \sqrt{v(t)}\right]dt + \sigma\sqrt{v(t)}dw_2(t). \tag{2.80}$$

---

[26]There are some incorrect statements on the double square root process in Longstaff's (1989) paper. More about the double square root process in Subsection 2.3.4

[27]Heston (1993) considered also the stochastic volatility model with double square root process in his appendix, but did not give an explicit solution for options. Following the method in his paper, we find that it leads to a rather cumbersome procedure and can not decompose the PDEs into several ordinary differential equations which should be solved successively. In this subsection, we will give an explicit solution by applying stochastic calculus.

Since two square root terms appear in this process, it is thus referred to as double square root process. The necessary condition for generating process (2.80) is the restriction $\sigma^2 = 4\kappa\theta$ with which some special expectations of $v(t)$ can be calculated analytically. Additionally, zero is an accessible boundary under this restriction.[28] Since the above process has the same random term as the process (2.56) in Section 2.2.2, we introduce an identical market price of risk as in the Heston model, i.e., $\lambda(t) = \lambda v(t)$. This interpretation of $\lambda$ leads to the following risk-neutral process:

$$dv(t) = \left[\frac{1}{4}\sigma^2 - \kappa\sqrt{v(t)} - \lambda v(t)\right] dt + \sigma\sqrt{v(t)}dw_2(t). \qquad (2.81)$$

Compared with process (2.53) in the Heston model, the double square root process has some distinct features. The mean level of variance here does not take an unambiguous value since the constant $\frac{1}{4}\sigma^2$ measures the long term level of $\kappa\sqrt{v(t)} + \lambda v(t)$. This mixed structure of the drift does not provides us with an exact information on future levels of both volatility and variance. Due to the restriction $\sigma^2 = 4\kappa\theta$, it seems that $\frac{1}{4}\sigma^2$ as long term value of $(\kappa\sqrt{v(t)} + \lambda v(t))$ is small in many cases. For example, for $\sigma = 0.5$ and $v_0 = 0.2$, the reasonable values of $\kappa$ should not be larger than 1. This means that volatility shocks to stock price process are rather persistent and the process of volatility is stable. Another possible drawback of this model is that, as mentioned above, the generating process of (2.80) is a Brownian motion with drift and therefore is not stationary, hence such specifications of volatility and variance are not tenable from *a priori* theoretical consideration. On the other hand, we have one parameter less to estimate empirically because of the above parameter restriction.

It is not hard to obtain the following two CFs for the double square root process:

$$\begin{aligned}
&f_1(\phi) \\
&= \mathbb{E}\left[\frac{S(T)}{S_0 e^{rT}} \exp\left(i\phi\ln S(T)\right)\right]
\end{aligned}$$

---

[28] When $0 < \sigma^2 < \kappa\theta$, zero value of $v(t)$ is inaccessible and no boundary condition can be imposed at zero. When $0 < \kappa\theta < \sigma^2$, zero is accessible. See Longstaff (1992).

$$= \exp\left[i\phi(\ln S_0 + rT) - \frac{(1+i\phi)\rho}{\sigma}(v_0 + \kappa\theta T)\right] \times$$

$$\mathbb{E}\left[\exp\left(-\frac{(1+i\phi)}{2}\left(1 - (1+i\phi)(1-\rho^2) - \frac{2\lambda\rho}{\sigma}\right)\int_0^T v(t)dt + \right.\right.$$

$$\left.\left.\frac{(1+i\phi)\kappa\rho}{\sigma}\int_0^T \sqrt{v(t)}dt + \frac{(1+i\phi)\rho}{\sigma}v(T)\right)\right]$$

$$= \exp\left(i\phi(\ln S_0 + rT) - s_3(v_0 + \kappa\theta T)\right) \times$$

$$\mathbb{E}\left[\exp\left(-s_1\int_0^T v(t)dt - s_2\int_0^T \sqrt{v(t)}dt + s_3 v(T)\right)\right]$$

$$= \exp\left(i\phi(\ln S_0 + rT) - s_3(v_0 + \kappa\theta T)\right) \times$$

$$\exp\left(G(T; s_1, s_2, s_3)v_0 + H(T; s_1, s_2, s_3)\sqrt{v_0} + I(T; s_1, s_2, s_3)\right)$$

$$(2.82)$$

with

$$s_1 = \frac{(1+i\phi)}{2}\left(1 - (1+i\phi)(1-\rho^2) - \frac{2\lambda\rho}{\sigma}\right),$$

$$s_2 = -\frac{(1+i\phi)\kappa\rho}{\sigma}, \qquad s_3 = \frac{(1+i\phi)\rho}{\sigma}.$$

Thus, the whole problem is reduced to computing the expectation value in the last equality, which can be solved by our standard method. The functions $G(T)$, $H(T)$ and $I(T)$ are given in Appendix B The explicit form of $f_1(\phi)$ has a complex structure, but is expressed in a closed-form manner by elementary functions. Similarly, we have

$$f_2(\phi) = \mathbb{E}\left[\exp\left(i\phi\ln S(T)\right)\right]$$

$$= \exp\left[i\phi(\ln S_0 + rT) - \frac{i\phi\rho}{\sigma}(v_0 + \kappa\theta T)\right] \times$$

$$\mathbb{E}\left[\exp\left(-\frac{i\phi}{2}\left(1 - i\phi(1-\rho^2) - \frac{2\lambda\rho}{\sigma}\right)\int_0^T v(t)dt + \right.\right.$$

$$\left.\left.\frac{i\phi\kappa\rho}{\sigma}\int_0^T \sqrt{v(t)}dt + \frac{i\phi\rho}{\sigma}v(T)\right)\right]$$

$$= \exp\left(i\phi(\ln S_0 + rT) - s_3^*(v_0 + \kappa\theta T)\right) \times$$

$$\mathbb{E}\left[\exp\left(-s_1^*\int_0^T v(t)dt - s_2^*\int_0^T \sqrt{v(t)}dt + s_3^* v(T)\right)\right]$$

$$= \exp\left(i\phi(\ln S_0 + rT) - s_3^*(v_0 + \kappa\theta T)\right) \times$$

$$\exp\left(G(T; s_1^*, s_2^*, s_3^*)v_0 + H(T; s_1^*, s_2^*, s_3^*)\sqrt{v_0} + I(T; s_1^*, s_2^*, s_3^*)\right)$$

$$(2.83)$$

with

$$
\begin{aligned}
s_1^* &= \frac{i\phi}{2}\left(1 - i\phi(1-\rho^2) - \frac{2\lambda\rho}{\sigma}\right), \\
s_2^* &= -\frac{i\phi\kappa\rho}{\sigma}, \qquad s_3^* = \frac{i\phi\rho}{\sigma}.
\end{aligned}
$$

Therefore, the option pricing formula for the model, where stochastic volatilities follow a double square root process, can be given analogous to the above section. Not surprisingly, this model has the same expressions for hedge ratios as the above two cases. Therefore, we do not list them here.

The obtained pricing formula will be identical to Heston's if we set some special parameter values:

$$\kappa_{DSR} = 0, \qquad \theta_{SR} = 0, \qquad \kappa_{SR} = \lambda_{DSR},$$

where the subscripts $DSR$ and $SR$ stand for double square root process and square root process respectively. Obviously, such parameter values are not realistic. However, the pricing formula for the double square root process can not be reduced to its counterpart for the Ornstein-Uhlenbeck process in Subsection 2.2.3 and vice versa.

We discuss this model briefly via some numerical examples. In order to compare this stochastic volatility model with the Black-Scholes model, we need to calculate suitable BS benchmark values, as discussed in Subsection 2.2.3. For this purpose we choose two possible BS prices:[29] The first one called $BS_1$ is computed according to the mean level of stochastic volatilities $\theta$ that is implied by $\theta = \sigma^2/(4\kappa)$. The other one denoted by $BS_2$ is the BS price by choosing the spot volatility as constant volatility. Each panel below has its own $BS_2$ as benchmark. Table 2.6 shows three

---

[29]Because the expected average variance with a double square root process can not be given analytically, we can not calculate a benchmark according to the expected average variance, as with an O-U process in the above subsection. Additionally, due to the restriction $\sigma^2 = 4\kappa\theta$, we can not get a good benchmark by letting $\sigma \to 0$, as done in S&S (1991).

data panels based on formulae (2.82) and (2.83) to demonstrate the impact of $\rho$ on option values. We choose $\lambda = 1.0$ and $\kappa = 0.3$ which seems to be small compared with our previous two models.[30] and implies a $\theta$ being equal to 0.208. All panels in Table 2.6 display the similar properties as shown in Table 2.3 of Subsection 2.2.3. Firstly, we find again that options with different moneyness react to the correlation $\rho$ oppositely. For ITM options, their values decrease with the values of correlation. And OTM options display a wholly opposite relation with the correlation $\rho$ to ITM options. Secondly, the finding in Subsection 2.2.3 that the bias between the long term mean $\theta$ and the spot volatility is important for the prices of options is confirmed. In Panel K we have $\theta = 0.208$ and spot volatility as $\sqrt{0.04} = 0.2$, then option prices in this panel are overall near these two BS benchmarks regardless of moneyness and correlation. In contrast to Panel K, the panels L and M are calculated with a spot volatility of 0.1 and 0.3 respectively. Consequently, the option prices in these panels deviate from $BS_1$ and $BS_2$ significantly. Finally, as reported in Subsection 2.2.3, options with different moneyness present different sensitivity to the correlation $\rho$. While OTM options are generally sensitive to correlation, ITM options do not change remarkably with $\rho$. Not surprisingly, we can calibrate the implied volatilities from the data with the negative correlation in Table 2.6 to capture the empirical volatility smile and sneer pattern.

Table 2.7 shows the impact of $\kappa$ on option prices. Panel N gives all $BS_1$ values since every $\kappa$ corresponds to a $\theta$, and each $BS_1$ is then the benchmark for the option prices in the corresponding position in the panels O, P and Q. In the case of $\kappa = 0.1$, $\theta$ has an extraordinary high value of 0.625 and leads to unsuitable benchmarks. One obvious finding is that the option price is a decreasing function of $\kappa$ regardless of the moneyness of options. This phenomenon can be explained as follows: For a fixed $\sigma$, the values of the explicit $\theta = \sigma^2/(4\kappa)$ go up with the falling values of $\kappa$, and imply a larger mean level of the weighted sum $\kappa\sqrt{v(t)} + \lambda v(t)$. Hence, option prices increase correspondingly. A comparison of panels O, P and Q shows that the true values of options result from a trade-off between long-term mean and spot volatility. By

---

[30] The Longstaff's (1989) empirical study shows that the values of the parameters $\lambda$ and $\kappa$ in a term structure model of interest rates indeed are of an order of $10^{-2}$ or $10^{-3}$ respectively.

| $\rho$ \ $K$ | 90 | 95 | 100 | 105 | 110 | 115 | 120 |
|---|---|---|---|---|---|---|---|
| $BS_1(\theta)$ | 15.241 | 11.518 | 8.358 | 5.817 | 3.885 | 2.492 | 1.539 |
| $BS_2(v)$ | 15.118 | 11.342 | 8.142 | 5.584 | 3.658 | 2.293 | 1.377 |
| -1.00 | 15.563 | 11.529 | 7.811 | 4.539 | 1.928 | 0.359 | 0.003 |
| -0.75 | 15.435 | 11.407 | 7.753 | 4.646 | 2.305 | 0.891 | 0.274 |
| -0.50 | 15.296 | 11.276 | 7.688 | 4.727 | 2.576 | 1.265 | 0.588 |
| -0.25 | 15.144 | 11.128 | 7.605 | 4.786 | 2.789 | 1.569 | 0.873 |
| 0.00 | 14.977 | 10.956 | 7.501 | 4.826 | 2.987 | 1.831 | 1.132 |
| 0.25 | 14.791 | 10.753 | 7.371 | 4.848 | 3.150 | 2.062 | 1.371 |
| 0.50 | 14.582 | 10.505 | 7.206 | 4.853 | 3.292 | 2.271 | 1.595 |
| 0.75 | 14.353 | 10.184 | 6.993 | 4.839 | 3.420 | 2.465 | 1.806 |
| 1.00 | 14.188 | 9.681 | 6.681 | 4.813 | 3.546 | 2.655 | 2.013 |

K: $v = 0.04, \lambda = 1.0, \kappa = 0.3, \sigma = 0.5, T = 0.5, S = 100, r = 0.0953$

| $\rho$ \ $K$ | 90 | 95 | 100 | 105 | 110 | 115 | 120 |
|---|---|---|---|---|---|---|---|
| $BS_2(v)$ | 14.223 | 9.668 | 5.684 | 2.765 | 1.081 | 0.3335 | 0.083 |
| -1.00 | 14.814 | 10.524 | 6.498 | 3.018 | 0.612 | 0.008 | 0.00 |
| -0.75 | 14.736 | 10.417 | 6.449 | 3.131 | 0.972 | 0.188 | 0.034 |
| -0.50 | 14.647 | 10.314 | 6.378 | 3.197 | 1.228 | 0.411 | 0.141 |
| -0.25 | 14.555 | 10.200 | 6.289 | 3.241 | 1.431 | 0.614 | 0.275 |
| 0.00 | 14.460 | 10.070 | 6.179 | 3.269 | 1.600 | 0.797 | 0.416 |
| 0.25 | 14.364 | 9.924 | 6.042 | 3.280 | 1.743 | 0.963 | 0.557 |
| 0.50 | 14.274 | 9.757 | 5.870 | 3.273 | 1.866 | 1.115 | 0.694 |
| 0.75 | 14.207 | 9.572 | 5.643 | 3.247 | 1.971 | 1.255 | 0.828 |
| 1.00 | 14.188 | 9.421 | 5.298 | 3.190 | 2.065 | 1.388 | 0.959 |

L: $v = 0.01, \lambda = 1.0, \kappa = 0.3, \sigma = 0.5, T = 0.5, S = 100, r = 0.0953$

| $\rho$ \ $K$ | 90 | 95 | 100 | 105 | 110 | 115 | 120 |
|---|---|---|---|---|---|---|---|
| $BS_2(v)$ | 16.887 | 13.615 | 10.784 | 8.395 | 6.629 | 4.848 | 3.604 |
| -1.00 | 16.784 | 13.082 | 9.701 | 6.704 | 4.159 | 2.147 | 0.772 |
| -0.75 | 16.631 | 12.957 | 9.646 | 6.773 | 4.415 | 2.624 | 1.403 |
| -0.50 | 16.465 | 12.824 | 9.591 | 6.846 | 4.644 | 2.997 | 1.853 |
| -0.25 | 16.283 | 12.677 | 9.528 | 6.909 | 4.848 | 3.316 | 2.229 |
| 0.00 | 16.078 | 12.510 | 9.452 | 6.962 | 5.032 | 3.598 | 2.561 |
| 0.25 | 15.841 | 12.315 | 9.360 | 7.004 | 5.201 | 3.855 | 2.864 |
| 0.50 | 15.559 | 12.083 | 9.249 | 7.039 | 5.358 | 4.094 | 2.145 |
| 0.75 | 15.202 | 11.794 | 9.117 | 7.068 | 5.511 | 4.323 | 3.413 |
| 1.00 | 14.646 | 11.410 | 8.977 | 7.111 | 5.671 | 4.550 | 3.673 |

M: $v = 0.09, \lambda = 1.0, \kappa = 0.3, \sigma = 0.5, T = 0.5, S = 100, r = 0.0953$
$BS_2$ values are calculated according to $v = 0.04$.
$v$ is the squared volatility

Table 2.6. The impact of $\rho$ on option prices.

its very nature, the BS model can not reflect the dynamic effect of varying
volatilities on the option prices. Based on the above observations most

of which are identical to the models of square root process and O-U process, we conclude that modelling stochastic volatility with a double square root process also constitutes a promising way in improving the pricing and hedging performance in practice.

| $\kappa$ \\ $K$ | 90 | 95 | 100 | 105 | 110 | 115 | 120 |
|---|---|---|---|---|---|---|---|
| $\theta = 0.125$ | 14.327 | 9.976 | 6.258 | 3.470 | 1.683 | 0.711 | 0.262 |
| $\theta = 0.156$ | 14.573 | 10.480 | 7.017 | 4.344 | 2.479 | 1.304 | 0.633 |
| $\theta = 0.208$ | 15.237 | 11.511 | 8.350 | 5.809 | 3.877 | 2.485 | 1.533 |
| $\theta = 0.313$ | 17.150 | 13.928 | 11.131 | 8.760 | 6.794 | 5.197 | 3.925 |
| $\theta = 0.625$ | 24.288 | 21.784 | 19.506 | 17.441 | 15.577 | 13.898 | 12.389 |

N: $BS_1(\theta)$ are calculated according to $\theta = \sigma^2/(4\kappa)$.

| $\kappa$ \\ $K$ | 90 | 95 | 100 | 105 | 110 | 115 | 120 |
|---|---|---|---|---|---|---|---|
| $BS_2(v)$ | 14.223 | 9.668 | 5.684 | 2.765 | 1.081 | 0.335 | 0.083 |
| 0.5 | 14.508 | 10.129 | 6.199 | 3.150 | 1.359 | 0.565 | 0.245 |
| 0.4 | 14.526 | 10.155 | 6.231 | 3.180 | 1.381 | 0.580 | 0.254 |
| 0.3 | 14.555 | 10.200 | 6.289 | 3.241 | 1.431 | 0.614 | 0.275 |
| 0.2 | 14.595 | 10.262 | 6.373 | 3.333 | 1.508 | 0.668 | 0.309 |
| 0.1 | 14.647 | 10.341 | 6.481 | 3.453 | 1.612 | 0.741 | 0.356 |

O: $v = 0.01, \lambda = 1.0, \rho = -0.25, \sigma = 0.5, T = 0.5, S = 100, r = 0.0953$

| $\kappa$ \\ $K$ | 90 | 95 | 100 | 105 | 110 | 115 | 120 |
|---|---|---|---|---|---|---|---|
| $BS_2(v)$ | 15.118 | 11.342 | 8.142 | 5.584 | 3.658 | 2.293 | 1.377 |
| 0.5 | 14.959 | 10.868 | 7.281 | 4.435 | 2.475 | 1.310 | 0.684 |
| 0.4 | 15.046 | 10.991 | 7.434 | 4.600 | 2.626 | 1.430 | 0.771 |
| 0.3 | 15.144 | 11.128 | 7.605 | 4.786 | 2.798 | 1.569 | 0.873 |
| 0.2 | 15.254 | 11.280 | 7.794 | 4.991 | 2.991 | 1.727 | 0.990 |
| 0.1 | 15.374 | 11.455 | 7.999 | 5.214 | 3.202 | 1.902 | 1.123 |

P: $v = 0.04, \lambda = 1.0, \rho = -0.25, \sigma = 0.5, T = 0.5, S = 100, r = 0.0953$

| $\kappa$ \\ $K$ | 90 | 95 | 100 | 105 | 110 | 115 | 120 |
|---|---|---|---|---|---|---|---|
| $BS_2(v)$ | 16.889 | 13.615 | 10.784 | 8.395 | 6.629 | 4.848 | 3.604 |
| 0.5 | 15.977 | 12.292 | 9.080 | 6.431 | 4.381 | 2.893 | 1.874 |
| 0.4 | 16.125 | 12.479 | 9.298 | 6.664 | 4.608 | 3.097 | 2.043 |
| 0.3 | 16.283 | 12.677 | 9.528 | 6.909 | 4.848 | 3.316 | 2.229 |
| 0.2 | 16.450 | 12.885 | 9.768 | 7.165 | 5.101 | 3.547 | 2.428 |
| 0.1 | 16.625 | 13.102 | 10.018 | 7.432 | 5.365 | 3.791 | 2.639 |

Q: $v = 0.09, \lambda = 1.0, \rho = -0.25, \sigma = 0.5, T = 0.5, S = 100, r = 0.0953$

BS$_2$ values are calculated according to spot volatility,
$v$ is the squared volatility.

Table 2.7 The impact of $\kappa$ on options prices.

## 2.3   Stochastic Interest Rates

### 2.3.1   An Introductory Survey

At the moment, stochastic interest rate models form a much larger theoretical field than stochastic volatility models, and even have a longer history because interest rates are the most important factor in economic life. Interest rates are classified in short-term, medium-term and long-term rates according to the time to maturity of the underlying bonds. Here we deal with only instantaneous short-term interest rates, or short rates, which obviously possesses some special properties: mean-reversion, stationarity, decreasing current shocks to future rates. All of these show that modelling the dynamics of instantaneous short rates should follow similar lines as modelling stochastic volatilities. In fact, most short-rate models are formulated by using the following stochastic differential equation:

$$dr(t) = \kappa[\theta - r(t)^a]dt + \sigma r(t)^b dw, \qquad (2.84)$$

with $a, b \geqslant 0$. The parameters $\kappa$ and $\theta$ have the same meaning as in stochastic volatility models. The general model (2.84) is referred to as the time-homogenous one-factor model since the parameters in this process are time-independent and the resulting bond prices are determined solely by the short rate $r(t)$. With a special choice of distinct values for the parameters $a$ and $b$, we can obtain different short-rate models which are given partially in Table 2.8.

| | | | |
|---|---|---|---|
| 1: $dr(t) = \mu dt + \sigma dw(t)$ | Merton (1978) | $a = 0$ | $b = 0$ |
| 2: $dr(t) = \kappa(\theta - r)dt + \sigma dw(t)$ | Vasicek (1977) | $a = 1$ | $b = 0$ |
| 3: $dr(t) = \sigma r dw(t)$ | Dothan (1978) | $a = 0$ | $b = 1$ |
| 4: $dr(t) = \kappa(\theta - r)dt + \sigma r dw(t)$ | Courtadon (1982) | $a = 1$ | $b = 1$ |
| 5: $dr(t) = \kappa(\theta - r)dt + \sigma\sqrt{r}dw(t)$ | CIR (1985) | $a = 1$ | $b = 0.5$ |
| 6: $dr(t) = \kappa(\theta - \sqrt{r})dt + \sigma\sqrt{r}dw(t)$ | Longstaff (1989) | $a = 0.5$ | $b = 0.5$ |

Table 2.8: Overview of Interest Rate Models

Short rates are not a directly traded good, hence the above models are not complete under the original measure. However, as long as the risk-neutral process of short rates is established by introducing a market price of risk, we can calculate the underlying zero-bond price by applying the local expectation hypothesis,[31] which postulates that the current bond price is the expected value of the discounted terminal value by rolling over the short-rate from now to the terminal time. Then a zero-bond with one dollar face value can be expressed by

$$B(0, T; r_0) = \mathbb{E}\left[\exp\left(-\int_0^T r(t)dt\right)B_T\right] \qquad (2.85)$$
$$= \mathbb{E}\left[\exp\left(-\int_0^T r(t)dt\right)\right]$$

for a terminal nominal payment $B_T = 1$. To obtain the pricing formula for $B(0, \tau; r_0)$, we can employ the Feynman-Kac formula again. The corresponding PDE reads

$$\frac{\partial B}{\partial \tau} = -rB + \kappa[\theta - r^a]\frac{\partial B}{\partial r} + \frac{1}{2}\sigma r^{2b}\frac{\partial^2 B}{\partial r^2}, \qquad (2.86)$$

with the boundary condition

$$B(0, 0; r_0) = 1.$$

The standard method to solve this PDE is to suggest an exponential solution structure, that is

$$B(0, \tau; r_0) = \exp(a_1(\tau) + a_2(\tau)r_0^a + a_3(\tau)r_0^{2b}). \qquad (2.87)$$

With this guess, a closed-form solution for the zero-bond price is given for all models except for model (4). With $B(0, T; r_0)$ known, the term-structure of interest rates is automatically available. Among the listed models, the Vasicek model and the CIR model are termed as affine models of the term structure and play a central role in modelling stochastic interest rates. Duffie and Kan (1996) provide the necessary and sufficient conditions on this representation in a multivariate setting.

Not all models in Table 2.8 are reasonable with respect to the nature of interest rates and only gain their significance in a historical context.

---

[31] This hypothesis is more explicit in a discrete-time setting. There are other two expectation hypotheses on short rates: return-to-maturity expectation hypothesis and yield-to-maturity expectation hypothesis. For a detailed discussion see Ingersoll (1987).

The models (1) and (3) have an unlimited variance if time goes to infinity whereas the model (4) is stationary only for $2\kappa > \sigma^2$. Additionally, the models (1) and (3) do not perform the feature of mean-reversion. The positive value of interest rate is guaranteed by all model except for the Vasicek model. However, for most parameters that are consistent with empirical values, the Vasicek model raises only a negligibly small probability of negative interest rates. Model (6) is also called "double square root process" model and has a closed-form solution for the zero-bond price only for the special case $4\kappa\theta = \sigma^2$. In the following three sections, we will concentrate on models (1), (5) and (6), all of which are popular in interest rate theory, and incorporate them into our option pricing models.

There are three other main directions in modelling interest rates: (i) Time-inhomogeneous processes are proposed to specify interest rate dynamics and lead to an inversion of the term structure of interest rates (Hull and White, 1990. 1993); (ii) Starting with the current term structure of spot rates or future rates, Ho and Lee (1986), Heath, Jarrow and Morton (1992) attempted to model the dynamics of the term structure; (iii) An interest rate process should be specified in a way that all parameters are matched as good as possible to the given current term structure of interest rates. (Brown and Dybvig, 1986). These approaches are strongly associated with the term structure and not directly with the dynamics of interest rates. Hence they are not considered in our MPO.

## 2.3.2   Square Root Process

Modeling interest rates as a square root process was for the first time suggested by CIR (1985b) in an equilibrium model. The advantage of this modelling is that the interest rates can never subsequently become negative if their initial values are nonnegative.[32] Formally, interest rate dynamics are given by

---

[32]Two key assumptions in the original work of CIR are (i) the utility function is logarithmic and thus the interest rate has a linear relationship to the state variable in a production economy, and (ii) the state variable (technological change) follows a square-root process. Consequently, interest rates follow also square-root process. In this sense, the result about interest rates is state-variable dependent, not derived from the equilibrium-coincide logic.

$$dr(t) = \kappa[\theta - r(t)]dt + \sigma\sqrt{r(t)}dw_3(t). \tag{2.88}$$

At first, we let $dw_3 dw_1 = 0$, that is, the short rates are uncorrelated with the stock returns in spite of some empirical objection to this simplified assumption. We will relax this assumption later. The market price of risk to $r(t)$ is determined endogenously by employing equilibrium arguments. Therefore, we regard (2.88) as risk-neutralized. As discussed in the above section, process (2.88) satisfies almost all properties that an interest rate model should have. Following the principle of constructing CFs, we have

$$g_1(T) = \exp\left(-\int_0^T r(t)dt\right)\frac{S(T)}{S_0} \tag{2.89}$$

and

$$g_2(T) = \exp\left(-\int_0^T r(t)dt\right)\frac{1}{B(0,T;r_0)}. \tag{2.90}$$

The CFs are calculated as follows:

$$
\begin{aligned}
f_1(\phi) &= \mathbb{E}\left[\exp\left(-\int_0^T r(t)dt\right)\frac{S(T)}{S_0}\exp\left(i\phi\ln S(T)\right)\right]\\
&= \mathbb{E}\left[\exp\left(-\int_0^T r(t)dt - \ln S_0 + (i\phi+1)x(T)\right)\right]\\
&= \mathbb{E}\left[\exp\left(i\phi\int_0^T r(t)dt + i\phi\ln S_0 + \right.\right.\\
&\qquad \left.\left.(i\phi+1)\left(-\frac{1}{2}\int_0^T v^2 dt + \int_0^T v\,dw_1\right)\right)\right],
\end{aligned}
$$

Since the interest rate is independent of $dw_1$ and $v$, we calculate the expected value associated with $r(t)$ separately. Thus,

$$
f_1(\phi) = \mathbb{E}\left[\exp\left(i\phi\int_0^T r(t)dt\right)\right]\times
$$
$$
\mathbb{E}\left[\exp\left(i\phi\ln S_0 + (i\phi+1)\left(-\frac{1}{2}\int_0^T v^2 dt + \int_0^T v\,dw_1\right)\right)\right]. \tag{2.91}
$$

The second expectation in the above equity should be computed according to the specification of volatility. In the Black-Scholes world, we can immediately obtain

$$
f_1(\phi) = \exp\left(i\phi\ln S_0 + \frac{1}{2}i\phi(i\phi + 1)v^2 T\right) \times
$$
$$
\mathbb{E}\left[\exp\left(i\phi\int_0^T r(t)dt\right)\right]. \tag{2.92}
$$

The remaining expectation $\mathbb{E}\left[\exp\left(i\phi\int_0^T r(t)dt\right)\right]$ is calculated by using formula (2.60) in Section 2.2.2. Following the same steps, we arrive at the expression for $f_2(\phi)$:

$$
f_2(\phi) = \exp\left(i\phi\ln S_0 + \frac{1}{2}i\phi(i\phi - 1)v^2 T\right) \times
$$
$$
\mathbb{E}\left[\exp\left((i\phi - 1)\int_0^T r(t)dt\right)/B(0,T;r_0)\right]. \tag{2.93}
$$

So far we have inserted the stochastic interest rates into the CFs and, therefore, are able to price options with stochastic interest rates for the case of zero correlation. A favorite property of this case is that the terms $\mathbb{E}[\cdot]$ are purely associated with the interest rate $r(t)$ and are not nested with the stochastic volatility $v$. This allows us to specify a stochastic $v$ arbitrarily and proceed in the same way as shown in Section 2.2 as long as the interest rate and the volatility are not mutually correlated. Unfortunately, when we let both stochastic factors be correlated, we can not derive tractable CFs even if the volatility $v$ is stochastically independent of stock returns. We will return to this topic in Section 2.5.

To extend zero correlation to the non-zero correlation case, we need a modification of the stock price process that is given by

$$
\frac{dS(t)}{S(t)} = r(t)dt + v\sqrt{r(t)}dw_1(t), \tag{2.94}
$$

where we allow $dw_1 dw_3 = \rho dt$. The appearance of the term $\sqrt{r(t)}$ in the volatility is due to Scott (1997), and as an advantageous feature, the modified process guarantees positive interest rates. We can justify this model by the following observations: (i) Interest rates are inversely correlated with stock returns, as reported in Scott (1997), this is in line with the relationship between volatilities and stock returns; (ii) Both interest rates and volatilities share similar properties such as mean-reversion, and both processes can be specified by the same class of SDE. Thus, we introduce a stock price process with stochastic interest rate and stochastic volatility by a single factor "$r(t)$". With $x(t) = \ln S(t)$, we have

$$
dx(t) = r(t)(1 - \frac{1}{2}v^2)dt + v\sqrt{r(t)}dw_1(t). \tag{2.95}
$$

Consequently, the CFs can be calculated as follows:

$$
\begin{aligned}
&f_1(\phi) \\
={}& \mathbb{E}\left[\exp\left(-\int_0^T r(t)dt\right)\frac{S(T)}{S_0}\exp\left(i\phi\ln S(T)\right)\right] \\
={}& \mathbb{E}\left[\exp\left(-\int_0^T r(t)dt\right) - \ln S_0 + (1+i\phi)x(T)\right] \\
={}& \mathbb{E}\left[\exp\left(\left(i\phi(1 - \frac{1}{2}v^2) - \frac{1}{2}v^2\right)\int_0^T r(t)dt\right) + \right. \\
& \left. i\phi\ln S_0 + v\int_0^T \sqrt{r(t)}dw_1 \right) \right] \\
={}& \mathbb{E}\left[\exp\left(\left(i\phi(1 - \frac{1}{2}v^2) - \frac{1}{2}v^2\right)\int_0^T r(t)dt\right) + i\phi\ln S_0\right. \\
& \left. +(1+i\phi)\left(\rho v\int_0^T \sqrt{r(t)}dw_3 + \sqrt{1-\rho^2}v\int_0^T \sqrt{r(t)}dw\right)\right)\right] \\
={}& \mathbb{E}\left[\exp\left(\left(i\phi(1 - \frac{1}{2}v^2) - \frac{1}{2}v^2 + \frac{1}{2}(1+i\phi)^2(1-\rho^2)v^2\right)\int_0^T r(t)dt\right.\right. \\
& \left.\left. +\frac{(1+i\phi)\rho v}{\sigma}[r(T) - r_0 - \kappa\theta T + \kappa\int_0^T r(t)dt] + i\phi\ln S_0\right)\right] \\
={}& \mathbb{E}\left[\exp\left(i\phi\ln S_0 + \frac{(1+i\phi)\rho v}{\sigma}r(T) - \frac{(1+i\phi)\rho v}{\sigma}(r_0 + \kappa\theta T) + \right.\right. \\
& \left(i\phi(1 - \frac{1}{2}v^2) - \frac{1}{2}v^2 + \frac{1}{2}(1+i\phi)^2(1-\rho^2)v^2\right. \\
& \left.\left. +\frac{(1+i\phi)\rho v\kappa}{\sigma}\right)\int_0^T r(t)dt\right)\right] \\
={}& \mathbb{E}\left[\exp\left(i\phi\ln S_0 - s_1\int_0^T r(t)dt + s_2 r(T) - s_2(r_0 + \kappa\theta T)\right)\right] \tag{2.96}
\end{aligned}
$$

with

$$s_1 = -i\phi(1 - \frac{1}{2}v^2) + \frac{1}{2}v^2 - \frac{1}{2}(1 + i\phi)^2(1 - \rho^2)v^2 - \frac{(1 + i\phi)\rho v\kappa}{\sigma},$$

$$s_2 = \frac{(1 + i\phi)\rho v}{\sigma}.$$

By using again formula (2.60) in Subsection 2.2.2, we obtain the final closed-form solution for $f_1(\phi)$ in the case of correlation. In the same fashion, $f_2(\phi)$ is given by

$$
\begin{aligned}
&f_2(\phi) \\
&= \mathbb{E}\left[ \frac{\exp\left(-\int_0^T r(t)dt\right)}{B(0,T;r_0)} \exp\left(i\phi \ln S(T)\right) \right] \\
&= \mathbb{E}\left[ \exp\left( \left( (i\phi(1 - \frac{1}{2}v^2) + \frac{i\phi v\rho\kappa}{\sigma} - \frac{1}{2}\phi^2 v^2(1 - \rho^2) - 1 \right) \int_0^T r(t)dt \right. \right. \\
&\qquad\qquad \left. + \frac{i\phi v\rho}{\sigma}r(T) \right] \times \exp\left( -\frac{i\phi v\rho}{\sigma}(\kappa\theta T + r_0) + \ln S_0 - \ln B \right) \\
&= \mathbb{E}\left[ \exp\left( \ln S_0 - \ln B - s_1^* \int_0^T r(t)dt + s_2^* r(T) - s_2^*(\kappa\theta T + r_0) \right) \right]
\end{aligned}
$$

$$(2.97)$$

with

$$s_1^* = -i\phi(1 - \frac{1}{2}v^2) - \frac{i\phi v\rho\kappa}{\sigma} + \frac{1}{2}\phi^2 v^2(1 - \rho^2) + 1, \qquad s_2^* = \frac{i\phi v\rho}{\sigma}.$$

Given these two CFs, we can evaluate option prices if stochastic interest rates are correlated with the stock returns. This model is certainly of interest when concerning the strong impact of short-rates on market liquidity and, hence, also on stock prices, especially stock indices.

## 2.3.3 Ornstein-Uhlenbeck Process

The drawback of modelling interest rates as a square root process in option pricing is that we need the alternative stock price process (2.94) for the case of non-zero correlation, otherwise the closed-form solution can not be derived. In order to overcome this drawback, as suggested by

Rabinovitch (1989), we can introduce the Vasicek (1977) model where interest rates follow a risk-neutralized mean-reverting O-U process:

$$dr(t) = \kappa[\theta - r(t)]dt + \sigma dw_3(t). \tag{2.98}$$

At the same time, stock price process is still modelled by the usual geometric Brownian motion. The correlation is permitted, i.e., $dw_1 dw_3 = \rho dt$. The CFs in this case have identical forms to these in the above subsection. We calculate $f_1(\phi)$ and $f_2(\phi)$ in detail:

$$
\begin{aligned}
f_1(\phi) &= \mathbb{E}\left[\exp\left(-\int_0^T r(t)dt\right)\frac{S(T)}{S_0}\exp\left(i\phi \ln S(T)\right)\right] \\
&= \mathbb{E}\left[\exp\left(i\phi \int_0^T r(t)dt + i\phi \ln S_0 + \right.\right. \\
&\qquad \left.\left. (i\phi + 1)\left(-\frac{1}{2}\int_0^T v^2 dt + \int_0^T v dw_1\right)\right)\right] \\
&= \exp\left(i\phi \ln S_0 - \frac{1}{2}(i\phi + 1)v^2 T\right) \times \\
&\quad \mathbb{E}\left[\exp\left(i\phi \int_0^T r(t)dt + (i\phi + 1)\rho v \int_0^T dw_3 + \right.\right. \\
&\qquad \left.\left. (i\phi + 1)\sqrt{1 - \rho^2}v \int_0^T dw\right)\right] \\
&= \exp\left(i\phi \ln S_0 - \frac{(i\phi + 1)}{2}v^2 T\right. \\
&\qquad \left. -\frac{(i\phi + 1)v\rho}{\sigma}(r_0 + \kappa\theta T) + \frac{1}{2}(i\phi + 1)^2 v^2(1 - \rho^2)T\right) \times \\
&\quad \mathbb{E}\left[\exp\left(\left(i\phi + \frac{(1 + i\phi)v\rho\kappa}{\sigma}\right)\int_0^T r(t)dt + \frac{(1 + i\phi)v\rho}{\sigma}r(T)\right)\right] \\
&= \exp\left(i\phi \ln S_0 - \frac{(i\phi + 1)}{2}v^2 T\right. \\
&\qquad \left. -\frac{(i\phi + 1)v\rho}{\sigma}(r_0 + \kappa\theta T) + \frac{1}{2}(i\phi + 1)^2 v^2(1 - \rho^2)T\right) \times \\
&\quad \mathbb{E}\left[\exp\left(-s_1 \int_0^T r(t)dt + s_2 r(T)\right)\right] \tag{2.99}
\end{aligned}
$$

with

$$s_1 = -i\phi - \frac{(1 + i\phi)v\rho\kappa}{\sigma}, \qquad s_2 = \frac{(1 + i\phi)v\rho}{\sigma}.$$

To get the expectation in the last equality of (2.99), we can use the Feynman-Kac formula to obtain a PDE as follows:

$$\frac{\partial y}{\partial \tau} = -s_1 r y + \kappa(\theta - r)\frac{\partial y}{\partial r} + \frac{1}{2}\sigma^2\frac{\partial^2 y}{\partial r^2}, \qquad (2.100)$$

subject to the boundary condition

$$y(r_0, 0) = \exp(s_2 r_0).$$

By applying the standard method, we obtain the general result:

$$\mathbb{E}\left[\exp\left(-s_1\int_0^T r(t)dt + s_2 r(T)\right)\right] = \exp(J(T)r_0 + K(T)) \qquad (2.101)$$

with

$$J(T) = \frac{s_1 - (s_2\kappa + s_1)e^{-\kappa T}}{-\kappa},$$

$$K(T) = \left(\frac{\sigma^2 s_1^2}{2\kappa^2} - s_1\theta\right)T + \left(\frac{\sigma^2 s_1}{\kappa^3} - \frac{\theta}{\kappa}\right)(s_2\kappa + s_1)(e^{-\kappa T} - 1)$$
$$- \frac{\sigma^2}{4\kappa^3}(s_2\kappa + s_1)^2(e^{-2\kappa T} - 1).$$

The calculation of $f_2(\phi)$ follows the same steps:

$$f_2(\phi) = \mathbb{E}\left[\frac{\exp\left(-\int_0^T r(t)dt\right)}{B(0,T;r_0)}\exp\left(i\phi\ln S(T)\right)\right]$$

$$= \exp\left(i\phi\ln S_0 - \frac{i\phi}{2}v^2 T - \frac{i\phi v\rho}{\sigma}(r_0 + \kappa\theta T)\right.$$
$$\left. - \frac{1}{2}\phi^2 v^2(1 - \rho^2)T - \ln B(0,T;r_0)\right) \times$$
$$\mathbb{E}\left[\exp\left(\left(i\phi + \frac{i\phi v\rho\kappa}{\sigma} - 1\right)\int_0^T r(t)dt + \frac{i\phi v\rho}{\sigma}r(T)\right)\right]$$

$$= \exp\left(i\phi\ln S_0 - \frac{i\phi}{2}v^2 T - s_2^*(r_0 + \kappa\theta T)\right.$$
$$\left. - \frac{1}{2}\phi^2 v^2(1 - \rho^2)T - \ln B(0,T;r_0)\right) \times$$
$$\mathbb{E}\left[\exp\left(-s_1^*\int_0^T r(t)dt + s_2^* r(T)\right)\right] \qquad (2.102)$$

with

$$s_1^* = -i\phi - \frac{i\phi\upsilon\rho\kappa}{\sigma} + 1, \qquad s_2^* = \frac{i\phi\upsilon\rho}{\sigma}.$$

As long as both CFs are known analytically, the closed-form option pricing formula is given by the Fourier inversion for the case where stochastic interest rates are correlated with stock returns, and is identical to Rabinovitch (1989).This model may provide us with some new insights into the impact of stochastic interest rates on option prices. Scott (1997) developed a jump-diffusion model with stochastic interest rates which are separated in two state variables. A difficult issue in the practical implementation of his model is to identify these two variables. In Subsection 2.5.2, we will study this model in more detail and attempt to answer the following question: Which correlation with stock returns is more crucial for a correct valuation of options? Correlation of stock returns with interest rates or with volatilities?

By setting $\rho = 0$, we obtain two simplified CFs which are essentially similar to (2.92) and (2.93) and allow us to have stochastic volatilities.

## 2.3.4   Double Square Root Process

Longstaff (1989) set up an alternative general equilibrium model of the term structure within the CIR theoretical framework by assuming that the state variable for technological change follows a random walk. He incorrectly claimed that the square root of the interest rate $r(t)$ follows a process reflected at $r(t) = 0$. Beaglehole and Tenney (1992) showed by simulation that Longstaff's solution for the zero-bond price is not identical to the one in the reflecting case of the double square root process. As shown in Subsection 2.2.4, a double square root process is generated by a normal Brownian motion without imposing any boundary condition on both processes.

Since interest rates are governed by the square of a state variable following a Brownian motion with drift, one can easily obtain a double square root process by applying Ito's lemma. Thus, the dynamics of the equilibrium interest rates are given by

$$dr(t) = \kappa \left[ \theta - \sqrt{r(t)} \right] dt + \sigma\sqrt{r(t)}dw_3(t), \qquad (2.103)$$

where the restriction $4\kappa\theta = \sigma^2$ is imposed on this model and zero value of $r(t)$ is accessible as discussed in Subsection 2.2.4. Process (2.103) shares most of the properties of the CIR square root process except that interest rates revert to the square root of itself in a double square root process. This implausible asymptotic property raises doubts to this model. However, a double square root process has two potential advantages: (i) only two parameters are required to be estimated because of the parameter restriction, and (ii) the yields of the zero-bond derived from this model are nonlinear, more precisely, are a function with the terms $r$ and $\sqrt{r}$. As reported in Longstaff (1989), this so-called nonlinear term structure outperforms the CIR square root process in describing actual Treasury Bill yields for the period of 1964-1986 where he used the GMM to obtain the parameter estimates. Here, we adopt his double square root process to specify the interest rates. Similarly to the CIR model, with a market price of risk proportional to $r(t)$, we have the following risk-neutral process:

$$dr(t) = \left[\kappa\theta - \kappa\sqrt{r(t)} - \lambda r(t)\right]dt + \sigma\sqrt{r(t)}dw_3(t). \qquad (2.104)$$

The stock prices are assumed to have the same dynamics as given by process (2.94) and allowed to be correlated with the interest rates, that is $dw_1 dw_3 = \rho dt$. Thus, the corresponding CFs are calculated as follows:

$$
\begin{aligned}
&f_1(\phi) \\
&= \mathbb{E}\left[\exp\left(-\int_0^T r(t)dt\right)\frac{S(T)}{S_0}\exp\left(i\phi\ln S(T)\right)\right] \\
&= \mathbb{E}\left[\exp\left(-\int_0^T r(t)dt\right) - \ln S_0 + (1+i\phi)x(T)\right] \\
&= \mathbb{E}\left[\exp\left(\left(i\phi(1-\tfrac{1}{2}v^2) - \tfrac{1}{2}v^2\right)\int_0^T r(t)dt\right) + \right.\\
&\qquad \left. i\phi\ln S_0 + v\int_0^T \sqrt{r(t)}dw_1\right] \\
&= \mathbb{E}\left[\exp\left(\left(i\phi(1-\tfrac{1}{2}v^2) - \tfrac{1}{2}v^2\right)\int_0^T r(t)dt\right) + i\phi\ln S_0 \right.\\
&\qquad \left. +(1+i\phi)\left(\rho v\int_0^T \sqrt{r(t)}dw_3 + \sqrt{1-\rho^2}v\int_0^T \sqrt{r(t)}dw\right)\right] \\
&= \mathbb{E}\left[\exp\left(\left(i\phi(1-\tfrac{1}{2}v^2) - \tfrac{1}{2}v^2 + \tfrac{1}{2}(1+i\phi)^2(1-\rho^2)v^2\right)\int_0^T r(t)dt\right)\right.
\end{aligned}
$$

$$+\frac{(1+i\phi)\rho v}{\sigma}\left(r(T)-r_0-\kappa\theta T+\lambda\int_0^T r(t)dt+\kappa\int_0^T \sqrt{r(t)}dt\right)$$

$$+i\phi\ln S_0]$$

$$=\ \mathbb{E}\left[\exp\left(\left(i\phi(1-\frac{1}{2}v^2)-\frac{1}{2}v^2+\frac{1}{2}(1+i\phi)^2(1-\rho^2)v^2\right.\right.\right.$$

$$\left.+\frac{(1+i\phi)\rho v\lambda}{\sigma}\right)\int_0^T r(t)dt+\frac{(1+i\phi)\rho v\kappa}{\sigma}\int_0^T \sqrt{r(t)}dt$$

$$\left.\left.+\frac{(1+i\phi)\rho v}{\sigma}r(T)+i\phi\ln S_0-\frac{(1+i\phi)\rho v}{\sigma}(r_0+\kappa\theta T)\right]\right]$$

$$=\ \mathbb{E}\left[\exp\left(i\phi\ln S_0-s_3(r_0+\kappa\theta T)\right.\right.$$

$$\left.\left.-s_1\int_0^T r(t)dt-s_2\int_0^T \sqrt{r(t)}dt+s_3r(T)\right)\right]$$

$$\hspace{10cm}(2.105)$$

$$s_1\ =\ -i\phi(1-\frac{1}{2}v^2)+\frac{1}{2}v^2-\frac{1}{2}(1+i\phi)^2(1-\rho^2)v^2-\frac{(1+i\phi)\rho v\lambda}{\sigma},$$

$$s_2\ =\ -\frac{(1+i\phi)v\rho\kappa}{\sigma},\qquad s_3=\frac{(1+i\phi)v\rho}{\sigma}.$$

and

$$f_2(\phi)$$

$$=\ \mathbb{E}\left[\frac{\exp\left(-\int_0^T r(t)dt\right)}{B(0,T;r_0)}\exp\left(i\phi\ln S(T)\right)\right]$$

$$=\ \exp\left(\frac{i\phi v\rho}{\sigma}(\kappa\theta T+r_0)-\ln B(0,T;r_0)\right)\times$$

$$\mathbb{E}\left[\exp\left(\left(i\phi(1-\frac{1}{2}v^2)+\frac{i\phi v\rho\lambda}{\sigma}-\frac{1}{2}\phi^2v^2(1-\rho^2)-1\right)\int_0^T r(t)dt\right.\right.$$

$$\left.\left.+\frac{i\phi v\rho\kappa}{\sigma}\int_0^T \sqrt{r(t)}dt+\frac{i\phi v\rho}{\sigma}r(T)\right)\right]$$

$$=\ \exp\left(-s_3^*(\kappa\theta T+r_0)-\ln B(0,T;r_0)\right)\times$$

$$\mathbb{E}\left[\exp\left(-s_1^*\int_0^T r(t)dt-s_2^*\int_0^T \sqrt{r(t)}dt+s_3^*r(T)\right)\right]\hspace{1cm}(2.106)$$

with

$$s_1^* = -\left(i\phi(1 - \frac{1}{2}v^2) + \frac{i\phi v\rho\lambda}{\sigma} - \frac{1}{2}\phi^2 v^2(1 - \rho^2) - 1\right),$$

$$s_2^* = -\frac{i\phi v\rho\kappa}{\sigma}, \qquad s_3^* = \frac{i\phi v\rho}{\sigma}.$$

By using the results in Appendix B of Subsection 2.2.4, we can immediately obtain the closed-form solutions for the CFs and the pricing formula for the zero-bond price $B(0, T; r_0)$. Hence, the closed-form formula for options in this case is derived.

# 2.4  Random Jumps

## 2.4.1  An Introductory Survey

Brownian motion is not the only way to specify a stock price process, at least not a complete way. Another fundamental continuous-time process in stochastic theory, the Poisson process,[33] is perhaps a good alternative to describe some abnormal events in financial markets. Merton (1976) derived an option pricing formula based on a stock price process generated by a mixture of Brownian motion and the Poisson process. In his interpretation, the normal price changes are due, for example, to a temporary non-equilibrium between supply and demand, changes in capitalization rates, changes in the economic outlook, all of which have a marginal impact on prices. Thus, this normal component is modelled by a Brownian motion. The "abnormal" component is produced by the irregular arrival of important new information specific to a firm, an industry or a country, and has a nonmarginal effect on prices. This component is then modelled by a Poisson process. The best known abnormal event in finance history is the great crash of 1987. Empirical distributions of stock returns have displayed an obvious leptokurtosis, and the implied volatilities for options on the most widely used stock market index have performed a remarkable "smile" pattern. It seems that adding a random jump to the stock price process is important in deriving more realistic option valuation formulae and in fitting the empirical leptokurtic distribution of stock returns. In this sense, models with a jump component are competing with stochastic

---

[33] The Poisson process is a continuous-time but not continuous-path process due to its jump property.

volatility models. Jorion (1988) reported that 96% of the total exchange risk and 36% of the total stock risk are caused by the respective jump components. He also concluded that a jump-diffusion process outperforms GARCH, a discrete version of some stochastic volatility models, in describing the exchange rate process. Bates (1996) showed that in many cases it is sufficient to reduce the volatility smile by using a jump-diffusion model. BCC (1997) arrived at a similar result. All of these support the argument that jump processes are important in option pricing theory. We define the Poisson process formally:

**Definition**: *A Poisson process is an adapted counting process $Y(t)$ with the following properties:*

*(a) $Y(0) = 0$ almost surely;*

*(b) for every $t > s \geqslant 0$, $Y(t) - Y(s)$ is Poisson distributed with the parameter $\lambda$, i.e., $P(Y(t) - Y(s) = n) = e^{-\lambda(t-s)} \frac{(\lambda(t-s))^n}{n!}$;*

*(c) for each fixed $\omega \in \Omega$, $Y(\omega, t)$ is continuous in $t$;*

*(d) for $0 \leqslant t_1 \leqslant t_2 \leqslant \cdots \leqslant t_n \leqslant \infty$, $Y(t_1), Y(t_2) - Y(t_1), \cdots, Y(t_n) - Y(t_{n-1})$ are stochastically independent.*

When compared with the Brownian motion, we can see that the only difference between both processes is the probability law: One is governed by the normal distribution which is suitable for the description of continuous events, and the other one is governed by the Poisson distribution which is good for counting discontinuous events. Both processes have the properties known as independent and stationary increments, and then belong to the class of Levy process.[34] The first two central moments of $Y(t)$ are identical and given as follows

$$\mathbb{E}[Y(t)] = Var[Y(t)] = \lambda t. \qquad (2.107)$$

Consequently, both $Y(t) - \lambda t$ and $Y(t)^2 - \lambda t$ are martingales with an expectation of zero. The process $Y(t) - \lambda t$ is referred to as the compensated Poisson process in stochastic literature and plays a crucial role in constructing risk-neutral jump-diffusion processes. Since the Poisson process is Markovian, we compute the covariance between $Y(t)$ and $Y(s), t > s$, as follows:

$$Cov[Y(t), Y(s)] = \mathbb{E}[\{Y(t) - \lambda t\}\{Y(s) - \lambda s\}]$$

---

[34]For more about the Levy process see Protter (1995).

$$
\begin{aligned}
&= \mathbb{E}\left[Y(t)Y(s)\right] - \lambda^2 ts \\
&= \mathbb{E}\left[\{Y(t-s) + Y(s)\}Y(s)\right] - \lambda^2 ts \quad (2.108) \\
&= \mathbb{E}\left[Y(s)Y(s)\right] - \lambda^2 ts \\
&= \lambda s + \lambda^2 s^2 - \lambda^2 ts = \lambda s[1 - \lambda(t-s)].
\end{aligned}
$$

An even more interesting property of the Poisson process is that the probability that a jump occurs only once in an infinitesimal time-increment is just the parameter $\lambda$ times $dt$, that is

$$
\lim_{t \to 0} \frac{1}{t} P(Y(t) = 1) = \lambda \qquad \text{or} \qquad P(dY(t) = 1) = \lambda dt. \quad (2.109)
$$

At the same time, the probability that a jump occurs more than once in the time interval $dt$ can be regarded as zero, i.e., $P(Y(t) \geqslant 2)$ is of the order $o(t)$. Because of these two special features, we can express the Poisson process in the continuous-time limit case as follows:

$$
\text{Jump in } dt = JdY(t) \quad (2.110)
$$

with

$$
dY(t) \sim \delta_1 \lambda dt + \delta_0 (1 - \lambda)dt,
$$

where $J$ denotes the jump size and is uncorrelated with $Y(t)$. $\delta_n$ denotes the indicator function with $\delta_n = \mathbf{1}(dY(t) = n) = n$ for $n = 0, 1$. Hence, jump process is strongly connected with binomial distribution. Cox, Ross and Rubinstein (1979) even showed that a binomial model can converge to a jump process under special conditions.[35] Assuming that the Poisson process and the Brownian motion are mutually stochastically independent, we can combine these two components and immediately obtain a mixed process

$$
\frac{dS(t)}{S(t)} = r(t)dt + v(t)dw_1(t) + JdY(t). \quad (2.111)
$$

Due to the new component $JdY(t)$, the process $g_1(t)$ in (1.5), which is necessary for constructing the CFs, is no longer a martingale with an

---

[35] It is also known that the Black-Scholes formula can be derived in a binomial setup. As shown as in Cox, Ross and Rubinstein (1979), one can obtain the option pricing formulas for the Brownian process and the Poisson process respectively in a continuous-time limit by setting different up- and down-probabilities.

expected value of one. To validate the risk-neutral pricing approach, the
stock price process (2.111) should be modified by using the martingale
property of the compensated Poisson process:

$$\frac{dS(t)}{S(t)} = [r(t) - \lambda\mathbb{E}[J]]\, dt + v(t)dw_1(t) + JdY(t). \tag{2.112}$$

One can easily verify that the required martingale property of $g_1(t)$
in (1.5) with an expected value of one is satisfied. In spite of this risk-
neutral process, there is a consensus that the risks associated to jumps
cannot be hedged away in the Black-Scholes's sense. In other words,
one cannot form a portfolio protecting against *any* price change at *any*
time. However, the martingale property implies that trading using the
Black-Scholes's hedge is a "fair game" over a long time in an expectation
sense even when jumps happen.[36] *"If an investor follows a Black-Scholes
hedge where he is long the stock and short the option, $\cdots\cdots$, the large
losses occur just frequently enough so as to, on average, offset the almost
steady "excess" return"* (Merton, 1976). Additionally, there are some
assumptions imposed on the option pricing model, in order to overcome
the hedge problem in connection with jump risks. For example, suppose
that the capital asset pricing model (CAPM) holds for asset returns, and
that jumps occurring in the stock prices are completely firm-specific,[37]
then the jump component is uncorrelated with market movements and
represents unsystematic risks.

In the following sections we study three cases. The first one termed
as pure jumps is a case where jump size $J$ is constant, the second one
termed as lognormal jumps means that the jump size $J$ is lognormally
distributed and independent of $Y(t)$ and $w_1(t)$. Finally, we consider a
case where the jump size is governed by a Pareto distribution. We will
incorporate all three different types of jumps into the option valuation
theory by using CFs.

---

[36] In their seminal work, Cox and Ross (1976) argued that risk-neutral pricing is
valid for the jump process without any additional restriction and a risk-free portfolio
can be found by the Black-Scholes trading strategy. We think that their arguments
could be understood only in the here mentioned long run sense.

[37] See also the interpretation of jumps at the beginning of this section.

## 2.4.2   Pure Jumps

In this subsection we at first briefly review a pure jump model that is
studied by Cox, Ross and Rubinstein (1979) and is an extension of the
work of Cox and Ross (1976). Assume that the stock price follows a
process of the following form

$$\frac{dS(t)}{S(t)} = qdt + JdY(t),\tag{2.113}$$

which is formally equivalent to the following description

$$
\begin{cases}
dS(t) = S(t)(u-1)dt & \text{if jumps occur in } dt \\[2ex]
dS(t) = S(t)qdt & \text{if jumps do not occur in } dt
\end{cases}
$$

Most of the time, stock prices grow with rate $q$; Occasionally, jumps
come with rate $\lambda$ and a jump size $J$. Taking the growth rate $q$ into
account, we have $q+J\lambda = (u-1)\lambda$. The necessary and sufficient condition
for a risk-neutral process of (2.113) is $q+J\lambda = r$, which leads to $(u-1)\lambda = r$.[38]

In the continuous-time case, jumps occur according to a Poisson process with intensity $\lambda$, and stock prices are log-Poisson distributed. For
$q < 0$ and $J > 0$,[39] the stock price distribution generated by pure jumps
has a left tail which is thinner than (a right tail fatter than) the counterpart of a corresponding lognormal one. With this setup, the European
call option price is given by

$$C = S_0\Psi(a; b) - Ke^{-rT}\Psi(a; b/u)\tag{2.114}$$

with

$$a = \left\{\frac{\ln(K/S_0) + qT}{\ln u}\right\}^+, \qquad b = \frac{(r+q)uT}{u-1}.$$

The symbol $\{x\}^+$ denotes the smallest nonnegative integer that is
greater than $x$. The function $\Psi(z; y)$ takes the following form

$$\Psi(z; y) = \sum_{i=z}^{\infty} \frac{e^{-y}y^i}{i!}.$$

---

[38] This condition is identical to that in Cox and Ross (1976), which allows them to
eliminate $\lambda$ from the option pricing formula.

[39] The original assumption of Cox, Ross and Rubinstein (1979) is $q < 0$ and $J > 0$,
which is unrealistic in that jumps can only be positive. Also see Hull (1997).

By setting $q = 0$ we obtain the identical formula for options with a so-called birth process (Cox and Ross,1976) that describes two states only: jump or nothing. Since the jump process is closely connected with binomial distribution in continuous-time limit, formula (2.114) can be derived in a binomial setup (Cox, Ross and Rubinstein, 1979).

In the light of the jump-diffusion process given by (2.112), we introduce the dynamics of stock prices with pure jumps as follows:

$$\frac{dS(t)}{S(t)} = [r(t) - \lambda J] \, dt + v(t) dw_1(t) + J dY(t). \tag{2.115}$$

Since here we only need to show what terms the jumps contribute to the CFs, we let the interest rates and volatilities to be constant. By using the lemma for the transformation of Poisson processes analog to Ito's lemma,[40] we obtain the process for $x(t) = \ln S(t)$,

$$
\begin{aligned}
dx(t) &= \left( r - \frac{1}{2}v^2 - \lambda J \right) x_S S dt + v dw_1(t) \\
&\quad + \mathbb{E}_x \left[ dY(t) \{ \ln(S(t)(1 + J)) - \ln S(t) \} \right] \\
&= \left( r - \frac{1}{2}v^2 - \lambda J \right) dt + v dw_1(t) + dY(t) \mathbb{E}_x \left[ \ln(1 + J) \right] \\
&= \left( r - \frac{1}{2}v^2 - \lambda J \right) dt + v dw_1(t) + \ln(1 + J) dY(t), \tag{2.116}
\end{aligned}
$$

where $\mathbb{E}_x$ stands for the expectation operator working only with the probability law of $x$. Recalling the principle for constructing CFs in Section 2.1, we find that this principle is essentially independent of the specification of the underlying process. The important point in constructing a CF is that the discounted process $\left( \exp(- \int_0^t r(t) dt) S(t)/S_0 \right)_{t>0}$ must be a martingale, which is obviously satisfied by (2.115). Hence, we start calculating the CFs for the Poisson process as follows:[41]

$$f_1(\phi)$$

---

[40] For more about this topic see Merton (1990), Malliaris and Brock (1991).

[41] Here we use the well-known result on the CF of a Poisson process $y(t)$, that is

$$f(\phi; ky) = \mathbb{E} \left[ e^{i\phi k y} \right] = \exp \left[ \lambda t (e^{i\phi k} - 1) \right],$$

where $k$ is an arbitrary real number.

$$
\begin{aligned}
&= \mathbb{E}\left[\frac{e^{-rT}S(T)}{S_0}\exp\left(i\phi\ln S(T)\right)\right] \\
&= \mathbb{E}\left[\exp(-rT - \ln S_0 + (1+i\phi)x(T))\right] \\
&= \mathbb{E}\left[\exp(-rT + i\phi\ln S_0 + (1+i\phi)\left(r - \frac{1}{2}v^2 - \lambda J\right)T \right.\\
&\qquad\left. + (1+i\phi)v dw_1 + (1+i\phi)\ln(1+J)\int_0^T dY(t)\right] \\
&= \exp\left(i\phi rT + i\phi\ln S_0 - (1+i\phi)\left(\frac{1}{2}v^2 + \lambda J\right)T + \frac{1}{2}(1+i\phi)^2 v^2 T \right.\\
&\qquad \lambda T\exp[(1+i\phi)\ln(1+J)] - \lambda T)
\end{aligned}
\tag{2.117}
$$

In a similar fashion, we obtain

$$
\begin{aligned}
&f_2(\phi) \\
&= \mathbb{E}\left[\exp\left(i\phi\ln S(T)\right)\right] \\
&= \mathbb{E}\left[\exp(i\phi rT + i\phi\ln S_0 - i\phi\left(\frac{1}{2}v^2 + \lambda J\right)T + \right.\\
&\qquad i\phi\ln(1+J)\int_0^T dY(t)\right] \\
&= \exp\left(i\phi rT + i\phi\ln S_0 - i\phi\left(\frac{1}{2}v^2 + \lambda J\right)T + \frac{1}{2}(1+i\phi)^2 v^2 T \right.\\
&\qquad + \lambda T\exp[i\phi\ln(1+J)] - \lambda T).
\end{aligned}
\tag{2.118}
$$

The most appealing attribute to $f_j(\phi)$ is that they are continuous functions of $\phi$ although the Poisson distribution is not continuous. The closed-form pricing formula for the European call options is then given in the standard way where the probabilities $F_j$ are expressed by Fourier inversion. If we omit the diffusion parts from these two CFs, that is, $v = 0$ and $r - \lambda J = q$, we obtain the same option pricing formula as given in (2.114). Obviously, this new formula is more easily computable and unified with other pricing formulae in a same Fourier transformation framework. In the following two subsections, we discuss two more complex jump models.

## 2.4.3  Lognormal Jumps

In line with Merton (1976), we go back to the process (2.112), the so-called jump-diffusion model where the jump size $J$ is no longer deterministic but lognormally distributed. The Brownian motion $w_1(t)$, the Poisson term $Y(t)$ and the jump size $J$ are mutually stochastically independent. Formally, we have [42]

$$\ln(1 + J) \sim N[\ln(1 + \mu_J) - \frac{1}{2}\sigma_J^2, \sigma_J^2], \qquad \mu_J \geqslant -1. \qquad (2.119)$$

This means that $J$ has a mean of $\mu_J$ and $\ln(1 + J)$ has a standard deviation of $\sigma_J$. Because of the normal distribution of the random variable $\ln(1 + J)$, this jump is referred to as a lognormal jump. We immediately obtain

$$dx(t) = [r(t) - \lambda\mu_J - \frac{1}{2}v^2(t)]dt + v(t)dw_1(t) + \ln(1 + J)dY(t), \quad (2.120)$$

where it is clear that the abnormal stock returns governed by the term $\ln(1 + J)dY(t)$ have a normally distributed jump size. Hence, the abnormal stock returns might be both positive and negative, and are modelled more realistically than in a pure jump model. Merton (1976) gave a pricing formula in terms of an infinite sum

$$C = \sum_{n=0}^{\infty} \frac{\exp[-\lambda T(1 + \mu_J)](\lambda T(1 + \mu_J))^n}{n!} C_n, \qquad (2.121)$$

with $C_n$ as the Black-Scholes price with an instantaneous variance $v^2 + \frac{n}{T}\sigma_J^2$ and the risk-free rate $r - \lambda\mu_J + \frac{n}{T}\ln(1 + \mu_J)$. Merton's formula includes infinite Black-Scholes formulae and therefore causes cumulative numerical errors. Again, we express formula (2.121) here in an alternative way and, for convenience, let the interest rate and volatility be constant. It follows

$$
\begin{aligned}
f_1(\phi) &= \mathbb{E}\left[\frac{e^{-rT}S(T)}{S_0}\exp\left(i\phi\ln S(T)\right)\right]\\
&= \mathbb{E}\left[\exp\left(i\phi(rT + \ln S_0) - (1 + i\phi)\lambda T\mu_J - (1 + i\phi)\frac{1}{2}v^2T\right.\right.\\
&\qquad\left.\left. + \frac{1}{2}(1 + i\phi)^2v^2T + (1 + i\phi)\ln(1 + J)\int_0^T dY(t)\right)\right]
\end{aligned}
$$

---

[42] Compare with Scott (1997) and BBC (1997).

$$
\begin{aligned}
= \quad & \mathbb{E}\left[\exp\left(\lambda T \exp((1+i\phi)\ln(1+J)) - \lambda T\right)\right] \times \\
& \exp\Big(i\phi(rT + \ln S_0) - (1+i\phi)\lambda T\mu_J - \\
& (1+i\phi)\frac{1}{2}v^2T + \frac{1}{2}(1+i\phi)^2 v^2 T\Big) \\
= \quad & \exp\Big(i\phi(rT+\ln S_0) - (1+i\phi)\lambda T\mu_J - (1+i\phi)\frac{1}{2}v^2T \\
& +\frac{1}{2}(1+i\phi)^2 v^2 T + \lambda T \cdot \mathbb{E}\left[\exp((1+i\phi)\ln(1+J))\right] - \lambda T\Big) \\
= \quad & \exp\Big(i\phi(rT+\ln S_0) - (1+i\phi)\lambda T\mu_J + \frac{1}{2}i\phi(1+i\phi)v^2T \\
& +\lambda T[(1+\mu_J)^{(1+i\phi)} e^{\frac{1}{2}i\phi(1+i\phi)\sigma_J^2} - 1]\Big),
\end{aligned}
$$

$$(2.122)$$

where, since $J$ and $dY(t)$ are independent of each other,[43] we can set
the expectation operator directly in front of $\exp\left[(1+i\phi)\ln(1+J)\right]$. In
a similar way, we obtain

$$
\begin{aligned}
f_2(\phi) = \quad & \mathbb{E}\left[\exp\left(i\phi\ln S(T)\right)\right] \\
= \quad & \exp\Big(i\phi(rT+\ln S_0) - i\phi\lambda T\mu_J + \frac{1}{2}i\phi(1+i\phi)v^2T \\
& +\lambda T[(1+\mu_J)^{i\phi} e^{\frac{1}{2}i\phi(i\phi-1)\sigma_J^2} - 1]\Big).
\end{aligned}
$$

$$(2.123)$$

The closed-form pricing formula is then given in the usual way by applying the Fourier inversion. Additionally, we can easily do comparative
statics with respect to the jump parameters $\lambda$ and $\mu_J$ while it is rather
cumbersome to do this with Merton's formula. If $\sigma_J$ is approaching zero,
then the jump size will converge to the deterministic one and the lognormal jump becomes a pure jump which is exactly the case addressed
above.

---

[43] The detailed calculation is as follows:

$$
\begin{aligned}
& \mathbb{E}\left[\exp((1+i\phi)\ln(1+J))\right] \\
= \quad & \exp\Big((1+i\phi)\ln(1+\mu_J) - \frac{1}{2}(1+i\phi)\sigma_J^2 + \frac{1}{2}(1+i\phi)^2\sigma_J^2\Big) \\
= \quad & (1+\mu_J)^{(1+i\phi)} \exp\Big(\frac{1}{2}i\phi(1+i\phi)\sigma_J^2\Big)
\end{aligned}
$$

## 2.4.4 Pareto Jumps

Another way to enhance the variants of jumps is to specify the jump size by an alternative distribution. In contrast to the above subsection, the logarithm of the random jump size can be suggested to be distributed as follows

$$\ln(1+J) \sim Ex[\mu_e], \qquad (2.124)$$

where the probability density function (p.d.f) of exponential distribution takes the following form

$$Ex[y; \mu_e] = \frac{1}{\mu_e} \exp\left(-\frac{y}{\mu_e}\right), \qquad 0 < y < \infty. \qquad (2.125)$$

Duffie, Pan and Singleton (1999) applied this type of distribution to model the jumps occurring in a volatility process. The mean and standard deviation of the exponentially distributed variable are identical and are given by

$$\mathbb{E}[y] = \mu_e, \qquad Std[y] = \mu_e. \qquad (2.126)$$

An exponential distribution is entirely characterized by a single parameter $\mu_e$. We can immediately derive from (2.125) that $J$ has a probability density function of the following form

$$\begin{aligned} p.d.f(J) &= \frac{1}{\mu_e(1+J)} \exp\left(-\frac{\ln(1+J)}{\mu_e}\right) \\ &= \frac{1}{\mu_e}(1+J)^{-\frac{1}{\mu_e}-1}, \qquad 0 < J < \infty, \qquad (2.127) \end{aligned}$$

which means that the jump size $J$ is Pareto distributed.[44] Hence, we call this a Pareto jump. The interchangeability between the exponential distribution and its Pareto counterpart is similar to the one between a normal distribution and its lognormal counterpart. One of the important implications of the Pareto distribution and the associated exponential distribution is that the random jump size $J$ and its logarithm $\ln(1+J)$ can only be positive and also have positive means. Given $0 < \mu_e < 1$, the mean of $J$ exists and is equal to

---

[44]For more details see Stuard and Ord (1994), or Johnson, Kotz and Balakrishnan (1994).

$$\mathbb{E}[J] = \frac{\mu_e}{1 - \mu_e}. \tag{2.128}$$

Therefore, if we specify the abnormality in the movement of stock prices using a single exponential jump, the jumps can only be positive. To overcome this drawback, we can introduce two exponential jumps with different expected jump size and jump intensity. More precisely, we have the following dynamics for stock returns:

$$
\begin{aligned}
dx(t) &= \left[r - \mu - \frac{1}{2}v^2\right] dt + v\,dw_1(t) \\
&\quad + \ln(1 + J_1)dY_1(t) - \ln(1 + J_2)dY_2(t), \tag{2.129}
\end{aligned}
$$

with

$$
\begin{aligned}
\mu &= \frac{\lambda_1 \mu_{J_1}}{1 - \mu_{J_1}} - \frac{\lambda_2 \mu_{J_2}}{1 - \mu_{J_2}}, \\
\ln(1 + J_1) &\sim \frac{1}{\mu_{J_1}} \exp\left(-\frac{\ln(1 + J_1)}{\mu_{J_1}}\right), \qquad 0 < J_1 < \infty, \\
\ln(1 + J_2) &\sim \frac{1}{\mu_{J_2}} \exp\left(-\frac{\ln(1 + J_2)}{\mu_{J_2}}\right), \qquad 0 < J_2 < \infty.
\end{aligned}
$$

The jump $Y_1(t)$ with jump intensity $\lambda_1$ characterizes the positive abnormal movements in stock prices while $Y_2(t)$ with jump intensity $\lambda_2$ characterizes the negative abnormal movements. Their joint impact on the drift of the risk-neutral process is then $\mu = \lambda_1 \mathbb{E}[J_1] - \lambda_2 \mathbb{E}[J_2]$. Based on the risk-neutralized process, the two CFs can be given as follows:[45]

$$
\begin{aligned}
f_1(\phi) &= \mathbb{E}\left[\frac{e^{-rT}S(T)}{S_0} \exp\left(i\phi \ln S(T)\right)\right] \\
&= \mathbb{E}\Big[\exp(i\phi(rT + \ln S_0) - (1 + i\phi)\mu T - \\
&\quad (1 + i\phi)\frac{1}{2}v^2 T + \frac{1}{2}(1 + i\phi)^2 v^2 T +
\end{aligned}
$$

---

[45] The following equation is employed in the calculations:

$$\mathbb{E}[e^{ky}] = \frac{1}{1 - k\mu_e},$$

if $y$ is exponentially distributed with a mean $\mu_e$ for a real or complex number $k$.

$$(1 + i\phi) \ln(1 + J_1) \int_0^T dY_1(t) -$$

$$(1 + i\phi) \ln(1 + J_2) \int_0^T dY_2(t) \Bigg) \Bigg]$$

$$= \exp(i\phi(rT + \ln S_0) - (1 + i\phi)\mu T -$$

$$(1 + i\phi)\frac{1}{2}v^2 T + \frac{1}{2}(1 + i\phi)^2 v^2 T\Bigg) \times$$

$$\mathbb{E}[\exp[(\lambda_1 T \exp((1 + i\phi)\ln(1 + J_1)) - \lambda_1 T)$$

$$- (\lambda_2 T \exp((1 + i\phi)\ln(1 + J_2)) - \lambda_2 T)]]$$

$$= \exp(i\phi(rT + \ln S_0) - (1 + i\phi)\mu T -$$

$$(1 + i\phi)\frac{1}{2}v^2 T + \frac{1}{2}(1 + i\phi)^2 v^2 T +$$

$$\lambda_1 T \cdot \mathbb{E}\left[\exp((1 + i\phi)\ln(1 + J_1))\right] - \lambda_1 T -$$

$$\lambda_2 T \cdot \mathbb{E}\left[\exp((1 + i\phi)\ln(1 + J_2))\right] + \lambda_2 T)$$

$$= \exp\left(i\phi(rT + \ln S_0) - (1 + i\phi)\mu T + \frac{1}{2}i\phi(1 + i\phi)v^2 T + \right.$$

$$\left. \lambda_1 T[(1 - (1 + i\phi)\mu_{J_1})^{-1} - 1] - \lambda_2 T[(1 - (1 + i\phi)\mu_{J_2})^{-1} - 1]\right)$$

$$\tag{2.130}$$

and

$$f_2(\phi) = \mathbb{E}\left[\exp\left(i\phi \ln S(T)\right)\right]$$

$$= \exp\left(i\phi(rT + \ln S_0) - i\phi\mu T + \frac{1}{2}i\phi(1 + i\phi)v^2 T \right.$$

$$\left. + \lambda_1 T[(1 - i\phi\mu_{J_1})^{-1} - 1] - \lambda_2 T[(1 - i\phi\mu_{J_2})^{-1} - 1]\right)$$

$$\tag{2.131}$$

With these two CFs for Pareto jumps we close this section.

## 2.5   Integrating the Modules

### 2.5.1   Scheme of Integration

So far, we have studied some basic option pricing models with stochastic interest rates (SI), stochastic volatilities (SV) and random jumps (RJ) where SI, SV and RJ are mutually independent, and have also given the corresponding CFs. Now we begin to assemble a framework with these three modules by using Fourier inversion. According to the scheme outlined in Table 2.1, we can establish $4 \times 4 \times 4 = 64$ different pricing variants for options including numerous existing models. Some new interesting pricing models are therefore perceivable in our assemblage work. BCC (1997) have developed a complex pricing formula involving SI, SV and RJ. In fact, by using the parsimonious expression of CFs (1.10) and (1.11), we can obtain the final form of the CFs more efficiently since the expectation of a certain form under a certain process always has a certain structure, as shown in the previous sections. Consequently, we take the expectations of SI, SV and RJ, respectively, and then integrate them in a single CF. This approach certainly provides us with a very convenient way to establish more complicated models without losing an overview on the entire structure of pricing models. Furthermore, it can be easily implemented on a computer since this essentially is a modular programming approach.

The assemblage work begins with SVs which are possibly correlated with stock returns. Let $SV_j, j = 1, 2.$, denote the CF that is derived from a stochastic volatility model while SI and RJ remain unspecified. Hence, we have the following choices:[46]

$$
SV_1 = \begin{cases} (1.33), & v(t) \text{ is constant (BS)} \\ (2.58), & v(t)^2 \text{ as square-root process} \\ (2.70), & v(t) \text{ as Ornstein-Uhlenbeck process} \\ (2.82), & v(t)^2 \text{ as double square root process} \end{cases}
$$

---

[46]Here $v(t)$ denotes volatility. Hence, for example, variance $v(t)^2$ is specified as square-root process. But, in subsections 3.2.2 and 3.2.4, we use $v(t)$ as variance.

and

$$SV_2 = \begin{cases} (1.34), & v(t) \text{ is constant (BS)} \\ (2.61), & v(t)^2 \text{ as square-root process} \\ (2.71), & v(t) \text{ as Ornstein-Uhlenbeck process} \\ (2.83), & v(t)^2 \text{ as double square root process} \end{cases}$$

Let $SI_j$ denote the component in CFs $f_j(\phi), j = 1.2$, from a stochastic interest rate model, where interest rates are uncorrelated with stock returns, so we have

$$SI_1 = \begin{cases} \exp(i\phi rT), & r(t) \text{ is constant (BS);} \\ \mathbb{E}[\exp(i\phi \int_0^T r(t)dt)], & r(t) \text{ as in CIR;} \\ \mathbb{E}[\exp(i\phi \int_0^T r(t)dt)], & r(t) \text{ as in Vasicek;} \\ \mathbb{E}[\exp(i\phi \int_0^T r(t)dt)], & r(t) \text{ as in Longstaff;} \end{cases}$$

and

$$SI_2 = \begin{cases} \exp(i\phi rT), & r(t) \text{ is constant (BS);} \\ \mathbb{E}[\exp((i\phi - 1) \int_0^T r(t)dt)]/B(0,T;r_0), & r(t) \text{ as in CIR;} \\ \mathbb{E}[\exp((i\phi - 1) \int_0^T r(t)dt)]/B(0,T;r_0), & r(t) \text{ as in Vasicek;} \\ \mathbb{E}[\exp((i\phi - 1) \int_0^T r(t)dt)]/B(0,T;r_0), & r(t) \text{ as in Longstaff;} \end{cases}$$

If interest rates are correlated with stock returns, we have

$$SI_1 = \begin{cases} (2.96), & r(t) \text{ as in CIR;} \\ & \text{stock process is modified as in (2.94) ;} \\ (2.99), & r(t) \text{ as in Vasicek;} \\ & \text{stock process is as usual;} \\ (2.105), & r(t) \text{ as in Longstaff;} \\ & \text{stock process is modified as in (2.94);} \end{cases}$$

and

$$SI_2 = \begin{cases} (2.93), & r(t) \text{ as in CIR;} \\ & \text{stock process is modified as in (2.94);} \\ (2.102), & r(t) \text{ as in Vasicek;} \\ & \text{stock process is as usual;} \\ (2.106), & r(t) \text{ as in Longstaff;} \\ & \text{stock process is modified as in (2.94).} \end{cases}$$

For jumps, we have the following components in CFs:

$$RJ_1 = \begin{cases} nil, & \text{not specified (BS);} \\ (2.117), & JdY(t) \text{ as in Cox and Ross;} \\ (2.122), & JdY(t) \text{ as in Merton;} \\ (2.130), & \text{jump size } J \text{ Pareto distributed,} \end{cases}$$

and

$$RJ_1 = \begin{cases} nil, & \text{not specified (BS);} \\ (2.118), & JdY(t) \text{ as in Cox and Ross;} \\ (2.123), & JdY(t) \text{ as in Merton;} \\ (2.131), & \text{jump size } J \text{ Pareto distributed,} \end{cases}$$

where the number in parenthesis stands for the equation number. Hence, in general the CFs of an option pricing formula can be expressed by

$$f_j(\phi) = SV_j \times SI_j \times RJ_j, \quad j = 1, 2., \qquad (2.132)$$

since the CF of a sum of independent random variables is simply the product of the CFs of each random variable. It should be emphasized that this scheme of integration is based on the following two conditions:

(1). Either SV or SI is correlated with the underlying stock returns, i.e., with $w_1(t)$. If SI does, then SV has to be constant. This means that the SI correlated with stock returns can only be nested with constant volatilities. In addition, the stock price process has to be modified to (2.94) for the cases that SI follows square root or double square root process.

(2). SV, SI and RJ are mutually stochastically independent.

These two conditions are not restrictive because most of the existing option pricing models are not beyond this framework. The scheme in (2.132) provides us with the basic idea of MPO in establishing more sophisticated option pricing models. Therefore, by MPO each stochastic independent factor can be arbitrarily inserted into or withdrawn from the pricing formula depending on the users. Practitioners will profit from this modular pricing by building a flexible pricing formula to adopt changing market environments.

Here we list some new special models for options to illustrate the concept of MPO. An interesting new one is a model including SV, SI and lognormal RJ where first two factors are characterized by a mean-reverting O-U process. This model is completely parallel to the BCC model (1997) which specifies SV and SI as mean-reverting square-root processes. In accordance with our scheme of integrating, we immediately obtain the following CFs for this model:

$$f_1(\phi) = SV_1(2.70) \times SI_1(2.99) \times RJ_1(2.122), \qquad (2.133)$$

and

$$f_2(\phi) = SV_2(2.71) \times SI_2(2.102) \times RJ_2(2.123), \qquad (2.134)$$

To give another example, an option valuation model involving SV specified as a double square root process, pure jump as well as a constant interest rate has the following CFs:

$$f_1(\phi) = SV_1(2.82) \times RJ_1(2.117), \qquad (2.135)$$

and

$$f_2(\phi) = SV_2(2.83) \times RJ_2(2.118). \qquad (2.136)$$

By MPO, more new special options pricing formulae can be continuously listed in this way. We do not deal with all of the possible models. In Table 2.9, 36 of 64 possible models are given and computed for different moneyness. In a practical implementation, every element in the CFs $f_j(\phi)$ can be programmed as module or procedure. By assembling these modules, we can compute the probabilities $F_j$ in all possible option pricing models via Fourier inversion where a step-by-step Gaussian Quadrature Routine with 96 bases produces very precise and robust results.[47] The integral routine is stopped until the contribution of last step becomes smaller than, say $10^{-15}$. This procedure works fast and can be implemented on normal desktop-computers. Heston (1993) as well as BCC (1997) did not report their numerical procedures in detail. Bates (1996) evaluated the integrals in his formula using Gaussian Quadrature software and obtained sufficiently accurate results except for extreme and

---

[47]The weights and abscissas for a Gaussian Quadrature Routine with 96 bases are taken from Abramowitz and Stegun (1965, page 919)

implausible jump parameters. Scott (1997) compared the Fourier inversion method with Monte Carlo simulations and finite difference methods and reported that the Fourier inversion is superior with respect to accuracy and computing time. My program supports his conclusion.[48]

The most challengeable issue in implementing the Fourier inversion is the logarithm of complex numbers, which is a multi-valued function. If one only uses the principal value of the complex logarithm (similar to many commercial software packages like GAUSS, Mathematica, Mathcad and others), this results in a wrong integration of the CFs. The uncontrolled usage of the principal value possibly leads to discontinuity in the value of the complex logarithm along the integration path. By keeping track of the complex logarithm along the integration path, we obtain a smooth CF and the correct values of the probabilities. This problem is especially severe for extreme parameter values.[49]

Table 2.9 does not serve for the purpose of making comparison between alternative option pricing models, but just for the purpose of showing the effect of adding an alternative specification of a stochastic factor in the options pricing models. It is especially difficult to compare the different stochastic models because SR and DSR processes are associated with the squared volatilities. Given the parameter values listed in Table 2.9, the option prices of different models do not diverge significantly except these with pure or lognormal random jumps (Parts 4-9 in Table 2.9). This result is not surprising because the specified jumps are positive and then overall increase the values of call options. The Pareto jumps consist of two components: one for positive jumps and the other for negative jumps. Therefore in the cases of Pareto jumps (Parts 10-12), there are no considerable differences when compared with the cases of no jumps (Parts 1-3).

---

[48]Carr and Madan (1998) suggested using the Fast Fourier Transform (FFT) to value options numerically. This method improves the computing performance only when calculating a number of options with different moneyness.

[49]I thank Hartmut Nagel for letting me consider this issue. Nagel (1999) also discussed the behavior of the complex logarithm.

| No. | SV | SI | RJ | K=90 | K=95 | K=100 | K=105 | K=110 | K=115 | K=120 |
|---|---|---|---|---|---|---|---|---|---|---|
| 1 | SR | SR | Nil | 14.170 | 10.661 | 7.719 | 5.371 | 3.591 | 2.307 | 1.426 |
| | OU | SR | Nil | 14.120 | 10.621 | 7.698 | 5.375 | 3.615 | 2.346 | 1.470 |
| | DSR | SR | Nil | 14.802 | 11.047 | 7.750 | 5.062 | 3.092 | 1.816 | 1.061 |
| 2 | SR | OU | Nil | 14.179 | 10.675 | 7.737 | 5.392 | 3.612 | 2.326 | 1.442 |
| | OU | OU | Nil | 14.129 | 10.635 | 7.717 | 5.395 | 3.636 | 2.364 | 1.485 |
| | DSR | OU | Nil | 14.805 | 11.057 | 7.769 | 5.089 | 3.122 | 1.841 | 1.078 |
| 3 | SR | DSR | Nil | 14.263 | 10.765 | 7.829 | 5.481 | 3.694 | 2.397 | 1.500 |
| | OU | DSR | Nil | 14.214 | 10.726 | 7.809 | 5.484 | 3.717 | 2.434 | 1.542 |
| | DSR | DSR | Nil | 14.882 | 11.141 | 7.862 | 5.190 | 3.224 | 1.929 | 1.143 |
| 4 | SR | SR | Pure | 14.697 | 11.387 | 8.620 | 6.393 | 4.659 | 3.224 | 2.380 |
| | OU | SR | Pure | 14.659 | 11.361 | 8.611 | 6.400 | 4.679 | 3.375 | 2.409 |
| | DSR | SR | Pure | 15.155 | 11.590 | 8.557 | 6.162 | 4.393 | 3.118 | 2.195 |
| 5 | SR | OU | Pure | 14.707 | 11.401 | 8.637 | 6.411 | 4.676 | 3.363 | 2.393 |
| | OU | OU | Pure | 14.669 | 11.375 | 8.628 | 6.418 | 4.696 | 3.390 | 2.422 |
| | DSR | OU | Pure | 15.161 | 11.603 | 8.577 | 6.186 | 4.414 | 3.134 | 2.208 |
| 6 | SR | DSR | Pure | 14.790 | 11.487 | 8.723 | 6.492 | 4.750 | 3.427 | 2.447 |
| | OU | DSR | Pure | 14.752 | 11.462 | 8.714 | 6.499 | 4.769 | 3.454 | 2.476 |
| | DSR | DSR | Pure | 15.239 | 11.689 | 8.671 | 6.280 | 4.498 | 3.202 | 2.261 |
| 7 | SR | SR | LogN | 14.713 | 11.414 | 8.660 | 6.446 | 4.724 | 3.422 | 2.459 |
| | OU | SR | LogN | 14.675 | 11.388 | 8.652 | 6.454 | 4.745 | 3.450 | 2.489 |
| | DSR | SR | LogN | 15.167 | 11.608 | 8.584 | 6.202 | 4.450 | 3.194 | 2.288 |
| 8 | SR | OU | LogN | 14.723 | 11.428 | 8.677 | 6.463 | 4.741 | 3.437 | 2.472 |
| | OU | OU | LogN | 14.685 | 11.403 | 8.668 | 6.472 | 4.762 | 3.465 | 2.502 |
| | DSR | OU | LogN | 15.173 | 11.621 | 8.604 | 6.225 | 4.470 | 3.210 | 2.301 |
| 9 | SR | DSR | LogN | 14.806 | 11.514 | 8.763 | 6.545 | 4.815 | 3.501 | 2.526 |
| | OU | DSR | LogN | 14.769 | 11.489 | 8.754 | 6.553 | 4.835 | 3.528 | 2.555 |
| | DSR | DSR | LogN | 15.251 | 11.708 | 8.698 | 6.320 | 4.555 | 3.278 | 2.354 |

continuing in the next page

Table 2.9 Theoretical call prices of different pricing models in MPO

continuing from the last page.

| No. | SV | SI | RJ | K=90 | K=95 | K=100 | K=105 | K=110 | K=115 | K=120 |
|-----|-----|-----|--------|--------|--------|-------|-------|-------|-------|-------|
| 10 | SR | SR | Pareto | 14.284 | 10.821 | 7.921 | 5.601 | 3.827 | 2.529 | 1.613 |
|    | OU | SR | Pareto | 14.237 | 10.785 | 7.904 | 5.606 | 3.851 | 2.564 | 1.653 |
|    | DSR | SR | Pareto | 14.873 | 11.156 | 7.915 | 5.294 | 3.381 | 2.114 | 1.317 |
| 11 | SR | OU | Pareto | 14.293 | 10.836 | 7.939 | 5.620 | 3.847 | 2.546 | 1.628 |
|    | OU | OU | Pareto | 14.246 | 10.800 | 7.922 | 5.626 | 3.871 | 2.582 | 1.668 |
|    | DSR | OU | Pareto | 14.877 | 11.167 | 7.934 | 5.321 | 3.409 | 2.136 | 1.332 |
| 12 | SR | DSR | Pareto | 14.378 | 10.925 | 8.029 | 5.708 | 3.926 | 2.615 | 1.685 |
|    | OU | DSR | Pareto | 14.331 | 10.890 | 8.013 | 5.712 | 3.949 | 2.650 | 1.723 |
|    | DSR | DSR | Pareto | 14.953 | 11.251 | 8.027 | 5.421 | 3.507 | 2.219 | 1.392 |

The parameter values for calculating option prices are following:

| $S = 100$ | $T = 0.5$ | $r = 0.05$ | $v = 0.2$ |
|-----------|-----------|------------|-----------|
| SV: $\kappa_{SR} = 4$ | $\theta_{SR} = 0.06$ | $\sigma_{SR} = 0.1$ | $\lambda_{SR} = 0$ |
| $\rho_{SR} = -0.5$ | | | |
| $\kappa_{OU} = 4$ | $\theta_{OU} = 0.245$ | $\sigma_{OU} = 0.1$ | $\lambda_{OU} = 0$ |
| $\rho_{OU} = -0.5$ | | | |
| $\kappa_{DSR} = 0.4$ | $\theta_{DSR} = 0.4$ | $\sigma_{DSR} = 0.8$ | $\lambda_{DSR} = 0.05$ |
| $\rho_{DSR} = -0.5$ | | | |
| SI: $\kappa_{SR} = 2$ | $\theta_{SR} = 0.06$ | $\sigma_{SR} = 0.1$ | $\lambda_{SR} = 0$ |
| $\kappa_{OU} = 2$ | $\theta_{OU} = 0.06$ | $\sigma_{OU} = 0.1$ | $\lambda_{OU} = 0$ |
| $\kappa_{DSR} = 0.4$ | $\theta_{DSR} = 0.306$ | $\sigma_{DSR} = 0.7$ | $\lambda_{DSR} = 0.5$ |
| RJ: $\lambda = 0.5$ | $\mu_{Pure} = 0.2$ | | |
| $\lambda = 0.5$ | $\mu_{LogN} = 0.2$ | $\sigma_{LogN} = 0.05$ | |
| $\lambda_1 = 0.5$ | $\mu_{Pareto1} = 0.2$ | $\lambda_2 = 0.3$ | $\mu_{Pareto2} = 0.25$ |

Table 2.9. Theoretical call prices of different pricing models in MPO

## 2.5.2 Pricing Kernels for Options and Bonds

In previous sections, we have amplified how to incorporate stochastic factors, especially SV and SI, into a comprehensive option pricing model. To some surprise, similar functions are repeatedly used for this procedure as long as SV and SI are specified to follow the same stochastic process. More interestingly, these functions display the same structure as zero-bond pricing formulae. This indicates that the pricing kernels for options are nested with the pricing kernels for bonds. To see this, we summarize the similarity between these kernels case by case:

(1) Mean-reverting square-root process $z(t)$:

The key function in pricing both options and bonds is

$$y(z_0, T) = \mathbb{E}\left[\exp\left(-s_1 \int_0^T z(t)dt + s_2 z(T)\right)\right]. \tag{2.137}$$

Setting $s_1 = 1$ and $s_2 = 0$ yields the CIR (1985) bond pricing formula while $y(z_0, T)$ plays a central role in deriving the CFs for options in the Heston model, as shown in subsections 2.2.2 and 2.3.2.

(2) Mean-reverting O-U process $z(t)$:

In this case, the following function is crucial for pricing options and bonds:

$$y(z_0, T) = \mathbb{E}\left[\exp\left(-s_1 \int_0^T z^2(t)dt - s_2 \int_0^T z(t)dt + s_3 z^2(T)\right)\right]. \tag{2.138}$$

Once again, setting $s_1 = 0$, $s_2 = 1$ and $s_3 = 0$ reduces $y(z_0, T)$ to the well-known Vasicek (1977) bond pricing formula while $y(z_0, T)$ is a key function to arrive at a closed-form solution for CFs in the option pricing formula as in Schöbel and Zhu (1999).

(3) Mean-reverting double square root process $z(t)$:

In this case, we have a function that takes the following form:

$$y(z_0, T) = \mathbb{E}\left[\exp\left(-s_1 \int_0^T z(t)dt - s_2 \int_0^T \sqrt{z(t)}dt + s_3 z(T)\right)\right]. \tag{2.139}$$

We obtain the Longstaff (1989) bond pricing formula by setting $s_1 = 1$, $s_2 = 0$ and $s_3 = 0$, and the closed-form solution for CFs and options by using the general formula of $y(z_0, T)$.

All three functions $y(z_0, T)$ correspond to a PDE in accordance with the Feynman-Kac formula and are available analytically. This makes MPO feasible. While zero bond prices naturally are the expected value of the exponential function of $r(t)$ (here, $z(t)$) by the argument of the local expectations hypothesis, the CFs also are the expected value of the exponential function of $r(t)$ or $v(t)$ by Fourier transformation. In the light of spanning, as discussed in Section 2.2, the pricing kernels for bonds and options are nested in different spanned market spaces. While the pricing kernels for bonds with an exponential form are located in the original market space, the pricing kernels for options with the function $y(z_0, T)$ are generated in the transformed space. Both spaces are interchangeable by applying simple operators such as differentiation or translation (see Bakshi and Madan, 1999). The last step in option pricing in our new framework is the Fourier inversion which transports the valuation of options from the transformed space into the original one. Thus, at the end of whole pricing procedure, option prices return to the market space spanned by underlying assets, and options are valued in the original market spaces.

Regardless of whether in the original market space or in the Fourier transformed one, the backward Kolmolgov's equation works, this means, the probabilities $F_j$ and the corresponding CFs satisfy the same backward equation. This conjunction can be seen in Section 1.5, and forms the mathematical basis for the identical pricing kernel for options and bonds. Thus, it is no longer surprising that as long as we can obtain a closed-form formula for a zero-bond by applying a particular process, we can also obtain a closed-form formula for options in a stochastic volatility model by applying the same process.[50]

## 2.5.3 Correlation with Stock Returns: SI versus SV

In contrast to stochastic volatilities, few attention is paid to the impact of the correlation between SI and stock returns on the pricing issue of options. Using the results in Subsection 2.3.3, we can establish some option pricing models focusing on this impact. Here we expand on these models.

---

[50]see also Goldstein (1997).

Incorporating correlation between stock returns and stochastic interest rates into option valuation is justified by the empirical evidence that this correlation is statistically significantly negative. For example, Scott (1997) reported that the monthly correlation between the S&P 500 index returns and the rates on three-month Treasury bills over the period 1970 to 1987 is -0.158. If the crash in October 1987 is included, then this correlation over the period 1979 to 1990 is -0.096. A negative correlation can be explained in economic terms: If interest rates are high, then market liquidity becomes lower and opportunity costs will be higher. As a consequence, stock prices will also move downward. For the same reason, stock prices tend to go up if interest rates become lower. A negative correlation changes the terminal distribution of stock prices in a way that both tails of the distribution are thinner than a lognormal distribution if given a same mean and a same standard deviation. This is because stock prices tend to grow slowly if spot stock price is high in a framework of risk-neutral pricing, and vice versa. Consequently, call and put options will be overvalued by the Black-Scholes formula regardless of ITM or OTM. By contrast, a positive correlation between stock returns and SI causes the fatter tails of the true distribution of stock prices. Thus, in this case, the Black-Scholes formula undervalues call and put options regardless of moneyness. In Section 2.2, we have discussed stochastic volatility models in detail and found that the Black-Scholes formula overprices OTM call options and undervalues ITM call options if a negative correlation between stock returns and SV is present. A positive correlation results in an opposite relation in a stochastic volatility model. The choice of two alternative correlations in a practical application of MPO is then dependent on which pattern of stock price distribution fits the true distribution better. This requires empirical investigation and perhaps changes from case to case.

Rabinovitch (1989) gave an option pricing formula in a Gaussian model where interest rates follow a mean-reverting O-U process and correlation between stock returns and interest rates is allowed. In a single-factor model of interest rates, the zero-bond pricing formula is generally given by

$$B(0, T; r_0) = \exp[A(T)r_0 + C(T)],$$

Based on this result, a call option can be valued by the following formula:[51]

$$C = S_0 N(d_1) - K B(0, T; r_0) N(d_2) \qquad (2.140)$$

with

$$d_{1,2} = \frac{\ln(S_0/K) - \ln B(0, T; r_0) \pm \frac{1}{2}\eta^2(T)}{\eta(T)} \qquad (2.141)$$

and

$$\eta^2(T) = v^2 T + \int_0^T [\sigma^2 A(t)^2 - 2\rho v \sigma A(t)] dt. \qquad (2.142)$$

Thus, we can take stochastic interest rates and their correlation with stock returns $\rho$ into account when the variance $v^2 T$ in the Black-Scholes formula is replaced by the term $\eta^2(T)$. Note that the function $A(T)$ in the Vasicek model is deterministic, equation (2.142) can be integrated. Formula (2.140) is simple and easy to implement. If we use $A(T)$ in the Vasicek model, we obtain the same pricing formulae as given by (2.99) and (2.102) both of which are expressed by CFs. The only drawback is that one can not embody stochastic volatility in this formula even for $\rho = 0$. Another alternative model considering such non-zero correlation was developed by Scott (1997). In his model, stochastic interest rates and stochastic volatilities share a common state variable which is correlated with stock returns. Obviously, this implies the unappealing feature that correlations of stock returns with interest rates and with volatilities are same. In addition, it is difficult to identify the two state variables specified in his model.

Back to formulae (2.99) and (2.102) in Subsection 2.3.2, we present some numerical examples which demonstrate the effects of correlation between stock returns and interest rates on option prices. Here we calculate only one BS benchmark price by setting the discounter factor to be the corresponding zero-bond price. The BS values given in Panel U are benchmarks for the SI option prices in the corresponding position across Panel V to Panel X in Table 2.11. Table 2.10 shows the impact of $\rho$ on stock prices. The first finding is that the prices of call options are

---

[51]It is assumed that the volatility $v$ is a bounded deterministic function (see Rabinovich (1989), or Proposition 15.1.2 in Musiela and Rutkowski, (1997)). Hence, stochastic volatilities can not be incorporated into this pricing formula.

an increasing function of correlation regardless of moneyness. In fact, the prices of put options are also increasing with correlation and are not reported in Table 2.10 to save space; Secondly, we observe in Panel R that the BS option values best fit to the model values if we set $\rho = 0$ and $\theta_r = r$ (the long-term level is equal to the spot rate). In connection with the first finding, the Black-Scholes formula overvalues (undervalues) options in presence of negative (positive) correlation between stochastic interest rates and stock returns regardless of moneyness. This result is different from what we gain from the SV models presented in Section 2.2. The overvaluation or undervaluation due to correlations in the SV models depends on moneyness; Thirdly, we find that long-term level of interest rate $\theta_r$ is important for pricing options, especially for long-term options. Across the panels R to T, options prices change significantly with $\theta_r$. Table 2.11 also supports this finding. Hence, this model performs the same sensitivity of option prices to long-term level as the stochastic volatility models. In Table 2.11, we see that option prices are also an increasing function of $\theta_r$. This is not surprising because option prices go up with increasing interest rates even in the BS model. The option values in Panel V are generally very close to the option values in Panel W where the correlation between the stock returns and interest rates is zero. This confirms that the SI option prices can be very closely approximated by the BS option prices in the case of zero-correlation. In this respect the SI models resemble the SV models.

The SI model differs from the SV model mainly in that ITM options in the SI model increase in value with the correlation $\rho$. Given a negative correlation, what we need to know to choose between these two alternative models is whether the actual market prices of ITM options are undervalued by the BS formula. If this is the case, we prefer the SV model, and otherwise we prefer the SI model. An empirical study made by Rubinstein (1978) shows that the relative pricing biases of the BS formula do not display a persistent pattern over time and change from period to period. If his study presents a true picture of options markets, then the SI model might provide us with a potential application for pricing options.

| $\rho$ ＼ $K$ | 90 | 95 | 100 | 105 | 110 | 115 | 120 |
|---|---|---|---|---|---|---|---|
| BS | 15.114 | 11.338 | 8.138 | 5.581 | 3.656 | 2.291 | 1.376 |
| -1.00 | 14.918 | 11.048 | 7.774 | 5.184 | 3.274 | 1.961 | 1.115 |
| -0.75 | 14.968 | 11.125 | 7.871 | 5.290 | 3.376 | 2..048 | 1.183 |
| -0.50 | 15.019 | 11.201 | 7.967 | 5.395 | 3.477 | 2.135 | 1.251 |
| -0.25 | 15.071 | 11.276 | 8.061 | 5.497 | 3.575 | 2.220 | 1.319 |
| 0.00 | 15.122 | 11.351 | 8.154 | 5.597 | 3.672 | 2.305 | 1.387 |
| 0.25 | 15.174 | 11.425 | 8.245 | 5.696 | 3.768 | 2.389 | 1.455 |
| 0.50 | 15.226 | 11.498 | 8.335 | 5.793 | 3.862 | 2.472 | 1.523 |
| 0.75 | 15.277 | 11.571 | 8.426 | 5.889 | 3.955 | 2.555 | 1.590 |
| 1.00 | 15.329 | 11.643 | 8.510 | 5.986 | 4.046 | 2.636 | 1.657 |

R: $\theta_r = 0.0953, r = 0.0953, \kappa_r = 4, \sigma_r = 0.1, v = 0.2, T = 0.5, S = 100$

| $\rho$ ＼ $K$ | 90 | 95 | 100 | 105 | 110 | 115 | 120 |
|---|---|---|---|---|---|---|---|
| BS | 14.189 | 10.494 | 7.414 | 4.997 | 3.215 | 1.977 | 1.165 |
| -1.00 | 13.971 | 10.183 | 7.036 | 4.600 | 2.845 | 1.666 | 0.927 |
| -0.75 | 14.028 | 10.265 | 7.137 | 4.706 | 2.943 | 1.748 | 0.989 |
| -0.50 | 14.084 | 10.347 | 7.237 | 4.811 | 3.041 | 1.830 | 1.051 |
| -0.25 | 14.141 | 10.428 | 7.334 | 4.913 | 3.136 | 1.910 | 1.113 |
| 0.00 | 14.198 | 10.508 | 7.430 | 5.014 | 3.231 | 1.990 | 1.175 |
| 0.25 | 14.255 | 10.586 | 7.524 | 5.113 | 3.324 | 2.070 | 1.238 |
| 0.50 | 14.312 | 10.664 | 7.617 | 5.210 | 3.415 | 2.149 | 1.300 |
| 0.75 | 14.369 | 10.742 | 7.708 | 5.306 | 3.506 | 2.227 | 1.362 |
| 1.00 | 14.426 | 10.818 | 7.798 | 5.400 | 3.595 | 2.304 | 1.425 |

S: $\theta_r = 0.05, r = 0.0953, \kappa_r = 4, \sigma_r = 0.1, v = 0.2, T = 0.5, S = 100$

| $\rho$ ＼ $K$ | 90 | 95 | 100 | 105 | 110 | 115 | 120 |
|---|---|---|---|---|---|---|---|
| BS | 15.416 | 11.617 | 8.381 | 5.779 | 3.808 | 2.400 | 1.451 |
| -1.00 | 15.228 | 11.334 | 8.021 | 5.383 | 3.423 | 2.064 | 1.183 |
| -0.75 | 15.276 | 11.409 | 8.117 | 5.489 | 3.526 | 2.153 | 1.253 |
| -0.50 | 15.326 | 11.483 | 8.211 | 5.593 | 3.627 | 2.241 | 1.323 |
| -0.25 | 15.375 | 11.557 | 8.304 | 5.695 | 3.726 | 2.329 | 1.393 |
| 0.00 | 15.425 | 11.629 | 8.396 | 5.795 | 3.824 | 2.415 | 1.462 |
| 0.25 | 15.475 | 11.702 | 8.486 | 5.894 | 3.920 | 2.500 | 1.532 |
| 0.50 | 15.525 | 11.773 | 8.575 | 5.991 | 4.015 | 2.585 | 1.601 |
| 0.75 | 15.575 | 11.845 | 8.652 | 6.086 | 4.108 | 2.668 | 1.670 |
| 1.00 | 15.625 | 11.915 | 8.748 | 6.179 | 4.200 | 2.751 | 1.739 |

T: $\theta_r = 0.11, r = 0.0953, \kappa_r = 4, \sigma_r = 0.1, v = 0.2, T = 0.5, S = 100$

BS values are calculated by setting the
discounter factor to be zero-bond price.

Table 2.10. The impact of $\rho$ on option prices in SI model.

| $\theta_r$ \ $K$ | 90 | 95 | 100 | 105 | 110 | 115 | 120 |
|---|---|---|---|---|---|---|---|
| 0.03 | 13.061 | 9.039 | 5.756 | 3.349 | 1.775 | 0.858 | 0.380 |
| 0.06 | 13.724 | 9.642 | 6.253 | 3.713 | 2.012 | 0.996 | 0.451 |
| 0.09 | 14.392 | 10.259 | 6.770 | 4.101 | 2.272 | 1.150 | 0.534 |
| 0.12 | 15.064 | 10.888 | 7.307 | 4.513 | 2.554 | 1.323 | 0.628 |

U: BS benchmark values are calculated according to $\theta_r$.

| $\theta_r$ \ $K$ | 90 | 95 | 100 | 105 | 110 | 115 | 120 |
|---|---|---|---|---|---|---|---|
| 0.03 | 13.155 | 9.197 | 5.962 | 3.564 | 1.961 | 0.994 | 0.466 |
| 0.06 | 13.809 | 9.796 | 6.453 | 3.930 | 2.206 | 1.142 | 0.547 |
| 0.09 | 14.468 | 10.398 | 6.964 | 4.318 | 2.472 | 1.307 | 0.640 |
| 0.12 | 15.132 | 11.016 | 7.493 | 4.729 | 2.760 | 1.489 | 0.744 |

V: $\rho = 0.5, \kappa_r = 4, \sigma_r = 0.1, v = 0.15, T = 0.5, S = 100, r = 0.0953$

| $\theta_r$ \ $K$ | 90 | 95 | 100 | 105 | 110 | 115 | 120 |
|---|---|---|---|---|---|---|---|
| 0.03 | 13.070 | 9.055 | 5.777 | 3.371 | 1.794 | 0.872 | 0.388 |
| 0.06 | 13.733 | 9.657 | 6.273 | 3.735 | 2.032 | 1.010 | 0.461 |
| 0.09 | 14.400 | 10.273 | 6.790 | 4.123 | 2.292 | 1.166 | 0.544 |
| 0.12 | 15.070 | 10.901 | 7.326 | 4.535 | 2.575 | 1.339 | 0.640 |

W: $\rho = 0.0, \kappa_r = 4, \sigma_r = 0.1, v = 0.15, T = 0.5, S = 100, r = 0.0953$

| $\theta_r$ \ $K$ | 90 | 95 | 100 | 105 | 110 | 115 | 120 |
|---|---|---|---|---|---|---|---|
| 0.03 | 12.987 | 8.910 | 5.584 | 3.169 | 1.622 | 0.749 | 0.314 |
| 0.06 | 13.657 | 9.522 | 6.086 | 3.532 | 1.852 | 0.878 | 0.377 |
| 0.09 | 14.334 | 10.148 | 6.609 | 3.920 | 2.105 | 1.024 | 0.452 |
| 0.12 | 15.013 | 10.786 | 7.153 | 4.333 | 2.382 | 1.187 | 0.538 |

X: $\rho = -0.5, \kappa_r = 4, \sigma_r = 0.1, v = 0.15, T = 0.5, S = 100, r = 0.0953$

Table 2.11. The impact of $\theta_r$ on options prices in SI model.

# 2.6 Appendices

## 2.6.1 A: Derivation of the CFs with O-U Process

The CF $f_1(\phi)$ can be calculated as follows:

$$f_1(\phi)$$
$$= \mathbb{E}\left[\exp(-rT - \ln S_0 + (1 + i\phi)\ln S(T))\right]$$
$$= \mathbb{E}[\exp(-(rT + \ln S_0)$$

$$= \mathbb{E}\Big[\exp\big(-(rT + \ln S_0)$$

$$+ (1 + i\phi)\Big(\ln S_0 + \int_0^T r\,dt - \frac{1}{2}\int_0^T v^2(t)dt + \int_0^T v(t)dw_1\Big)\Big)\Big]$$

$$= \exp(i\phi(rT + \ln S_0)) \times$$

$$\mathbb{E}\Big[\exp\Big((1 + i\phi)\Big(-\frac{1}{2}\int_0^T v^2(t)dt + \int_0^T v(t)dw_1\Big)\Big)\Big]$$

$$= \exp(i\phi(rT + \ln S_0))\mathbb{E}\big[\exp((1 + i\phi) \times$$

$$\Big(-\frac{1}{2}\int_0^T v^2(t)dt + \rho\int_0^T v(t)dw_2 + \sqrt{1 - \rho^2}\int_0^T v(t)dw\Big)\big)\Big]$$

Note $\quad dw$ is uncorrelated with $dw_2$.

$$= \exp(i\phi(rT + \ln S_0)) \times$$

$$\mathbb{E}\Big[\Big(\exp\Big((1 + i\phi)\Big(-\frac{1}{2}\int_0^T v^2(t)dt + \rho\int_0^T v(t)dw_2\Big)\Big)\Big)$$

$$\times \exp\Big(\frac{1}{2}(1 + i\phi)^2(1 - \rho^2)\int_0^T v^2(t)dt\Big)\Big]$$

$$= \exp(i\phi(rT + \ln S_0)) \times$$

$$\mathbb{E}\Big[\exp\Big(\frac{1}{2}(1 + i\phi)(i\phi - \rho^2 - i\phi\rho^2)\int_0^T v^2(t)dt$$

$$+ (1 + i\phi)\rho\int_0^T v(t)dw_2\Big)\Big]$$

$$= \exp(i\phi(rT + \ln S_0)) \times$$

$$\mathbb{E}\Big[\exp\Big(\frac{1}{2}(1 + i\phi)(i\phi - \rho^2 - i\phi\rho^2)\int_0^T v^2(t)dt +$$

$$(1 + i\phi)\rho\Big(\frac{v^2(T)}{2\sigma} - \frac{v_0}{2\sigma} - \frac{\sigma}{2}T -$$

$$\frac{\kappa\theta}{\sigma}\int_0^T v(t)dt + \frac{\kappa}{\sigma}\int_0^T v^2(t)dt\Big)\Big)\Big]$$

$$= \exp(i\phi(rT + \ln S_0)) \times$$

$$\mathbb{E}\Big[\exp\Big([\frac{1}{2}(1 + i\phi)(i\phi - \rho^2 - i\phi\rho^2 + \frac{2\rho\kappa}{\sigma}]\int_0^T v^2(t)dt$$

$$- \frac{\rho\kappa\theta}{\sigma}(1 + i\phi)\int_0^T v(t)dt + \frac{\rho}{2\sigma}(1 + i\phi)v^2(T)$$

$$- \frac{\rho}{2\sigma}(1 + i\phi)v_0 - \frac{\rho\sigma T}{2}(1 + i\phi)\Big)\Big]$$

$$= \exp\Big(i\phi(rT + \ln S_0) - \frac{\rho}{2\sigma}(1 + i\phi)v_0 - \frac{\rho\sigma T}{2}(1 + i\phi)\Big) \times$$

$$\mathbb{E}\left[\exp\left(-s_1\int_0^T v^2(t)dt - s_2\int_0^T v(t)dt + s_3 v^2(T)\right)\right].$$

The expansion of $f_2(x)$ follows the same way. What we need to do is calculate the expectation value

$$
\begin{aligned}
y(v_0, T) &= \mathbb{E}\left[\exp\left(-s_1\int_0^T v^2(t)dt - s_2\int_0^T v(t)dt + s_3 v^2(T)\right)\right]\\
&= \mathbb{E}\left[\exp\left(\int_0^T (-s_1 v^2(t) - s_2 v(t))dt\right)\exp(s_3 v^2(T))\right]
\end{aligned}
$$

for arbitrary complex numbers $s_1, s_2$ and $s_3$. and $s_1 v^2(t) + s_2 v(t)$ is lower bounded. According to the Feynman-Kac formula, $y$ satisfies the following differential equation [see Karlin and Taylor (1975) and Øksendal (1995)]

$$\frac{\partial y}{\partial \tau} = -(s_1 v^2 + s_2 v)y + \kappa(\theta - v)\frac{\partial y}{\partial v} + \frac{1}{2}\sigma^2\frac{\partial^2 y}{\partial v^2}$$

with the boundary condition

$$y(v_0, 0) = \exp(s_3 v_0^2).$$

It can be shown that the above differential equation always has a solution of the form

$$
\begin{aligned}
y(v_0, \tau) &= \exp\left(\frac{1}{2}\widetilde{D}(\tau)v_0^2 + E(\tau)v_0 + F(\tau) + s_3 v_0^2\right)\\
&= \exp\left(\frac{1}{2}(\widetilde{D}(\tau) + 2s_3)v_0^2 + E(\tau)v_0 + F(\tau)\right)\\
&= \exp\left(\frac{1}{2}(D(\tau)v_0^2 + E(\tau)v_0 + F(\tau)\right)
\end{aligned}
$$

with $D(\tau) = \widetilde{D}(\tau) + 2s_3$. Substituting this into the differential equation, we can obtain three differential equations that determine $D(\tau)$, $E(\tau)$ and $F(\tau)$ :

$$
\begin{aligned}
\frac{1}{2}D_\tau &= -s_1 - \kappa D + \frac{1}{2}\sigma^2 D^2,\\
E_\tau &= -s_2 + \kappa\theta D - \kappa E + \sigma^2 E D,\\
F_\tau &= \kappa\theta E + \frac{1}{2}\sigma^2 E^2 + \frac{1}{2}\sigma^2 D,
\end{aligned}
$$

where $D(0) = 2s_3$, $E(0) = 0$ and $F(0) = 0$. Solving these equations is straightforward but tedious.

$$D(\tau) = \frac{\kappa}{\sigma^2} - \frac{\gamma_1}{\sigma^2} \frac{\sinh(\gamma_1 \tau) + \gamma_2 \cosh(\gamma_1 \tau)}{\gamma_4},$$

$$E(\tau) = \frac{(\kappa\theta\gamma_1 - \gamma_2\gamma_3)(1 - \cosh(\gamma_1 \tau)) - (\kappa\theta\gamma_1\gamma_2 - \gamma_3)\sinh(\gamma_1 \tau)}{\gamma_1\gamma_4\sigma^2},$$

$$F(\tau) = -\frac{1}{2}\ln\gamma_4 + \frac{[(\kappa\theta\gamma_1 - \gamma_2\gamma_3)^2 - \gamma_3^2(1 - \gamma_2^2)]\sinh(\gamma_1\tau)}{2\gamma_1^3\gamma_4\sigma^2}$$

$$+ \frac{(\kappa\theta\gamma_1 - \gamma_2\gamma_3)\gamma_3(\gamma_4 - 1)}{\gamma_1^3\sigma^2\gamma_4} + \frac{\tau}{2\gamma_1^2\sigma^2}[\kappa\gamma_1^2(\sigma^2 - \kappa\theta^2) + \gamma_3^2].$$

with

$$\gamma_1 = \sqrt{2\sigma^2 s_1 + \kappa^2}, \quad \gamma_3 = \kappa^2\theta - s_2\sigma^2,$$

$$\gamma_2 = \left(\frac{\kappa - 2\sigma^2 s_3}{\gamma_1}\right), \quad \gamma_4 = \cosh(\gamma_1\tau) + \gamma_2\sinh(\gamma_1\tau).$$

## 2.6.2   B: Derivation of the CFs with Double Square Root Process

Here we do the same thing as in Appendix A. Let $y$ be the related expectation value, namely

$$y(v_0, T) = \mathbb{E}\left[\exp\left(-s_1\int_0^T v(t)dt - s_2\int_0^T \sqrt{v(t)}dt + s_3v(T)\right)\right],$$

we have the following PDE by applying the Feynman-Kac formula

$$\frac{\partial y}{\partial \tau} = -(s_1 v + s_2\sqrt{v})y + (\kappa\theta - \kappa\sqrt{v} - \lambda v)\frac{\partial y}{\partial v} + \frac{1}{2}\sigma^2 v\frac{\partial^2 y}{\partial v^2}$$

where $\tau$ denotes time to maturity. The boundary condition is

$$y(v_0, 0) = \exp(s_3 v_0).$$

For $4\kappa\theta = \sigma^2$, we think of a solution which takes the form of

$$y(v_0, \tau) = \exp(G(\tau)v_0 + H(\tau)\sqrt{v_0} + I(\tau))$$

with $G(0) = s_3 v_0$. Setting the corresponding derivatives into the above PDE, we obtain a system of ordinary differential equations:

$$G_\tau = -s_1 - \lambda G + \frac{1}{2}\sigma^2 G^2,$$

$$H_\tau = -s_2 - \kappa G - \frac{1}{2}\lambda H + \frac{1}{2}\sigma^2 GH,$$

$$I_\tau = \frac{1}{4}\sigma^2 G - \frac{1}{2}\kappa H + \frac{1}{8}\sigma^2 H^2.$$

This leads to the following solutions:

$$G(\tau) = \frac{\lambda}{\sigma^2} - \frac{2\gamma_1}{\sigma^2}\left(\frac{2\gamma_1 \sinh(\gamma_1\tau) + \gamma_2 \cosh(\gamma_1\tau)}{2\gamma_1 \cosh(\gamma_1\tau) + \gamma_2 \sinh(\gamma_1\tau)}\right),$$

$$H(\tau) = \frac{2\sinh(\frac{1}{2}\gamma_1\tau)}{\gamma_1\gamma_4\sigma^2} \times$$
$$\left((\kappa\gamma_2 - 2\gamma_3)\cosh(\frac{1}{2}\gamma_1\tau) + (2\kappa\gamma_1 - \gamma_2\gamma_3/\gamma_1)\sinh(\frac{1}{2}\gamma_1\tau)\right),$$

$$I(\tau) = -\frac{1}{2}\ln\gamma_4 + \frac{1}{4}\lambda\tau + \frac{\tau(\gamma_3^2 - \kappa^2\gamma_1^2)}{2\gamma_1^2\sigma^2} + \frac{(\gamma_2\gamma_3 - 2\kappa\gamma_1^2)\gamma_3}{2\gamma_1^4\sigma^2}(\frac{1}{\gamma_4} - 1)$$
$$+\frac{\sinh(\gamma_1\tau)(\kappa^2\gamma_1^2 - \kappa\gamma_2\gamma_3 - \gamma_3^2 + 0.5(\gamma_2\gamma_3/\gamma_1)^2)}{2\gamma_1^3\sigma^2\gamma_4},$$

where

$$\gamma_1 = \frac{1}{2}\sqrt{\lambda^2 + 2\sigma^2 s_1}, \qquad \gamma_2 = \lambda - \sigma^2 s_3,$$

$$\gamma_3 = \frac{1}{2}(\lambda\kappa + \sigma^2 s_2), \qquad \gamma_4 = \cosh(\gamma_1\tau) + \frac{\gamma_2}{2\gamma_1}\sinh(\gamma_1\tau).$$

# 3 Extensions of MPO to Exotic Options

## 3.1 Introduction

Exotic options are a common name for a number of options either with an unconventional payoff structure or with a complicated probability structure (i.e., path-dependent options). There is a long list of financial derivatives belonging to this class: barrier options, Asian options, correlation options, spread options, quanto options, exchange options etc. Most of them are generated in the course of the expansion of the financial derivative business since the 1970s, and are referred to as second generation options although some exotic options, for example barrier options, are as old as standard options. Normally, exotic options are traded in OTC markets. Recently, this situation has somehow changed. The American Stock Exchange trades quanto options while the New York Mercantile Exchange provides spread options. With financial risks being understood better, exotic options are more and more widely employed by financial institutions, big corporations and fund managers. Some exotic options have already become commonplace in risk management due to their case-orientated properties. According to whether they possess an exotic payoff or probability structure, exotic options are valued in a different manner. Generally speaking, options with a complicated probability are path-dependent and therefore difficult to price. However, in the Black-Scholes world, closed-form pricing formulae for almost all exotic options have been derived.[52]

In this chapter, we incorporate stochastic volatilities, stochastic interest rates and random jumps into the pricing formulae for exotic options

---

[52] See Zhang (1997) for a comprehensive collection.

by MPO. We do not handle all possible variants of exotic options and concentrate mainly on some typical representatives such as barrier options and Asian options. Section 3.2 deals with Barrier options. Then lookback options follow in Section 3.3. Next, we handle Asian options in Section 3.4. Section 3.5 discusses correlation options including exchange options, quotient options and product options. In Section 3.5 we briefly address how to deal with other exotic options with an unconventional payoff structure. In most cases we only take stochastic volatilities as an example to show how to apply MPO. However, it must be pointed out that not all stochastic factors can be embedded in the considered cases. Hence, we should be careful in the extension of MPO and distinguish case by case. Because the square root process and the double square root process share most of their properties in many respects, we neglect the double square root process in the following chapters to save space.

## 3.2   Barrier Options

### 3.2.1   Introduction

Barrier options are path-dependent and can be classified as knock-in or knock-out based on the ratio of the initial asset price to the barrier level. For knock-out barrier options, if the prices of the underlying asset during the option's lifetime reach a certain prevailing barrier, then the option becomes worthless. Although barrier options have been traded in the OTC marketplace since the 1960s, their innovative features had not been uncovered among the financial investors until the late 1980s. Hedging strategies using barrier options are normally associated with the purpose of protecting against extreme downside or upside risk. A possible application might take place in a portfolio insurance strategy for a well-endowed investor who only need to hedge against big unexpected price risks.[53] For this purpose, buying knock-out calls is a cheaper and more efficient hedging tool than using plain vanilla options. Additionally, the knock-out or knock-in components embedded in bonds may serve to reduce the costs related to costly bond covenants (Cox and Rubinstein, 1985).

---

[53]The so-called stop-loss strategy for portfolio insurance can be duplicated by knock-out barrier options.

In the framework of the Black-Scholes model, a closed-form solution for barrier options can be derived. Merton (1973) was the first to give a closed-form pricing formula for European knock-out options. Rubinstein and Reiner (1991), and Rich (1994) dealt with barrier options systematically and covered all possible variants of barrier options. A barrier option is cheaper than the corresponding plain-vanilla options because the possibility of knock-out or knock-in is priced explicitly as a rebate. This price rebate is the so-called knock-out (in) discount. Pricing the knock-out discount is essentially a problem of evaluating the probability that the option hits the predetermined barrier. Obviously, this probability depends on the volatilities of the underlying asset. Under the usual assumption of constant volatility, the volatility has a stable impact on these hitting probabilities. However, if the volatility itself follows a stochastic process, a sudden change of its value might considerably affect the hitting probabilities. For instance, in the case where stock prices and volatilities are negatively correlated, the left tail of the distribution of stock prices will be thinner than a lognormal distribution. Thus, the hitting probabilities of knock-out options will tend to be smaller compared to constant volatilities. Consequently, the knock-out discount will be smaller. At the same time, stochastic volatilities have a significant effect on the values of plain vanilla options. Therefore, with these two effects together, stochastic volatilities have a more complicated impact on prices of knock-out options than on prices of plain vanilla options. To our knowledge, an exact analytical pricing model for barrier options with stochastic volatilities is not available yet. This section gives a partial answer to this gap.

We take out-of-the-money knock-out options as an example to highlight the issue of evaluating the hitting probabilities. A general form of an out-of-the-money knock-out call option is

$$
\begin{aligned}
C_{KO} &= e^{-rT}\left[(S(T) - K)\Pr(X(T) \geqslant \ln K, m_T^X \geqslant \ln H)\right] \\
&= e^{-rT}\left[(S(T) - K)\Pr(X(T) \geqslant \ln K)\right] \\
&\quad - e^{-rT}\left[(S(T) - K)\Pr(X(T) \geqslant \ln K, m_T^X < \ln H)\right],
\end{aligned}
$$

$$(3.143)$$

where $H$ is the downside barrier and smaller than $K$. $m_T^X$ is defined by $\min_{u \in [0,T]} X(u)$ and stands for the minimum of $X(u)$ up to time $T$.

Formula (3.143) implies that an out-of-the-money knock-out call option
is composed of two parts: a normal European call and a call involving
the probability $\Pr(X(T) \geqslant \ln K, m_T^X < \ln H)$. If the volatility $v(t)$ is
constant, then the joint distribution of $(X(T), m_T^X)$ satisfies

$$
\Pr(X(T) \geqslant x, m_T^X \geqslant y) = N\left(\frac{-x + rT - \frac{1}{2}v^2 T}{v\sqrt{T}}\right)
$$
$$
- e^{(2rv^{-2}-1)y} N\left(\frac{2y - x + rT - \frac{1}{2}v^2 T}{v\sqrt{T}}\right) \quad (3.144)
$$

for every $x, y$ such that $y \leqslant x$. This probability is the key to derive a
closed-form solution for out-of-the-money knock-out call options, which
is given by [54]

$$
C_{KO} = C - C_{discount}
$$
$$
(3.145)
$$
$$
= C - S_0 e^{(2rv^{-2}+1)y} N(d_1^*) + Ke^{-rT} e^{(2rv^{-2}-1)y} N(d_2^*),
$$

where $C$ denotes a normal European-style call option price and

$$
d_j^* = \frac{2y - x + rT \pm \frac{1}{2}v^2 T}{v\sqrt{T}}, \quad y = \ln(H/S_0), \quad x = \ln(K/S_0), \quad j = 1, 2.
$$

The formula (3.145) was given for the first time by Merton (1973).
The probability (3.144) shows two different points which are specific to
barrier options: Firstly, the probability is two-dimensional and involves
two events: the first one is the terminal value $X(T)$ at time $T$, the other
one is the minimum $m_T^X$ over the period up to time $T$; Secondly, the
minimum involves the stopping time. Usually, the reflecting principle of
the standard Brownian motion is applied to solve this problem. But, in
the presence of stochastic volatilities in a stock price process, calculating
the probability $\Pr(X(T) \geqslant \ln K, m_T^X < \ln H)$ becomes explosively complicated. It is not theoretically assured that the heuristic argument of the
reflecting principle is still valid in stochastic volatility models. Instead
of generally dealing with barrier options in stochastic volatility models,

---

[54]See Goldman, Sosin and Gatto (1979), or Merton (1973). Harrison (1985),
Musiela and Rutkowski (1997) give a detailed derivation of the joint distribution
of $(X_T, m_T^X)$ with $m_T^X = \min_{u \in [0,T]} X(u)$.

we address only two special cases where we can indeed arrive at exact closed-form solutions.

The following subsections are organized as follows: In Subsection 3.1.2 we handle two special cases and give two closed-form solutions for barrier options respectively. The pricing formulae for other types of barrier options can be obtained correspondingly. In Subsection 3.1.3, some numerical examples are given to demonstrate the special features of our solutions.

## 3.2.2  Two Special Cases

Our first case is an out-of the-money knock-out option on futures. Although they are not commonplace in financial markets, barrier options on futures provide investors with a potentially efficient insurance tool in trading futures. If futures prices fall under a certain level, investors will get a margin call and are required to fullfil a maintenance margin. In this case, one can hedge unexpected cash shortcomings by using a long position in barrier put options. Within the framework of the risk-neutral pricing, we have the following relation

$$F^T(t) = \mathbb{E}[S(T)] = e^{r(T-t)}S(t), \qquad t \leqslant T. \qquad (3.146)$$

where $F^T(t)$ denotes the futures price of spot price $S(T)$ at time $t$. Under this assumption we obtain the dynamics of futures price

$$dF^T(t) = F^T(t)v(t)dw_1(t), \qquad t \leqslant T. \qquad (3.147)$$

or

$$dX(t) = -\frac{1}{2}v(t)^2dt + v(t)dw_1(t), \quad \text{with } X_0 = 0, \qquad (3.148)$$

where $X(t) = \ln(F^T(t)/F_0^T)$. Obviously, $F^T(t)$ is a martingale. Black (1976b) derived the pricing formula for options on futures, which differs from the Black-Scholes formula only in replacing $S_0$ by $e^{-rT}F_0^T$. We specify here either the volatility $v(t)$ as a mean-reverting O-U process or the squared volatility $v(t)^2$ as a mean-reverting (double) square root process. However, it is assumed that these volatilities are not correlated with stock returns. In this subsection, we take the O-U process for demonstrating our results and have the following proposition:

**Proposition 1** *If $X(t)$ follows the process (3.148) and the volatility $v(t)$ follows a mean-reverting O-U process, and they are mutually not correlated, then the probabilities of $\Pr(m_T^X \leqslant z_1)$ and $\Pr(X(T) \geqslant x, m_T^X \geqslant z_2)$ are given respectively by*

$$\Pr(m_T^X \leqslant z_1) = \frac{1}{2} - \frac{1}{\pi} \int_0^\infty \mathrm{Re}\left(f_2(\phi)\frac{\exp(-i\phi z_1)}{i\phi}\right) d\phi$$

$$+ e^{-z_1}\left[\frac{1}{2} + \frac{1}{\pi}\int_0^\infty \mathrm{Re}\left(f_2(\phi)\frac{\exp(i\phi z_1)}{i\phi}\right) d\phi\right].$$

(3.149)

*with $z_1 \leqslant 0$, and*

$$\Pr(X(T) \geqslant z_1, m_T^X \geqslant z_2) = \frac{1}{2} + \frac{1}{\pi}\int_0^\infty \mathrm{Re}\left(f_2(\phi)\frac{\exp(-i\phi z_1)}{i\phi}\right) d\phi$$

$$- e^{-z_2}\left[\frac{1}{2} + \frac{1}{\pi}\int_0^\infty \mathrm{Re}\left(f_2(\phi)\frac{\exp(-i\phi(z_1 - 2z_2))}{i\phi}\right) d\phi\right]$$

(3.150)

*with $z_1 \geqslant z_2$ and $z_2 \leqslant 0$. $f_2(\phi)$ is defined by $f_2(\phi) = \mathbb{E}[\exp(i\phi X(T))]$.*

The proof is given in Appendix C. By applying the results in Proposition 1, we can derive a pricing formula for out-of-the money knock-out options on futures, which is expressed by

$$
\begin{aligned}
C_{KO} &= e^{-rT}\mathbb{E}\left[(F^T(T) - K)\cdot\mathbf{1}_{(X(T)\geqslant x, m_T^X\geqslant y)}\right] \\[2mm]
&= e^{-rT}F_0^T\mathbb{E}\left[\frac{F^T(T)}{F_0^T}\cdot\mathbf{1}_{(X(T)\geqslant x, m_T^X\geqslant y)}\right] \\[2mm]
&\quad - e^{-rT}K\Pr(X(T)\geqslant x, m_T^X\geqslant y)
\end{aligned}
$$

(3.151)

with $x = \ln(K/F_0^T)$, $y = \ln(H/F_0^T)$. Note that $F^T(T)/F_0^T$ implies a measure transformation by which the original process (3.148) is switched to be

$$dX(t) = \frac{1}{2}v(t)^2 dt + v(t)d\widehat{w}_1(t), \qquad \text{with } X_0 = 0.$$

This fact immediately leads to the following pricing formula for barrier options

$$C_{KO} = e^{-rT}F_0^T F_1 - e^{-rT}K F_2$$

(3.152)

with

$$F_1 = \frac{1}{2} + \frac{1}{\pi} \int_0^\infty \mathrm{Re}\left( f_1(\phi)\frac{\exp(-i\phi x)}{i\phi} \right) d\phi$$

$$-e^y \left[ \frac{1}{2} + \frac{1}{\pi} \int_0^\infty \mathrm{Re}\left( f_1(\phi)\frac{\exp(-i\phi(x-2y))}{i\phi} \right) d\phi \right] \qquad (3.153)$$

and

$$F_2 = \frac{1}{2} + \frac{1}{\pi} \int_0^\infty \mathrm{Re}\left( f_2(\phi)\frac{\exp(-i\phi x)}{i\phi} \right) d\phi$$

$$-e^{-y} \left[ \frac{1}{2} + \frac{1}{\pi} \int_0^\infty \mathrm{Re}\left( f_2(\phi)\frac{\exp(-i\phi(x-2y))}{i\phi} \right) d\phi \right], \qquad (3.154)$$

where $f_1(\phi) = \mathbb{E}[\exp((1+i\phi)X(T))]$ and $f_2(\phi) = \mathbb{E}[\exp(i\phi X(T))]$. Apparently, the discounted factor $e^{-rT}$ can be replaced by the price of a zero-bond à *la* CIR (1985b) or Vasicek (1977). For in-the-money knock-out options, strike price $K$ is smaller than or equal to barrier level $H$, and barrier level is again smaller than the current future price, that is, $K \leqslant H$ and $H < F_0^T$. In this case, we have a simplified probability $\Pr(X(T) \geqslant x, m_T^X \geqslant y) = \Pr(m_T^X \geqslant y)$, and the call option has the following reduced form

$$C_{KO} = F_0^T e^{-rT} F_1(m_T^X \geqslant y) - K e^{-rT} F_2(m_T^X \geqslant y) \qquad (3.155)$$

where

$$F_1 = \frac{1}{2} + \frac{1}{\pi} \int_0^\infty \mathrm{Re}\left( f_1(\phi)\frac{\exp(-i\phi y)}{i\phi} \right) d\phi$$

$$-e^y \left[ \frac{1}{2} + \frac{1}{\pi} \int_0^\infty \mathrm{Re}\left( f_1(\phi)\frac{\exp(i\phi y)}{i\phi} \right) d\phi \right]$$

and

$$F_2 = \frac{1}{2} + \frac{1}{\pi} \int_0^\infty \mathrm{Re}\left( f_2(\phi)\frac{\exp(-i\phi y)}{i\phi} \right) d\phi$$

$$-e^{-y} \left[ \frac{1}{2} + \frac{1}{\pi} \int_0^\infty \mathrm{Re}\left( f_2(\phi)\frac{\exp(i\phi y)}{i\phi} \right) d\phi \right].$$

The formulae (3.152) and (3.155) together give the pricing formula for knock-out barrier options on futures under the assumption that the volatilities and the stock returns are not correlated.

In the second case, we consider barrier options on equity instruments. For this purpose, we adopt the stock price process as in (2.95), that is

$$dX(t) = r(t)\left(1 - \frac{1}{2}v^2\right)dt + v\sqrt{r(t)}dw_1(t), \qquad X(t) = \ln(S(t)/S_0).$$
(3.156)

Here the volatility is the term $v\sqrt{r(t)}$ times a constant $v$, and is then accompanied by the risk of interest rates. In other words, volatilities vary through time because they bear the same risk as interest rates that are specified as a mean-reverting square root process

$$dr(t) = \kappa(\theta - r(t))dt + \sigma\sqrt{r(t)}dw_2(t),$$
(3.157)

where two processes are uncorrelated, $dw_1(t)dw_2(t) = 0$. Under these two specifications, we have the following proposition on the hitting probabilities:

**Proposition 2** *If $X(t)$ and $r(t)$ follow the processes (3.156) and (3.157) respectively, then the probabilities of $\Pr(m_T^X \leqslant z_1)$ and $\Pr(X(T) \geqslant z_1, m_T^X \geqslant y)$ are given by*

$$\Pr(m_T^X \leqslant z_1) = \frac{1}{2} - \frac{1}{\pi}\int_0^\infty \operatorname{Re}\left(f_2(\phi)\frac{\exp(-i\phi z_1)}{i\phi}\right)d\phi$$

$$+e^{-z_1\left(1-2v^{-2}\right)}\left[\frac{1}{2} + \frac{1}{\pi}\int_0^\infty \operatorname{Re}\left(f_2(\phi)\frac{\exp(i\phi z_1))}{i\phi}\right)d\phi\right].$$
(3.158)

*with $z_1 \leqslant 0$, and*

$$\Pr(X(T) \geqslant z_1, m_T^X \geqslant z_2) = \frac{1}{2} + \frac{1}{\pi}\int_0^\infty \operatorname{Re}\left(f_2(\phi)\frac{\exp(-i\phi z_1)}{i\phi}\right)d\phi$$

$$-e^{-z_2\left(1-2v^{-2}\right)}\left[\frac{1}{2} + \frac{1}{\pi}\int_0^\infty \operatorname{Re}\left(f_2(\phi)\frac{\exp(-i\phi(z_1-2z_2))}{i\phi}\right)d\phi\right]$$
(3.159)

*with $z_1 \geqslant z_2$ and $z_2 \leqslant 0$. $f_2(\phi)$ is defined by $f_2(\phi) = \mathbb{E}[\exp(i\phi X(T))]$.*

The detailed proof is given in Appendix C in Section 3.7. Following the same steps applied above, we obtain a pricing formula for knock-out barrier options on an equity with modified equity price process and stochastic interest rates.

The pricing formula takes the following form

$$
\begin{aligned}
C_{KO} &= \mathbb{E}\left[\exp\left(-\int_0^T r(t)dt\right)\left((S(T)-K)\cdot\mathbf{1}_{(X(T)\geqslant x,\,m_T^X\geqslant y)}\right)\right] \\
&\qquad\qquad\qquad\qquad\qquad\qquad\qquad\qquad\qquad\qquad (3.160) \\
&= S_0 F_1 - B(0,T;r_0)K F_2
\end{aligned}
$$

with

$$
\begin{aligned}
F_1 &= \frac{1}{2}+\frac{1}{\pi}\int_0^\infty \operatorname{Re}\left(f_1(\phi)\frac{\exp(-i\phi x)}{i\phi}\right)d\phi \\
&\qquad\qquad\qquad\qquad\qquad\qquad\qquad\qquad\qquad (3.161) \\
&\quad -e^{x\left(1+2v^{-2}\right)}\left[\frac{1}{2}+\frac{1}{\pi}\int_0^\infty \operatorname{Re}\left(f_1(\phi)\frac{\exp(-i\phi(x-2y))}{i\phi}\right)d\phi\right]
\end{aligned}
$$

and

$$
\begin{aligned}
F_2 &= \frac{1}{2}+\frac{1}{\pi}\int_0^\infty \operatorname{Re}\left(f_2(\phi)\frac{\exp(-i\phi x)}{i\phi}\right)d\phi \\
&\qquad\qquad\qquad\qquad\qquad\qquad\qquad\qquad\qquad (3.162) \\
&\quad -e^{-x\left(1-2v^{-2}\right)}\left[\frac{1}{2}+\frac{1}{\pi}\int_0^\infty \operatorname{Re}\left(f_2(\phi)\frac{\exp(-i\phi(x-2y))}{i\phi}\right)d\phi\right].
\end{aligned}
$$

The pricing formula for in-the-money knock-out options is correspondingly given by

$$
C_{KO} = S_0 F_1(m_T^X \geqslant y) - B(0,T;r_0)K F_2(m_T^X \geqslant y) \qquad (3.163)
$$

where

$$
\begin{aligned}
F_1 &= \frac{1}{2}+\frac{1}{\pi}\int_0^\infty \operatorname{Re}\left(f_1(\phi)\frac{\exp(-i\phi y)}{i\phi}\right)d\phi \\
&\qquad\qquad\qquad\qquad\qquad\qquad\qquad\qquad\qquad (3.164) \\
&\quad -e^{x\left(1+2v^{-2}\right)}\left[\frac{1}{2}+\frac{1}{\pi}\int_0^\infty \operatorname{Re}\left(f_1(\phi)\frac{\exp(i\phi y)}{i\phi}\right)d\phi\right]
\end{aligned}
$$

and

$$F_2 = \frac{1}{2} + \frac{1}{\pi} \int_0^\infty \mathrm{Re}\left( f_2(\phi) \frac{\exp(-i\phi y)}{i\phi} \right) d\phi$$

$$-e^{-x\left(1-2v^{-2}\right)} \left[ \frac{1}{2} + \frac{1}{\pi} \int_0^\infty \mathrm{Re}\left( f_2(\phi) \frac{\exp(i\phi y)}{i\phi} \right) d\phi \right]. \tag{3.165}$$

The two CFs are defined respectively by

$$f_1(\phi) = \mathbb{E}\left[ \frac{\exp\left(-\int_0^T r(t)dt\right) S(T)}{S_0} \exp(i\phi X(T)) \right] \tag{3.166}$$

and

$$f_2(\phi) = \mathbb{E}\left[ \frac{\exp\left(-\int_0^T r(t)dt\right)}{B(0,T;r_0)} \exp(i\phi X(T)) \right]. \tag{3.167}$$

All of the above closed-form solutions display the same structure as Merton's solution given in (3.145), and consists of two components: the first one is the same as the standard European call options; the second is the so-called knock-out discount or price rebate. The implementation of these formulae presents no special difficulty since all CFs are known and are given in the above chapter. The put-call parity for barrier options is different from that for plain vanilla options. Because of the following relation

$$\mathrm{Pr}(X(T) \geqslant x, m_T^X \geqslant y) + \mathrm{Pr}(X(T) < x, m_T^X < y) = 1,$$

we have the parity for knock-out calls and knock-in puts:

$$C_{KO} + Ke^{-rT} = P_{KI} + S_0, \tag{3.168}$$

which enables us to obtain the pricing formula for knock-in put options. Other variants of barrier options can be evaluated by applying the schemes given in Rubinstein and Reiner (1991), or Rich (1994)

### 3.2.3   Numerical Examples

In this subsection, we present some numerical examples to demonstrate the special features of the above derived pricing formulae and to show how the stochastic volatilities or stochastic interest rates influence the values of knock-out options. At first, we examine the knock-out options on futures with two different stochastic volatility models, namely, the volatility as a mean-reverting O-U process and the squared volatility as a mean-reverting square-root process. The CFs for these two processes have already been given in the subsections 2.2.2 and 2.2.3, respectively. For the implementation of the formulae (3.152) and (3.155), we simply set $\rho$ equal to zero in the corresponding CFs.

Table 3.1 reports the case where the stochastic volatilities follow an O-U process, and includes three panels with different values of the long-run mean $\theta$ of volatility. In every panel, we calculate the values of the knock-out call options by combining the different strike price $K$ and the barrier $H$. Thus, both in-the-money (ITM) knock-out options ($K < H$) and out-of-the-money (OTM) knock-out options ($K > H$) are considered. For the purpose of carrying out a comparison with the case of constant volatility, we evaluate the benchmark values of the knock-out options using Merton's formula with the expected average variance as given in (2.78). The price differences between the model values and the benchmarks are denoted by $PD$. In order to give a better understanding of the following tables, we briefly discuss a special feature associated with knock-out options on futures: If $H = K \leqslant F_0$, we always have the call prices equal to $e^{-rT}(F_0 - K)$, regardless of how the volatilities are specified. This feature can be explained as follows: Since the barrier $H$ is set to be $K$, the options can not gain a premium for the case $F^T(t) < K, 0 \leqslant t \leqslant T$. Furthermore, $F^T(t)$ is a martingale, therefore such particular options have no time value and their values are simply the discounted positive difference between the current futures price $F_0$ and the strike price $K$. Consequently, the values of $PD$ on the diagonal from Panel A to Panel C are zero. Another feature of knock-out options is that the options are worthless if $H = F_0$. This is apparent regardless of whether the underlying assets are futures or equity. Thus, both call prices and the $PD$ in the last column in panels A, B and C are equal to zero.

Some observations are summarized as follows: Firstly, all exact theo-

retical values of the OTM knock-out options $(H < K)$ are greater than
the corresponding benchmark values, and we have $PD > 0$. At the same
time, the exact theoretical values and the corresponding benchmark for
the ITM knock-out options perform an opposite relation with $PD < 0$.
This finding is valid for all panels in Table 3.1 and independent of the
values of $\theta$. Thus, Merton's solution seems to undervalue (overvalue) the
OTM (ITM) knock-out options on futures. Secondly, the more the spot
volatility differs from its long-run mean $\theta$, the larger the magnitude of the
undervaluation and overvaluation becomes. In Panel B and Panel C, we
can see that the mispricing due to constant volatility is significant. If we
calculate the call prices by simply using spot volatility, the price biases
are much more remarkable. To save space, we do not list these values
here. Moreover, the price biases $PD$ do not display a simple increasing
or decreasing relationship with both $H$ and $K$. The pattern of mispricing seems to be hump-shaped. Finally, by comparing the data across
panels, we reveal that a higher long-run mean $\theta$ leads to higher prices
of the OTM knock-out options and lower prices of the ITM knock-out
options. Similarly, a lower long-run mean $\theta$ leads to lower prices of the
OTM knock-out options and higher prices of the ITM knock-out options.

In Table 3.2, we give the theoretical values of the knock-out options
with the squared volatility $v(t)^2$ (variance) as a square root process. To
calculate a similar benchmark as in Table 3.1, the expected average variance has to be evaluated and is given by

$$
\begin{aligned}
AV &= \mathbb{E}\left[\frac{1}{T}\int_0^T v(t)^2 dt\right] \\
&= \frac{1}{\kappa T}(v^2 - \theta)(1 - e^{-\kappa T}) + \theta.
\end{aligned} \tag{3.169}
$$

As expected, these two stochastic volatility models perform the almost identical features, as shown in Table 3.2. All findings in Table 3.1
are confirmed again by Table 3.2 except that the magnitude of the mispricing due to constant volatility is not so considerable as in the model
with an O-U process.

Table 3.3 lists the theoretical values of the knock-out options on spot
calculated by using the formulae (3.160) and (3.163). As discussed above,
this model is based on a modified process of stock prices and a specification of interest rates as a square root process. This raises a problem in

finding out a suitable benchmark for the purpose of comparison. In order to make Merton's solution to match this model, we replace the constant interest rate and the squared volatility by the expected average interest rate and the expected average variance, respectively. These two expected values can be calculated by (3.169) and have the following form

$$r_{const} = \frac{1}{\kappa_r T}(r - \theta_r)(1 - e^{-\kappa_r T}) + \theta_r, \qquad (3.170)$$

$$v_{const} = v\sqrt{r_{const}} = v\sqrt{\frac{1}{\kappa_r T}(r - \theta_r)(1 - e^{-\kappa_r T}) + \theta_r}. \quad (3.171)$$

The benchmark values evaluated in this way best fit the values of our model in the case where the spot interest rate $r$ is equal to $\theta_r$, as shown in Panel G. But if the current interest rate $r$ diverges from the long-run mean $\theta_r$, the considerable prices biases occur. Since the underlying asset of the options is not futures but equity, it is not expected that the option prices in Table 3.3 are zero for $K = H$. The pattern of the price biases does not have a clear structure as in the model for barrier options on futures. This might be due to the choice of the benchmark. Apart from this exception, knock-out options on spot share all the features of these on futures. Thus, the model specified by (3.156) and (3.157) could be regarded as a reliable model for barrier options.

| H \ K | | 80 | 85 | 90 | 95 | 100 | 105 | 110 |
|---|---|---|---|---|---|---|---|---|
| 80 | Call | 19.506 | 15.336 | 11.480 | 8.170 | 5.531 | 3.571 | 2.211 |
| | PD | 0.000 | -0.012 | -0.031 | -0.052 | -0.060 | -0.049 | -0.026 |
| 85 | Call | 18.181 | 14.630 | 11.146 | 8.019 | 5.464 | 3.542 | 2.199 |
| | PD | 0.041 | 0.000 | -0.039 | -0.066 | -0.072 | -0.058 | -0.031 |
| 90 | Call | 14.854 | 12.304 | 9.753 | 7.261 | 5.072 | 3.347 | 2.104 |
| | PD | 0.114 | 0.057 | 0.000 | -0.051 | -0.077 | -0.071 | -0.045 |
| 95 | Call | 8.803 | 7.494 | 6.185 | 4.877 | 3.600 | 2.487 | 1.623 |
| | PD | 0.120 | 0.080 | 0.040 | 0.000 | -0.036 | -0.052 | -0.045 |
| 100 | Call/PD | 0.000 | 0.000 | 0.000 | 0.000 | 0.000 | 0.000 | 0.000 |

A: $v = 0.2, \theta = 0.2, \kappa = 2, \sigma = 0.1, T = 0.5, F_0 = 100, r = 0.05$

| H \ K | | 80 | 85 | 90 | 95 | 100 | 105 | 110 |
|---|---|---|---|---|---|---|---|---|
| 80 | Call | 19.506 | 15.510 | 11.810 | 8.614 | 6.027 | 4.056 | 2.637 |
| | PD | 0.000 | -0.087 | -0.166 | -0.223 | -0.248 | -0.236 | -0.198 |
| 85 | Call | 17.963 | 14.630 | 11.354 | 8.388 | 5.917 | 4.004 | 2.612 |
| | PD | 0.054 | 0.000 | -0.051 | -0.086 | -0.098 | -0.088 | -0.062 |
| 90 | Call | 14.453 | 12.103 | 9.753 | 7.450 | 5.393 | 3.721 | 2.463 |
| | PD | 0.120 | 0.060 | 0.000 | -0.055 | -0.088 | -0.091 | -0.071 |
| 95 | Call | 8.449 | 7.258 | 6.067 | 4.877 | 3.710 | 2.672 | 1.834 |
| | PD | 0.210 | 0.140 | 0.070 | 0.000 | -0.065 | -0.107 | -0.119 |
| 100 | Call/PD | 0.000 | 0.000 | 0.000 | 0.000 | 0.000 | 0.000 | 0.000 |

B: $v = 0.2, \theta = 0.25, \kappa = 2, \sigma = 0.1, T = 0.5, F_0 = 100, r = 0.05$

| H \ K | | 80 | 85 | 90 | 95 | 100 | 105 | 110 |
|---|---|---|---|---|---|---|---|---|
| 80 | Call | 19.506 | 15.173 | 11.164 | 7.736 | 5.043 | 3.102 | 1.813 |
| | PD | 0.000 | -0.083 | -0.174 | -0.253 | -0.288 | -0.267 | -0.207 |
| 85 | Call | 18.404 | 14.630 | 10.932 | 7.642 | 5.006 | 3.088 | 1.807 |
| | PD | 0.145 | 0.000 | -0.139 | -0.243 | -0.288 | -0.269 | -0.209 |
| 90 | Call | 15.298 | 12.525 | 9.753 | 7.054 | 4.728 | 2.962 | 1.751 |
| | PD | 0.335 | 0.168 | 0.000 | -0.154 | -0.245 | -0.254 | -0.206 |
| 95 | Call | 9.213 | 7.767 | 6.322 | 4.877 | 3.473 | 2.284 | 1.402 |
| | PD | 0.334 | 0.223 | 0.111 | 0.000 | -0.101 | -0.154 | -0.150 |
| 100 | Call/PD | 0.000 | 0.000 | 0.000 | 0.000 | 0.000 | 0.000 | 0.000 |

C: $v = 0.2, \theta = 0.15, \kappa = 2, \sigma = 0.1, T = 0.5, F_0 = 100, r = 0.05$

Table 3.1. Values of Knockout Calls on Futures with SV as an O-U Process

| H \ K | | 80 | 85 | 90 | 95 | 100 | 105 | 110 |
|---|---|---|---|---|---|---|---|---|
| 80 | Call | 19.506 | 15.310 | 11.439 | 8.123 | 5.480 | 3.515 | 2.150 |
| | PD | 0.000 | -0.003 | -0.008 | -0.013 | -0.015 | -0.013 | -0.007 |
| 85 | Call | 18.194 | 14.630 | 11.133 | 7.995 | 5.429 | 3.496 | 2.143 |
| | PD | 0.011 | 0.000 | -0.010 | -0.017 | -0.019 | -0.015 | -0.008 |
| 90 | Call | 14.850 | 12.302 | 9.753 | 7.261 | 5.065 | 3.326 | 2.067 |
| | PD | 0.030 | 0.015 | 0.000 | -0.013 | -0.020 | -0.019 | -0.012 |
| 95 | Call | 8.784 | 7.482 | 6.179 | 4.877 | 3.604 | 2.489 | 1.614 |
| | PD | 0.031 | 0.021 | 0.010 | 0.000 | -0.009 | -0.013 | -0.012 |
| 100 | Call/PD | 0.000 | 0.000 | 0.000 | 0.000 | 0.000 | 0.000 | 0.000 |

D: $v^2 = 0.04, \theta = 0.04, \kappa = 2, \sigma = 0.1, T = 0.5, F_0 = 100, r = 0.05$

| H \ K | | 80 | 85 | 90 | 95 | 100 | 105 | 110 |
|---|---|---|---|---|---|---|---|---|
| 80 | Call | 19.506 | 15.503 | 11.800 | 8.605 | 6.016 | 4.039 | 2.610 |
| | PD | 0.000 | -0.004 | -0.009 | -0.012 | -0.013 | -0.011 | -0.007 |
| 85 | Call | 17.955 | 14.630 | 11.361 | 8.397 | 5.922 | 3.998 | 2.593 |
| | PD | 0.010 | 0.000 | -0.009 | -0.015 | -0.016 | -0.014 | -0.008 |
| 90 | Call | 14.419 | 12.086 | 9.753 | 7.465 | 5.413 | 3.733 | 2.460 |
| | PD | 0.022 | 0.011 | 0.000 | -0.010 | -0.016 | -0.016 | -0.012 |
| 95 | Call | 8.409 | 7.232 | 6.054 | 4.877 | 3.722 | 2.688 | 1.845 |
| | PD | 0.022 | 0.015 | 0.007 | 0.000 | -0.007 | -0.010 | -0.010 |
| 100 | Call/PD | 0.000 | 0.000 | 0.000 | 0.000 | 0.000 | 0.000 | 0.000 |

E: $v^2 = 0.04, \theta = 0.0625, \kappa = 2, \sigma = 0.1, T = 0.5, F_0 = 100, r = 0.05$

| H \ K | | 80 | 85 | 90 | 95 | 100 | 105 | 110 |
|---|---|---|---|---|---|---|---|---|
| 80 | Call | 19.506 | 15.153 | 11.136 | 7.711 | 5.019 | 3.072 | 1.773 |
| | PD | 0.000 | -0.001 | -0.007 | -0.014 | -0.017 | -0.014 | -0.006 |
| 85 | Call | 18.410 | 14.630 | 10.927 | 7.633 | 4.992 | 3.063 | 1.770 |
| | PD | 0.011 | 0.000 | -0.011 | -0.019 | -0.021 | -0.016 | -0.007 |
| 90 | Call | 15.271 | 12.512 | 9.753 | 7.064 | 4.737 | 2.956 | 1.728 |
| | PD | 0.037 | 0.019 | 0.000 | -0.017 | -0.024 | -0.021 | -0.011 |
| 95 | Call | 9.165 | 7.736 | 6.306 | 4.877 | 3.486 | 2.296 | 1.402 |
| | PD | 0.042 | 0.028 | 0.014 | 0.000 | -0.012 | -0.017 | -0.013 |
| 100 | Call/PD | 0.000 | 0.000 | 0.000 | 0.000 | 0.000 | 0.000 | 0.000 |

F: $v^2 = 0.04, \theta = 0.0225, \kappa = 2, \sigma = 0.1, T = 0.5, F_0 = 100, r = 0.05$

Table 3.2. Values of Knockout Calls on Futures with Squared SV
As a Square Root Process

| H \ K | | 80 | 85 | 90 | 95 | 100 | 105 | 110 |
|---|---|---|---|---|---|---|---|---|
| 80 | Call | 21.529 | 17.176 | 13.103 | 9.534 | 6.608 | 4.364 | 2.751 |
| | PD | -0.003 | -0.006 | -0.010 | -0.015 | -0.016 | -0.012 | -0.005 |
| 85 | Call | 20.294 | 16.513 | 12.792 | 9.398 | 6.551 | 4.341 | 2.742 |
| | PD | 0.006 | -0.004 | -0.013 | -0.019 | -0.020 | -0.015 | -0.007 |
| 90 | Call | 16.933 | 14.137 | 11.342 | 8.599 | 6.140 | 4.141 | 2.650 |
| | PD | 0.024 | 0.010 | -0.004 | -0.017 | -0.023 | -0.020 | -0.012 |
| 95 | Call | 10.357 | 8.868 | 7.379 | 5.890 | 4.431 | 3.130 | 2.085 |
| | PD | 0.028 | 0.017 | 0.007 | -0.003 | -0.012 | -0.016 | -0.013 |
| 100 | Call/PD | 0.000 | 0.000 | 0.000 | 0.000 | 0.000 | 0.000 | 0.000 |

G: $r = 0.04, \theta_r = 0.04, \kappa_r = 2, \sigma_r = 0.1, T = 0.5, S_0 = 100, v = 1$

| H \ K | | 80 | 85 | 90 | 95 | 100 | 105 | 110 |
|---|---|---|---|---|---|---|---|---|
| 80 | Call | 21.783 | 17.584 | 13.645 | 10.170 | 7.279 | 5.007 | 3.316 |
| | PD | -0.288 | -0.464 | -0.619 | -0.727 | -0.766 | -0.733 | -0.640 |
| 85 | Call | 20.327 | 16.743 | 13.210 | 9.957 | 7.180 | 4.963 | 3.297 |
| | PD | -0.034 | -0.261 | -0.479 | -0.643 | -0.722 | -0.711 | -0.630 |
| 90 | Call | 16.741 | 14.130 | 11.520 | 8.952 | 6.615 | 4.661 | 3.142 |
| | PD | 0.230 | 0.013 | -0.204 | -0.408 | -0.549 | -0.598 | -0.564 |
| 95 | Call | 10.119 | 8.742 | 7.366 | 5.990 | 4.637 | 3.408 | 2.386 |
| | PD | 0.283 | 0.150 | 0.018 | -0.114 | -0.238 | -0.322 | -0.348 |
| 100 | Call/PD | 0.000 | 0.000 | 0.000 | 0.000 | 0.000 | 0.000 | 0.000 |

H: $r = 0.04, \theta_r = 0.0625, \kappa_r = 2, \sigma_r = 0.1, T = 0.5, S_0 = 100, v = 1$

| H \ K | | 80 | 85 | 90 | 95 | 100 | 105 | 110 |
|---|---|---|---|---|---|---|---|---|
| 80 | Call | 21.299 | 16.805 | 12.602 | 8.938 | 5.977 | 3.767 | 2.243 |
| | PD | 0.227 | 0.367 | 0.492 | 0.580 | 0.613 | 0.583 | 0.504 |
| 85 | Call | 20.279 | 16.301 | 12.392 | 8.857 | 5.948 | 3.757 | 2.239 |
| | PD | 0.021 | 0.208 | 0.386 | 0.520 | 0.582 | 0.568 | 0.498 |
| 90 | Call | 17.166 | 14.170 | 11.175 | 8.244 | 5.663 | 3.633 | 2.188 |
| | PD | -0.202 | -0.020 | 0.163 | 0.334 | 0.450 | 0.486 | 0.451 |
| 95 | Call | 10.642 | 9.027 | 7.411 | 5.796 | 4.219 | 2.845 | 1.786 |
| | PD | -0.247 | -0.134 | -0.021 | 0.091 | 0.197 | 0.266 | 0.285 |
| 100 | Call/PD | 0.000 | 0.000 | 0.000 | 0.000 | 0.000 | 0.000 | 0.000 |

I: $r = 0.04, \theta_r = 0.0225, \kappa_r = 2, \sigma_r = 0.1, T = 0.5, S_0 = 100, v = 1$

Table 3.3. Values of Knockout Call on Spot with SI as
a Square Root Process and a Modified Stock Price Process

## 3.3   Lookback Options

### 3.3.1   Introduction

Lookback options are financial derivatives which allow their owners to purchase (sell) a certain asset at expiry at the minimum (maximum) price during the option's lifetime. This type of option makes it possible for investors to buy at the lowest and sell at the highest. However, lookback options offer "no-free-lunch" for investors and, by the rule of thumb, are almost doubly expensive as the corresponding plain vanilla options. A possible application of lookback options might be related to some sophisticated portfolios. For example, one can minimize the regret of missing the best interest (exchange) rate if (currency linked) bonds are issued. Obviously, lookback options are path-dependent and involve evaluating the probability of the maximum or the minimum of the underlying asset again. In the previous section on barrier options, we have derived all the probabilities associated with a certain barrier, both maximum and minimum for two particular processes. Stochastic interest rates can be embodied into these probabilities if we introduce a modified stock price process as suggested in (2.94). In this section, we will discuss how to price lookback options with such stochastic factors.

We briefly review the valuation of a lookback option in the Black-Scholes's framework. The earliest study on this topic was done by Goldman, Sosin and Gatto (1979) who gave detailed arguments about the replication strategy, hedgeability and valuation associated with lookback options. Based on reasonable replication strategies, the risk-neutral pricing is well guaranteed. The pricing formula with constant volatility is given by

$$
\begin{aligned}
C_{LB} &= S_0 N(d) - m e^{-rT} N(d - v\sqrt{T}) - \frac{S_0 v^2}{2r} N(-d) \\
&\quad + e^{-rT} \frac{S_0 v^2}{2r} \left( \frac{m}{S_0} \right)^{2rv^{-2}} N(-d + 2rv^{-1}\sqrt{T}), \quad (3.172)
\end{aligned}
$$

where

$$
d = \frac{\ln(S_0/m) + (r + \frac{1}{2}v^2)T}{v\sqrt{T}}.
$$

$m$ denotes the realized minimum price until the current time. The first two terms in (3.172 ) represent the value of a standard European-style option whereas the last two terms in (3.172) can be interpreted as the strike-bonus since there is always a possibility that the actual strike price falls lower than the realized $m$. Hence, lookback options are always in-the-money and, thus, cost more than their standard counterparts.

## 3.3.2   Pricing Formulae with Stochastic Factors

We now attempt to value lookback options with stochastic volatilities or stochastic interest rates in the same economic setting as given in Section 3.1. We now consider a lookback call option on futures, whose terminal payoff is defined by

$$C_{LB}(T) = F_T^T - \min(m, m_T^F), \tag{3.173}$$

where $m_T^F = \min_{t \in [0,T]} F_t^T$ and $m$ is the realized minimum price during the past option's lifetime. By the risk-neutral pricing, we have

$$
\begin{aligned}
C_{LB} &= e^{-rT}\mathbb{E}[F_T^T - \min(m, m_T^F)] \\
&= e^{-rT}F_0^T - e^{-rT}\mathbb{E}\left[\min(m, m_T^F)\right] \\
&= e^{-rT}F_0^T - e^{-rT}\mathbb{E}\left[\min(m, F_0^T \exp(m_T^X)\right] \quad (3.174)
\end{aligned}
$$

where $m_T^X = \min X(t)$ and $X(t) = \ln(F_t^T/F_0^T)$. Following the above procedure, we obtain

$$
\begin{aligned}
e^{rT}C_{LB} &= F_0^T - \mathbb{E}\left[\min(m, F_0^T \exp(m_T^X)\right] \\
&= F_0^T - \mathbb{E}\left[F_0^T \exp(m_T^X) \cdot \mathbf{1}_{(F_0^T \exp(m_T^X) \leqslant m)}\right. \\
&\quad \left. + m \cdot \mathbf{1}_{(F_0^T \exp(m_T^X) > m)}\right] \\
&= F_0^T - F_0^T\mathbb{E}\left[\exp(m_T^X) \cdot \mathbf{1}_{(m_T^X \leqslant z)}\right] - m\mathbb{E}\left[\mathbf{1}_{(m_T^X > z)}\right] \\
&= F_0^T - F_0^T\mathbb{E}\left[\exp(m_T^X) \cdot \mathbf{1}_{(m_T^X \leqslant z)}\right] - m\Pr(m_T^X > z)
\end{aligned}
$$
$$\tag{3.175}$$

with $z = \ln(m/F_0^T)$. Therefore, the key to getting a closed form solution for lookback options is the minimum probability $\Pr(m_T^X > z)$.

According to Proposition 1 in Section 3.2, the probability $\Pr(m_T^X > z)$ can be calculated as follows

$$
\begin{aligned}
L_1 &= \Pr(m_T^X > z) \\
&= \frac{1}{2} + \frac{1}{\pi} \int_0^\infty \mathrm{Re}\left(f_2(\phi)\frac{\exp(-i\phi z)}{i\phi}\right) d\phi \\
&\quad - e^{-z}\left[\frac{1}{2} + \frac{1}{\pi} \int_0^\infty \mathrm{Re}\left(f_2(\phi)\frac{\exp(i\phi z)}{i\phi}\right) d\phi\right].
\end{aligned}
\tag{3.176}
$$

Differentiating $\Pr(m_T^X \leqslant u)$ with respect to $u$ yields the density function $p.d.f(u)$ of $m_T^X$:

$$
\begin{aligned}
p.d.f(u) &= \frac{1}{\pi} \int_0^\infty \mathrm{Re}\left(f_2(\phi)\exp(-i\phi u)\right) d\phi \\
&\quad - e^{-u}\left[\frac{1}{2} + \frac{1}{\pi} \int_0^\infty \mathrm{Re}\left(f_2(\phi)\frac{\exp(i\phi u)}{i\phi}\right) d\phi\right] \\
&\quad + e^{-u}\frac{1}{\pi} \int_0^\infty \mathrm{Re}\left(f_2(\phi)\exp(i\phi u)\right) d\phi.
\end{aligned}
$$

Rearranging, we get

$$
p.d.f(u) = \frac{1}{\pi} \int_0^\infty \mathrm{Re}\left[f_2(\phi)e^{-i\phi u} + h(u;\phi)e^{i\phi u}\right] d\phi - \frac{1}{2}e^{-u}
\tag{3.177}
$$

with

$$
h(u;\phi) = f_2(\phi)e^{-u}\frac{(i\phi - 1)}{i\phi}.
$$

We evaluate $\mathbb{E}\left[\exp(m_T^X) \cdot \mathbf{1}_{(m_T^X \leqslant z)}\right]$ by the Fourier transformation:

$$
\begin{aligned}
L_2 &= \mathbb{E}\left[\exp(m_T^X) \cdot \mathbf{1}_{(m_T^X \leqslant z)}\right] = \int_{-\infty}^z e^u\, p.d.f(u)du, \quad u = M_T^X, \\
&= \frac{1}{\pi}\int_{-\infty}^z \int_0^\infty \mathrm{Re}\{f_2(\phi)e^{u-i\phi u} + h(u;\phi)e^{u+i\phi u}\} d\phi du - \int_{-\infty}^z \frac{1}{2}du
\end{aligned}
$$

$$
= \frac{1}{\pi} \int_0^\infty \int_{-\infty}^z \operatorname{Re}\left( f_2(\phi) e^{(1-i\phi)u} \right) du\, d\phi +
$$

$$
\frac{1}{\pi} \int_0^\infty \int_{-\infty}^z \operatorname{Re}\left( f_2(\phi) e^{i\phi u} \frac{(i\phi - 1)}{i\phi} \right) du\, d\phi - \int_{-\infty}^z \frac{1}{2} du
$$

$$
= \frac{1}{\pi} \int_0^\infty \operatorname{Re}\left( f_2(\phi) \frac{1}{1 - i\phi} e^{(1-i\phi)z} \right) d\phi +
$$

$$
\frac{1}{\pi} \int_0^\infty \operatorname{Re}\left( f_2(\phi) \frac{e^{i\phi z} - e^{-i\phi \infty}}{i\phi} \right) d\phi -
$$

$$
\frac{1}{2} \int_{-\infty}^z d\phi - \frac{1}{\pi} \int_0^\infty \int_{-\infty}^z \operatorname{Re}\left( f_2(\phi) \frac{e^{i\phi u}}{i\phi} \right) du\, d\phi \qquad (3.178)
$$

Note the identity

$$
\frac{1}{2} + \frac{1}{\pi} \int_0^\infty \operatorname{Re}\left( f_2(\phi) \frac{e^{i\phi z}}{i\phi} \right) = \Pr(X(T) > -z),
$$

we have

$$
\frac{1}{\pi} \int_0^\infty \operatorname{Re}\left( f_2(\phi) \frac{e^{-i\phi \infty}}{i\phi} \right) = \Pr(X(T) > \infty) - \frac{1}{2} = -\frac{1}{2}.
$$

Additionally, in order to obtain a tractable expression for the third and fourth terms in (3.178), we use the well-known fact $\frac{2}{\pi} \int_0^\infty \frac{\sin(\phi u)}{\phi} d\phi = sign(u)$ to express $\frac{1}{2} \int_{-\infty}^z du$ as

$$
-\frac{1}{2} \int_{-\infty}^z du = \frac{1}{\pi} \int_0^\infty \int_{-\infty}^z \frac{\sin(\phi u)}{\phi} du\, d\phi.
$$

With these manipulations, we have

$$
\begin{aligned}
L_2 &= \frac{1}{2} + \frac{1}{\pi} \int_0^\infty \operatorname{Re}\left( f_2(\phi) \frac{e^{(1-i\phi)z}}{1 - i\phi} + \frac{e^{i\phi z}}{i\phi} \right) d\phi \\
&\quad - \frac{1}{\pi} \int_0^\infty \int_{-\infty}^z \operatorname{Re}\left( f_2(\phi) \frac{e^{i\phi u}}{i\phi} + \frac{\sin(\phi u)}{\phi} \right) du\, d\phi \\
&= \frac{1}{2} + \frac{1}{\pi} \int_0^\infty \operatorname{Re}\left( f_2(\phi) \frac{e^{(1-i\phi)z}}{1 - i\phi} + \frac{e^{i\phi z}}{i\phi} \right) d\phi + \\
&\quad \lim_{a \to -\infty} \frac{1}{\pi} \int_0^\infty \operatorname{Re}\left( f_2(\phi) \frac{e^{i\phi z} - e^{i\phi a}}{\phi^2} - \frac{\cos(\phi z) - \cos(\phi a)}{\phi^2} \right) d\phi.
\end{aligned}
$$

$$
(3.179)
$$

The numerical integrals in (3.179) display a well-behaved convergence for a sufficiently small $a$, say $-10$.[55] The pricing formula for lookback options takes then a form of

$$C_{LB} = e^{-rT}(F_0^T - mL_1 - F_0^T L_2).$$ (3.180)

The interpretation of this pricing formula is straightforward: $L_1$ is the probability that the expected minimum up to maturity is smaller than the realized minimum while $L_2$ gives the opposite probability but under another measure. The technique applied in the above procedure is somehow different from anywhere else in this book. We do not change measure to evaluate $\mathbb{E}\left[\exp(m_T^X) \cdot \mathbf{1}_{(m_T^X \leqslant z)}\right]$. Instead we calculate it by using the density function.

If $X(t)$ and $r(t)$ follow the processes (3.156) and (3.157) respectively, we can obtain a pricing formula for lookback options on spot in the same way:

$$
\begin{aligned}
C_{LB} &= \mathbb{E}\left[\exp\left(-\int_0^T r(t)dt\right)\left[S(T) - \min(m, S_0 \exp(m_T^X))\right]\right] \\
&= S_0 - B(0, T; r_0)(mL_1 + S_0 L_2)
\end{aligned}
$$ (3.181)

with

$$
\begin{aligned}
L_1 &= \Pr(m_T^X > z) \\
&= \frac{1}{2} + \frac{1}{\pi}\int_0^\infty \mathrm{Re}\left(f_2(\phi)\frac{\exp(-i\phi z)}{i\phi}\right)d\phi \\
&\quad - e^{-z(1-2v^{-2})}\left[\frac{1}{2} + \frac{1}{\pi}\int_0^\infty \mathrm{Re}\left(f_2(\phi)\frac{\exp(i\phi z)}{i\phi}\right)d\phi\right]
\end{aligned}
$$ (3.182)

and

$$L_2 = \frac{-1 + 2v^{-2}}{4v^{-2}}e^{2v^{-2}z}$$

---

[55] The number $a = -10$ for this integral can be regarded to be sufficiently small because we have $m = 4.54 \times 10^{-5} F_0^T$ ($\ln(m/F_0^T) = -10$) for this case and the probability $\Pr(m_T^X \leqslant -10)$ is actually zero. Thus, we only need to implement the integral over the interval $[a, z]$ instead of $[-\infty, z]$.

$$+\frac{1}{\pi}\int_0^\infty \mathrm{Re}\left(f_2(\phi)\left[\frac{e^{(1-i\phi)z}}{1-i\phi}+\frac{1-2v^{-2}-i\phi}{\phi^2-2v^{-2}i\phi}e^{(2v^{-2}+i\phi)z}\right]\right)d\phi$$

$$=\ e^{2v^{-2}z}[\mathrm{Pr}(X(T)>-z)-0.25v^2]$$

$$+\frac{1}{\pi}\int_0^\infty \mathrm{Re}\left(f_2(\phi)\left[\frac{e^{(1-i\phi)z}}{1-i\phi}+\frac{e^{(2v^{-2}+i\phi)z}}{\phi^2-2v^{-2}i\phi}\right]\right)d\phi \qquad (3.183)$$

where $f_2(\phi)$ is defined by

$$f_2(\phi)=\mathbb{E}\left[\frac{\exp\left(-\int_0^T r(t)dt\right)}{B(0,T;r_0)}\exp(i\phi X(T))\right].$$

A similar procedure can be applied to price lookback put options. However, one must know the probability distributions involving maximum. We have the following proposition:

**Proposition 3** *(a) If $X(t)$ follows the process (3.148) and the volatility $v(t)$ follows a mean-reverting O-U process, and they are mutually not correlated, then the probabilities of $\mathrm{Pr}(X(T)\leqslant z_1, M_T^X\geqslant y)$ and $\mathrm{Pr}(M_T^X\leqslant z_2)$ with $z_1\leqslant z_2$ and $z_2\geqslant 0$ are respectively given by*

$$\mathrm{Pr}(X(T)\ \leqslant\ z_1,M_T^X\geqslant z_2)$$

$$\tag{3.184}$$

$$=\ e^{z_2}\left[\frac{1}{2}-\frac{1}{\pi}\int_0^\infty \mathrm{Re}\left(f_2(\phi)\frac{\exp(-i\phi(z_1-2z_2))}{i\phi}\right)d\phi\right].$$

*and*

$$\mathrm{Pr}(M_T^X\ \leqslant\ z_2)=\frac{1}{2}-\frac{1}{\pi}\int_0^\infty \mathrm{Re}\left(f_2(\phi)\frac{\exp(-i\phi z_2)}{i\phi}\right)d\phi$$

$$\tag{3.185}$$

$$-e^{-z_2}\left[\frac{1}{2}-\frac{1}{\pi}\int_0^\infty \mathrm{Re}\left(f_2(\phi)\frac{\exp(i\phi z_2)}{i\phi}\right)d\phi\right].$$

*(b) If $X(t)$ and $r(t)$ follow the processes (3.156) and (3.157) respectively, then the probabilities of $\mathrm{Pr}(X(T)\leqslant z_1, M_T^X\geqslant z_2)$ and $\mathrm{Pr}(M_T^X\leqslant z_2)$ with $z_1\leqslant z_2$ and $z_2\geqslant 0$ are given by*

$$\mathrm{Pr}(X(T)\ \leqslant\ z_1,M_T^X\geqslant z_2)=e^{-z_2\left(1-2v^{-2}\right)}\times$$

$$\tag{3.186}$$

$$\left[\frac{1}{2}-\frac{1}{\pi}\int_0^\infty \mathrm{Re}\left(f_2(\phi)\frac{\exp(i\phi(z_1-2z_2))}{i\phi}\right)d\phi\right].$$

*and*

$$\Pr(M_T^X \leqslant z_2) = \frac{1}{2} - \frac{1}{\pi}\int_0^\infty \mathrm{Re}\left(f_2(\phi)\frac{\exp(-i\phi z_2)}{i\phi}\right) d\phi$$

$$-e^{-z_2\left(1-2v^{-2}\right)}\left[\frac{1}{2} - \frac{1}{\pi}\int_0^\infty \mathrm{Re}\left(f_2(\phi)\frac{\exp(i\phi z_2)}{i\phi}\right) d\phi\right]. \tag{3.187}$$

A detailed proof is given in Appendix C. Since the terminal payoff of lookback put options on futures is equal to $\max_{t\in[0,T]} F^T(t) - F^T(T)$, their theoretical prices can be evaluated by

$$\begin{aligned} P_{LB} &= e^{-rT}\mathbb{E}\left[\max F^T(t) - F^T(T)\right] \\ &= e^{-rT}\mathbb{E}\left[M\Pr\left(M_T^X \leqslant z\right) + F_0^T\exp(M_T^X)\cdot\mathbf{1}_{(M_T^X>z)} - F^T(T)\right] \\ &= e^{-rT}[M\cdot L_1 + F_0^T\cdot L_2 - F_0^T] \end{aligned} \tag{3.188}$$

where $M$ is the realized maximum up to now and $z$ is equal to $\ln(M/F_0^T)$. $L_1$ and $L_2$ are respectively given by

$$\begin{aligned} L_1 &= \frac{1}{2} - \frac{1}{\pi}\int_0^\infty \mathrm{Re}\left(f_2(\phi)\frac{\exp(-i\phi z)}{i\phi}\right) d\phi \\ &\quad -e^{-z}\left[\frac{1}{2} - \frac{1}{\pi}\int_0^\infty \mathrm{Re}\left(f_2(\phi)\frac{\exp(i\phi z)}{i\phi}\right) d\phi\right] \end{aligned}$$

and

$$\begin{aligned} L_2 &= \mathbb{E}[\exp(M_T^X)\cdot\mathbf{1}_{(M_T^X>z)}] \\ &= \frac{1}{2} - \frac{1}{\pi}\int_0^\infty \mathrm{Re}\left(f_2(\phi)\frac{\exp(i\phi z)}{i\phi}\right) d\phi \\ &\quad + \lim_{a\to\infty}\frac{1}{\pi}\int_0^\infty \mathrm{Re}\left(f_2(\phi)\frac{e^{(1-i\phi)a} - e^{(1-i\phi)z}}{1-i\phi}\right) d\phi \\ &\quad + \lim_{a\to\infty}\frac{1}{\pi}\int_0^\infty \mathrm{Re}\left(f_2(\phi)\frac{e^{i\phi a} - e^{i\phi z}}{\phi^2} - \frac{\cos(\phi a) - \cos(\phi z)}{\phi^2}\right) d\phi. \end{aligned}$$

In a practical implementation, setting the number $a$ as 10 offers us reasonably accurate results. The derivation of the pricing formula for lookback put options on equity instruments follows an analogous way. We have the following form:

$$P_{LB} = B(0, T; r_0)[M \cdot L_1 + S_0 \cdot L_1] - S_0 \qquad (3.189)$$

with

$$
\begin{aligned}
L_1 = {} & \frac{1}{2} - \frac{1}{\pi} \int_0^\infty \mathrm{Re}\left( f_2(\phi) \frac{\exp(-i\phi z)}{i\phi} \right) d\phi \\
& - e^{-z\left(1-2v^{-2}\right)} \left[ \frac{1}{2} - \frac{1}{\pi} \int_0^\infty \mathrm{Re}\left( f_2(\phi) \frac{\exp(i\phi z)}{i\phi} \right) d\phi \right]
\end{aligned}
$$

and

$$
\begin{aligned}
L_2 = {} & \lim_{a \to \infty} \frac{1}{\pi} \int_0^\infty \mathrm{Re}\left( f_2(\phi) \frac{e^{(1-i\phi)a} - e^{(1-i\phi)z}}{1 - i\phi} \right) d\phi \\
& + \frac{1}{1-b} \lim_{a \to \infty} \frac{1}{\pi} \int_0^\infty \mathrm{Re}\left( f_2(\phi) \frac{\left(e^{(1-b+i\phi)a} - e^{(1-b+i\phi)z}\right)}{1 - b + i\phi} \right) d\phi \\
& - \frac{b}{1-b} e^{(1-b)z} \left[ \frac{1}{2} - \frac{1}{\pi} \int_0^\infty \mathrm{Re}\left( f_2(\phi) \frac{\exp(i\phi z)}{i\phi} \right) d\phi \right]
\end{aligned}
$$

where $b = 1 - 2v^{-2}$. With these complex pricing formulae having been derived, we close this section.

# 3.4 Asian Options

## 3.4.1 Introduction

Asian options are referred to as a class of options whose payoff at maturity depends on a certain average of some prices of the underlying asset prior to the expiration. The average designed in a contract could be arithmetic or geometric. Asian options based on an arithmetic average dominate trading in the OTC markets. The exotic average feature of Asian options is especially designed for those thinly traded assets whose prices can be manipulated easily. Hence, the average component in Asian options allows their holders to control the risk of manipulation better. Another usage of Asian options, which is not emphasized in the literature, is the diversification of volatile market prices. In this section, we study the effect of stochastic volatilities on the pricing of Asian options and give closed-form pricing formulae for two cases: a mean-reverting Ornstein-Uhlenbeck process and a mean-reverting square-root process. This is a natural extension of our MPO by using the Fourier transformation. An Asian option is usually cheaper than its standard counterpart. Thus, it is also an economic alternative for hedging and other risk management.

A still unsolved problem in financial economics is that one can not find a closed-form solution for arithmetic average Asian options even in the Black-Scholes world. However, the closed-form solution for Asian options with a geometric average is available since the geometric average of stock prices is still lognormally distributed. If the time to maturity of an option has the same length as the average period specified in the option contract, we have the following formula for Asian options with continuous geometric average:

$$C_{asian} = S_0 e^{-(\frac{1}{2}rT+\frac{1}{12}v^2T)} N(d + \sqrt{T/3}v) - Ke^{-rT}N(d), \qquad (3.190)$$

where

$$d = \frac{\ln(S_0/K) + \frac{1}{2}T(r - \frac{1}{2}v^2)}{\sqrt{T/3}v}.$$

In comparison with the Black-Scholes formula for standard options, this formula has two additional correction terms: $1/2$ for $T(r - \frac{1}{2}v^2)$ and $\sqrt{1/3}$ for $\sqrt{T}v$. This is the reason why Asian options are cheaper than their standard counterparts. In the following subsections, at first, we explain how these two terms enter the valuation formula. Next, we incorporate stochastic factors including random jumps into the pricing formulae. The third subsection is about the approximation methods for arithmetic average Asian options. Finally, we deal with a pricing model for Asian interest rate options.

## 3.4.2 The Black-Scholes World

In this subsection, we give an alternative pricing formula to (3.190) by applying the Fourier inversion. This formula is equivalent to the existing one. The purpose of giving an alternative pricing formula, which, at first glance, is more complicated, is twofold. Firstly, we show why hedging with Asian options is different from hedging with plain vanilla options. In other words, why we need to modify the method of risk-neutral pricing used for plain vanilla options. Secondly, we make preparations for the valuation of Asian options with stochastic factors. Some notations are defined here:

$n_0$ : the number of total observation points in the whole average period.

$n$ : the number of remaining observation points for calculating the average stock price. For out-of-the-period (OTP) Asian options we have $n_0 = n$.

$T_0$ : time from the current time to the first observation point. For in-the-period (ITP) or at-the-period (ATP) Asian options $T_0 = 0$.

$h$ : observation frequency defined by the whole average period dividing $n$.

Instead of using the arithmetic average, we use the geometric average of the observed stock prices to price Asian options. The discrete geometric average is defined as follows:

$$GA(n) = \left(\prod_{j=1}^{n} S_j\right)^{1/n}. \tag{3.191}$$

where $S_j$ is the stock price at the $j$-th observation point. The price of an Asian option is then generally given by

$$
\begin{aligned}
C_{asian} &= e^{-rT}\mathbb{E}\left[\{(nGA(n) + A)/n_0 - K\} \cdot \mathbf{1}_{\{nGA(n)+A \geqslant K \cdot n_0\}}\right] \\
&\tag{3.192} \\
&= e^{-rT}\mathbb{E}\left[\{(nGA(n) + A)/n_0 - K\} \cdot \mathbf{1}_{\{GA(n) \geqslant (K \cdot n_0 - A)/n\}}\right],
\end{aligned}
$$

where $A$ is the sum of stock prices from the first day of the average period to the current time, and is equal to zero for the OTP- and ATP-Asian options. By defining $K_0 = (Kn_0 - A)/n$ and $K_1 = K - A/n_0$, we have

$$C_{asian} = e^{-rT}\mathbb{E}\left[\left(\frac{n}{n_0}GA(n) - K_1\right) \cdot \mathbf{1}_{\{GA(n) \geqslant K_0\}}\right] \tag{3.193}$$

$$= e^{-rT}\frac{n}{n_0}\mathbb{E}\left[GA(n)\cdot \mathbf{1}_{\{GA(n)\geqslant K_0\}}\right] - e^{-rT}K_1\mathbb{E}\left[\mathbf{1}_{\{GA(n)\geqslant K_0\}}\right].$$

What we need to do here is to calculate the CFs of $GA(n)$ under the risk-neutral measure. We consider the Black-Scholes world where the volatility is constant. The logarithm of $GA(n)$ can be expanded as follows:

$$\ln GA(n) = \frac{1}{n}\ln\left(\prod_{j=1}^{n}S_j\right) = \frac{1}{n}\sum_{j=1}^{n}\ln S_j = \frac{1}{n}\sum_{j=1}^{n}x_j$$

$$= x_0 + (r - \frac{1}{2}v^2)\frac{1}{n}\sum_{j=1}^{n}T_j + \frac{v}{n}\sum_{j=1}^{n}w_j$$

$$= x_0 + (r - \frac{1}{2}v^2)\left(T_0 + \frac{h(n+1)}{2}\right) + \frac{v}{n}\sum_{j=1}^{n}w_j.$$

$$(3.194)$$

So we have

$$\mathbb{E}[\exp(i\phi\ln GA(n)]$$

$$= \mathbb{E}\left[\exp\left(i\phi\left(x_0 + (r - \frac{1}{2}v^2)\left(T_0 + \frac{h(n+1)}{2}\right) + \frac{v}{n}\sum_{j=1}^{n}w_j\right)\right)\right]$$

$$= \mathbb{E}\left[\exp\left(i\phi x_0 + i\phi(r - \frac{1}{2}v^2)t_1 + \frac{i\phi v}{n}\sum_{j=1}^{n}w_j\right)\right]$$

$$= \exp\left(i\phi x_0 + i\phi(r - \frac{1}{2}v^2)t_1\right)\mathbb{E}\left[\exp\left(\frac{i\phi v}{n}\sum_{j=1}^{n}w_j\right)\right]$$

$$= \exp\left(i\phi x_0 + i\phi(r - \frac{1}{2}v^2)t_1\right)\exp\left(\frac{-\phi^2}{2}Var\left(\frac{v}{n}\sum_{j=1}^{n}w_j\right)\right)$$

$$(3.195)$$

with

$$t_1 = T_0 + \frac{h(n+1)}{2}.$$

Let $w(h)$ be a Brownian motion over an interval of length $h$. To calculate $Var\left(\frac{v}{n}\sum_{j=1}^{n}w_j\right)$, we can rewrite $w_j = w(T_0) + jw(h)$ since every increment of $w_j$ over an interval $[t, t+h]$ can be regarded to be identical to $w(h)$. Hence, we have the following equation

$$\frac{1}{n}\sum_{j=1}^{n} w_j = \frac{1}{n}\sum_{j=1}^{n}\left(w(T_0) + jw(h)\right) = w(T_0) + \sum_{j=1}^{n}\frac{j}{n}w(h).$$

Due to the Markovian property of the Brownian motion we immediately obtain

$$
\begin{aligned}
\exp\left(\frac{\phi^2}{2}Var\left(\frac{v}{n}\sum_{j=1}^{n}w_j\right)\right) &= \exp\left(\frac{v^2\phi^2}{2}\left(T_0 + \sum_{j=1}^{n}\frac{j^2}{n^2}h\right)\right) \\
&= \exp\left(\frac{v^2\phi^2}{2}\left(T_0 + \sum_{j=1}^{n}\frac{j^2}{n^2}h\right)\right) \\
&= \exp\left(\frac{v^2\phi^2}{2}\left(\frac{h(n+1)(2n+1)}{6n} + T_0\right)\right) \\
&= \exp\left(\frac{v^2\phi^2}{2}t_2\right)
\end{aligned}
$$

where

$$t_2 = \frac{h(n+1)(2n+1)}{6n} + T_0.$$

Therefore,

$$
\begin{aligned}
f_2(\phi; \ln GA(n)) &= \mathbb{E}[\exp(i\phi \ln GA(n)] \\
&= \exp\left(i\phi x_0 + i\phi(r - \frac{1}{2}v^2)t_1 - \frac{v^2\phi^2}{2}t_2\right).
\end{aligned}
$$

$$(3.196)$$

Now we consider the expectation

$$\mathbb{E}\left[GA(n)\cdot\mathbf{1}_{\{GA(n)\geqslant K_0\}}\right].$$

In order to guarantee the risk-neutral pricing and a suitable hedging, we have to find a suitable process $M(t)$ such that $GA(n)/S_0 M(t)$ is a likelihood process with an expected value of one. $M(t) = e^{rt}$, usually suggested for standard options, obviously can no longer satisfy the required condition since $\mathbb{E}\left[GA(n)\right] = \exp\left(x_0 + (r - \frac{1}{2}v^2)t_1 + \frac{v^2}{2}t_2\right)$. This means that the usual arbitrage argument for European options is no longer valid for Asian options. An appropriate $M(t)$ should be the term $\exp\left((r - \frac{1}{2}v^2)t_1 + \frac{v^2}{2}t_2\right)$, with which we have $\mathbb{E}\left[GA(n)/S_0M(t)\right] = 1$. Thus,

$$\mathbb{E}\left[GA(n) \cdot \mathbf{1}_{\{GA(n) \geq K_0\}}\right] = S_0M(t)\mathbb{E}\left[\frac{GA(n)}{S_0M(t)} \cdot \mathbf{1}_{\{GA(n) \geq K_0\}}\right] \quad (3.197)$$

with

$$M(t) = \exp\left((r - \frac{1}{2}v^2)t_1 + \frac{v^2}{2}t_2\right).$$

The expectation in the above equality implies a probability measure due to the special term $S_0M(t)$. It is well worth discussing $M(t)$ in more detail because it includes some useful informations for hedging. Due to the correlation among the sequence of stock prices, $t_2$ is somehow smaller than $t_1$ and $M(t)$ can not be reduced to $e^{rt}$. Hence, the volatility $v$ plays an important role in discounting $GA(n)$ to $S_0$, which is not the case for plain vanilla options. The larger the volatility $v$ is, the smaller the value of the "discounted" spot price $S_0 \exp\left((r - \frac{1}{2}v^2)t_1 + \frac{v^2}{2}t_2\right)$ is. This effect shows the usefulness and effectiveness of Asian options in eliminating the undesired impact of volatility on option prices. The CF of $\mathbb{E}\left[\frac{GA(n)}{S_0M(t)} \cdot \mathbf{1}_{\{GA(n) \geq K_0\}}\right]$ is given by

$$\begin{aligned} f_1(\phi; \ln GA(n)) &= \mathbb{E}\left[\frac{GA(n)}{S_0M(t)} \exp(i\phi \ln GA(n)\right] \\ &= \exp\left(i\phi x_0 + i\phi r - \frac{i\phi}{2}v^2 t_1 + \frac{v^2(2i\phi - \phi^2)}{2}t_2\right). \end{aligned} \quad (3.198)$$

Thus, the pricing formula for Asian stock options with the discrete geometric average is given by

$$C_{asian} = \exp\left(-rT + (r - \frac{1}{2}v^2)t_1 + \frac{v^2}{2}t_2\right)\frac{n}{n_0}S_0F_1 - e^{-rT}K_1F_2. \quad (3.199)$$

where

$$F_j = \frac{1}{2} + \frac{1}{\pi} \int_0^{\infty} \mathrm{Re}\left(\frac{f_j(\phi; \ln GA(n)) \exp(-i\phi \ln K_0)}{i\phi}\right) d\phi, \quad j = 1, 2.$$

(3.200)

If $n$ approaches infinity, we actually arrive at the pricing formula for options with the continuous geometric average. In the case of ATP-Asian options, we have $t_1 = \frac{1}{2}T$ and $t_2 = \frac{1}{3}T$. Consequently, the pricing formula for Asian options with a continuous geometric average is given by:

$$C_{asian} = \exp\left(-\frac{rT}{2} - \frac{v^2T}{12}\right)\frac{n}{n_0}S_0F_1 - e^{-rT}K_1F_2,$$

(3.201)

which is identical to formula (3.190).

### 3.4.3    Asian Options in a Stochastic World

In this subsection, we take stochastic volatilities and stochastic interest rates into account in pricing geometric average Asian options. Intuitively, $\ln GA(n)$ should follow a Brownian motion since $GA(n)$ is lognormally distributed. In order to obtain the concrete form of the process $\ln GA(n)$, we consider $\mathbb{E}[GA(n)]$ and hope to get a detailed information on the drift and volatility structure of the process $\ln GA(n)$. From the results in the above subsection, we rewrite

$$\begin{aligned}
\mathbb{E}[GA(n)] &= \mathbb{E}[\exp(\ln GA(n)] \\
&= \exp\left(x_0 + (r - \frac{1}{2}v^2)t_1 + \frac{v^2}{2}t_2\right) \\
&= \mathbb{E}\left[\exp\left(x_0 + \frac{t_1}{T}(r - \frac{1}{2}v^2)T + (\sqrt{t_2/T}v)w_T\right)\right] \\
&= \mathbb{E}\left[\exp\left(x_0 + \int_0^T \frac{t_1}{T}(r - \frac{1}{2}v^2)dt + \int_0^T (\sqrt{t_2/T}v)dw\right)\right].
\end{aligned}$$

(3.202)

This expression with stochastic integral implies a "visual" stochastic process of $\ln GA(n)$, which takes the following form

$$d \ln GA(t;n) = \frac{t_1}{T}\left(r - \frac{1}{2}v^2\right)dt + \sqrt{\frac{t_2}{T}}vdw,$$

$$= \varepsilon_1\left(r - \frac{1}{2}v^2\right)dt + (\sqrt{\varepsilon_2}v)dw, \qquad \ln GA(0;n) = x_0,$$

$$(3.203)$$

with

$$\varepsilon_1 = \frac{t_1}{T}, \qquad \text{and} \qquad \varepsilon_2 = \frac{t_2}{T}.$$

In the case of ATP-Asian options with infinity $n$, $t_1/T = 1/2$ and $t_1/T = 1/3$. The process can be rewritten as

$$d \ln GA(t) = \frac{1}{2}\left(r - \frac{1}{2}v^2\right)dt + \sqrt{\frac{1}{3}}vdw(t), \qquad \ln GA(0;n) = x_0.$$

$$(3.204)$$

We call such a process of $\ln GA(t)$ "visual" since this process can not be directly observed in the marketplaces and is derived from the stock price process. The derivation of the rigorous process of $GA(t;n)$ in the presence of stochastic volatilities and interest rates is mathematically very cumbersome and does not result in a tractable form. To ease incorporating stochastic factors into geometric average Asian options, we have the following assumption:

**Assumption:** The geometric average of $n$ sequential stock prices of Asian options $GA(t;n)$ follows the process (3.203) even in the presence of stochastic volatilities and stochastic interest rates.

If the pricing formula for Asian options implies no arbitrage, as mentioned above, then there exists a process $M(t)$ such that the following equation holds:

$$\mathbb{E}\left[\frac{GA(T)}{S_0M(T)}\right] = 1 \Leftrightarrow M(T) = \mathbb{E}\left[GA(T)\right]/S_0.$$

$$(3.205)$$

Consequently, the CFs $f_1(\phi)$ and $f_2(\phi)$ are given by

$$f_1(\phi) = \mathbb{E}\left[\frac{GA(n)}{S_0M(T)}\exp(i\phi \ln GA(n))\right] = \mathbb{E}\left[\frac{\exp((1+i\phi)\ln GA(n))}{S_0M(T)}\right]$$

$$= \mathbb{E}\left[\frac{\exp((1+i\phi)\ln GA(n))}{\mathbb{E}\left[GA(T)\right]}\right] = \mathbb{E}\left[\frac{g(1+i\phi)}{\mathbb{E}\left[g(1)\right]}\right]$$

$$(3.206)$$

and

$$f_2(\phi) = \mathbb{E}\left[g(i\phi)\right], \tag{3.207}$$

where the function $g(a) = \exp(a \ln GA(n))$. Again, in order to calculate the CFs, we classify the volatilities in two popular cases:

**Case 1**: A mean-reverting Ornstein-Uhlenbeck process:
Similar to the Schöbel and Zhu (1999) model:

$$
\begin{aligned}
\mathbb{E}\left[g(a)\right] &= \mathbb{E}\left[\exp(a \ln GA(n))\right] \\
&= \mathbb{E}\left[\exp\left(ax_0 + a \int_0^T \varepsilon_1(r - \frac{1}{2}v^2)dt + a \int_0^T \sqrt{\varepsilon_2}v\,dw\right)\right] \\
&= \mathbb{E}\left[\exp\left(ax_0 + a\varepsilon_1 rT - \frac{a\sqrt{\varepsilon_2}\rho}{2\sigma}v_0^2 - \frac{a\sqrt{\varepsilon_2}\rho\sigma T}{2}\right.\right. \\
&\quad - \left(\frac{a\varepsilon_1}{2} - \frac{a\sqrt{\varepsilon_2}\rho\kappa}{\sigma} - \frac{a^2\varepsilon_2(1-\rho^2)}{2}\right)\int_0^T v^2(t)dt \\
&\quad \left.\left. - \frac{a\sqrt{\varepsilon_2}\rho\kappa\theta}{\sigma}\int_0^T v(t)dt + \frac{a\sqrt{\varepsilon_2}\rho}{2\sigma}v^2(T)\right)\right]
\end{aligned}
\tag{3.208}
$$

**Case 2**: A mean-reverting square-root process:
Let $\omega(t)$ denote variance, as in the Heston (1993) model:

$$
\begin{aligned}
\mathbb{E}\left[g(a)\right] &= \mathbb{E}\left[\exp(a \ln GA(n))\right] \\
&= \mathbb{E}\left[\exp\left(ax_0 + a \int_0^T \varepsilon_1(r - \frac{1}{2}\omega(t))dt + a \int_0^T \sqrt{\varepsilon_2\omega(t)}\,dw\right)\right] \\
&= \mathbb{E}\left[\exp\left(ax_0 + a\varepsilon_1 rT - \frac{a\sqrt{\varepsilon_2}\rho}{\sigma}\omega(0) - \frac{a\sqrt{\varepsilon_2}\rho\kappa\theta T}{\sigma}\right.\right. \\
&\quad - \left(\frac{a\varepsilon_1}{2} - \frac{a\sqrt{\varepsilon_2}\rho\kappa}{\sigma} - \frac{a^2\varepsilon_2(1-\rho^2)}{2}\right)\int_0^T \omega(t)dt \\
&\quad \left.\left. + \frac{a\sqrt{\varepsilon_2}\rho}{\sigma}\omega(T)\right)\right].
\end{aligned}
\tag{3.209}
$$

As shown in Chapter 2, the expected value $\mathbb{E}\left[g(a)\right]$ has an analytical form for the above two cases. The values of $f_1(\phi)$, $f_2(\phi)$ and $M(T)$ can be computed for $a$ as $1 + i\phi, i\phi$ and 1, respectively. The pricing formula for Asian options with stochastic volatilities is therefore given by the following form:

$$C_{asian} = e^{-rT} \left( S_0 M(T) \frac{n}{n_0} F_1 - K_1 F_2 \right). \qquad (3.210)$$

For these two cases, we have integrated stochastic volatility into the geometric Asian options. Integrating stochastic interest rates follows a similar line. We now consider the issue of incorporating jumps into Asian options and demonstrate the method by applying lognormal jumps. From (2.120) and (3.203), we obtain a risk-neutralized process

$$
\begin{aligned}
d \ln GA(t; n) &= \varepsilon_1 \left( r - \lambda \mu_J - \frac{1}{2} v^2 \right) dt + (\sqrt{\varepsilon_2} v) dw(t) \\
&\quad + \ln(1 + J) \frac{1}{n} \sum_{j=1}^{n} dY_j
\end{aligned}
\qquad (3.211)
$$

with

$$Y_j = Y(T_0 + hj), \qquad \ln GA(0; n) = x_0.$$

By applying MPO, we only need to calculate one additional term caused by jumps for CF $f_1(\phi)$:

$$
\begin{aligned}
RJ_1 &= \mathbb{E}\left[ \exp\left( \ln(1 + J) \frac{1 + i\phi}{n} \sum_{j=1}^{n} Y_j \right) - (1 + i\phi) \lambda \mu_J t_1 \right] \\
&= \exp(-(1 + i\phi) \lambda \mu_J t_1) \times \\
&\quad \mathbb{E}\left[ \exp\left( \ln(1 + J) \frac{1 + i\phi}{n} [nY_0 + \sum_{j=1}^{n} (n - j + 1) \Delta Y_j] \right) \right] \\
&= \exp\left( \lambda T_0 [(1 + \mu_J)^{(1+i\phi)} e^{\frac{1}{2} i\phi(1+i\phi)\sigma_J^2} - 1] - (1 + i\phi) \lambda \mu_J t_1 \right) \times \\
&\quad \mathbb{E}\left[ \exp\left( \ln(1 + J) \frac{1 + i\phi}{n} \sum_{j=1}^{n} (n - j + 1) \Delta Y_j \right) \right]
\end{aligned}
$$

Note the Markovian property of the Poisson process

$$
\begin{aligned}
&= \exp\left( \lambda T_0 [(1 + \mu_J)^{(1+i\phi)} e^{\frac{1}{2} i\phi(1+i\phi)\sigma_J^2} - 1] - (1 + i\phi) \lambda \mu_J t_1 \right) \times \\
&\quad \exp\left( \sum_{j=1}^{n} \left( \lambda h [(1 + \mu_J)^{k_j} \exp(\frac{1}{2} k_j (k_j - 1) \sigma_J^2) - 1] \right) \right)
\end{aligned}
$$

$$
\begin{aligned}
&= \ \exp\left(\lambda T_0[(1+\mu_J)^{(1+i\phi)}e^{\frac{1}{2}i\phi(1+i\phi)\sigma_J^2} - 1] - (1+i\phi)\lambda\mu_J t_1\right) \times \\
&\quad \ \exp\left(\lambda h \sum_{j=1}^{n}(1+\mu_J)^{k_j}\exp(\frac{1}{2}k_j(k_j-1)\sigma_J^2) - \lambda(T-T_0)\right) \\
&= \ \exp\left(\lambda T_0(1+\mu_J)^{(1+i\phi)}e^{\frac{1}{2}i\phi(1+i\phi)\sigma_J^2} - \lambda T - (1+i\phi)\lambda\mu_J t_1\right) \times \\
&\quad \ \exp\left(\lambda h \sum_{j=1}^{n}(1+\mu_J)^{k_j}\exp(\frac{1}{2}k_j(k_j-1)\sigma_J^2)\right) \qquad (3.212)
\end{aligned}
$$

with

$$
k_j = \frac{(1+i\phi)(n+j-1)}{n}.
$$

For CF $f_2(\phi)$ we have a similar result but with another $k_j$:

$$
\begin{aligned}
RJ_2 &= \ \mathbb{E}\left[\exp\left(\ln(1+J)\frac{i\phi}{n}\sum_{j=1}^{n}Y_j\right) - i\phi\lambda\mu_J t_1\right] \\
&= \ \exp\left(\lambda T_0(1+\mu_J)^{i\phi}e^{\frac{1}{2}i\phi(i\phi-1)\sigma_J^2} - \lambda T - i\phi\lambda\mu_J t_1\right) \times \\
&\quad \ \exp\left(\lambda h \sum_{j=1}^{n}(1+\mu_J)^{k_j}\exp(\frac{1}{2}k_j(k_j-1)\sigma_J^2)\right) \qquad (3.213)
\end{aligned}
$$

with

$$
k_j = \frac{i\phi(n+j-1)}{n}.
$$

### 3.4.4 Approximations for Arithmetic Average Asian Options

Although Asian options based on the geometric average can be valued analytically by a closed-form formula, these options are not commonplace in the OTC markets. The most popular Asian options are based on the arithmetic average of the underlying asset, which, unfortunately, is no longer lognormally distributed. In other words, the arithmetic average does not follow a geometric Brownian motion. This raises a serious problem in pricing arithmetic average Asian options. In order to fill this gap, some approximation methods based on the pricing formula for geometric average Asian options are suggested. Boyle (1977) was the first to apply the Monte Carlo control-variate method to get the approximative values of arithmetic average Asian options. However, the Monte Carlo method is very time-consuming, inefficient and inaccurate for Asian options as reported in Fu, Madan and Wang (1995).

In this subsection, we briefly review the existing approximation methods that attempt to reduce the bias between the geometric average and arithmetic average, hoping that the previously derived formulae can be used. All these approximations are suggested in the framework of constant volatilities. Nevertheless, the methods presented below attempt to obtain better values for arithmetic average Asian options by correcting the moments of the geometric average, which can be calculated by the CFs. Therefore, the following corrections are also applicable for stochastic volatilities and stochastic interest rates.

(1). Zhang's approach (1997).

In his approach, the general mean is the key to associate arithmetic average with geometric average. The general mean is defined as follows:

$$GM(\gamma; a) = \left( \frac{1}{n} \sum_{i=1}^{n} a_i^{\gamma} \right)^{1/\gamma} \quad \text{for} \quad \gamma > 0. \quad (3.214)$$

We need the following two special properties of $GM(\gamma; a)$ for approximation:

$$GM(1; a) = \left( \frac{1}{n} \sum_{i=1}^{n} a_i \right) = AA(a) \quad (3.215)$$

and

$$\lim_{\gamma \to 0} GM(\gamma; a) = \lim_{\gamma \to 0} \left( \frac{1}{n} \sum_{i=1}^{n} a_i^{\gamma} \right)^{1/\gamma} = \left( \prod_{i=1}^{n} a_i \right)^{1/n} = GA(a). \quad (3.216)$$

Thus, we can consider the arithmetic average and the geometric average as two special values of the function $GM(\gamma; a)$ at the point $\gamma = 1$ and $\gamma = 0$, respectively. Additionally, $GM(\gamma; a)$ is an increasing continuous function in $\gamma$. Using Taylor's expansion, we have

$$AA(a) = GM(1) \approx GM(0) + GM'(0) = GA(a)[1 + \frac{1}{2} Var(\ln a)], \quad (3.217)$$

where $GM'(\varphi)$ is the first derivation of $GM$. Zhang's main result can be summarized as follows:

$$AA(S) \cong kGA(S) \tag{3.218}$$

with

$$k = 1 + \frac{1}{2}EV + \frac{1}{4}(VV + EV)^2, \tag{3.219}$$

where

$$EV = \frac{(n^2 - 1)h}{6}\left(\frac{1}{2}(r - \frac{1}{2}v^2)^2 h + \frac{1}{n}v^2\right)$$

and

$$VV = \frac{(n^2 - 1)(3n^2 - 2)}{15n^3}\left(1 - \frac{1}{2}v^2\right)^2 v^2 h^3.$$

Obviously, when $n$ approaches 1, the number $k$ will degenerate to 1. When $n$ approaches infinity, we obtain the limiting $k$ which is given by

$$k = 1 + \frac{1}{24}\left((r - \frac{1}{2}v^2)nh\right)^2 + \frac{1}{576}\left((r - \frac{1}{2}v^2)nh\right)^4. \tag{3.220}$$

By using the corrected geometric average, we can calculate the approximative prices of the arithmetic average Asian options.

(2). Vorst's approach (1990).

Instead of correcting the geometric average, Vorst suggests a simple method to correct the strike price by using the difference between $\mathbb{E}[GA(n)]$ and $\mathbb{E}[AA(n)]$. The new effective strike price is therefore given by

$$K_{new} = K + \mathbb{E}[GA(n)] - \mathbb{E}[AA(n)].$$

Because $\mathbb{E}[GA(n)] \leqslant \mathbb{E}[AA(n)]$, we always have $K_{new} \leqslant K$. This correction uses only the first moment whereas Zhang's correction uses not only the first but also the second moments. The expectation value $\mathbb{E}[AA(n)]$ can be obtained analytically by the standard tool.

(3). The modified geometric average (MGA).

This method is more accurate than Vorst's approach as reported by Levy and Turnbull (1992). The main idea of MGA is that if $\ln AA(n)$ is normally distributed according to $N(\mu, \sigma)$, then $\mathbb{E}\left[AA(n)\right] = \exp(\mu + \frac{1}{2}\sigma^2)$. It immediately follows that $\mu = \ln \mathbb{E}\left[AA(n)\right] - \frac{1}{2}\sigma^2$. In the framework of risk-neutral pricing, MGA implies the replacement of $r$ by $\ln \mathbb{E}\left[AA(n)\right]$, namely,

$$r_{new} = \ln \mathbb{E}\left[AA(n)\right]. \qquad (3.221)$$

Beside the above mentioned approximation approaches, a number of suggestions have been proposed to improve the performance of pricing arithmetic average options based on the available closed-form formula. These works include Levy (1990), Turnbull and Wakeman (1991).

### 3.4.5   A Model for Asian Interest Rate Options

In this subsection, we deal with a special interest rate derivative whose payoff at maturity depends on the average of interest rates in a specified period prior to maturity. Such financial instruments are called Asian interest rate options and, then are a direct function of interest rates. This feature is different from a bond option whose payoff is indirectly affected by the interest rate. We can consider Asian interest rate options as an innovation of the interest rate cap or floor with average attribute. Therefore, Asian interest rate call (put) options are also called cap (floor) on the average interest rates.

Longstaff (1995) addressed the issue of pricing and hedging this particular option in the framework of the Vasicek model and found that it is an important alternative hedging instrument for managing borrowing costs. As Asian stock options do, this type of derivative is always less costly than the corresponding full cap and less sensitive to changes in interest rates. Ju (1997) studied Asian interest rate options by applying the Fourier transformation. His idea is that if the density function of the underlying average is known, then the option based on this average can be given in an integral form. The unfavorable feature of his solution is that one does not have a solution form à la Black-Scholes and can not get the hedge ratios explicitly. Here we enhance Ju's idea and give a closed-form solution for Asian interest rate options by using the underlying CFs. The following results are valid both for the Vasicek (1977) model and the CIR (1985b) model.

Without loss of generality, we let the notional amount in the option contract be equal to one. Let $y(T) = \int_0^T r(t)dt$, the average rate is then $y(T)/T$. We consider a case where the time to maturity is shorter than or equal to the length of the average period, i.e., ATP- or ITP-Asian options. Let $A$ denote the sum of the interest rates from the first day of the average period to the current time. For the call option we have

$$
\begin{aligned}
C_{AIR} &= \mathbb{E}\left[\exp\left(-\int_0^T r(t)dt\right)\left(\frac{1}{T}\left(A + \int_0^T r(t)dt\right) - K\right)^+\right] \\
&= \mathbb{E}\left[\exp\left(-y(T)\right)\left(\frac{y(T)}{T} - K_0\right)^+\right], \quad K_0 = K - \frac{A}{T} \\
&= \mathbb{E}\left[\exp\left(-y(T)\right)\left(\frac{y(T)}{T} - K_0\right)\cdot \mathbf{1}_{(y \geqslant TK_0)}\right] \\
&= T^{-1}\mathbb{E}\left[e^{-y(T)}y(T)\cdot \mathbf{1}_{(y \geqslant TK_0)}\right] - K_0\mathbb{E}\left[e^{-y(T)}\cdot \mathbf{1}_{(y \geqslant TK_0)}\right] \\
&= \frac{V(T)}{T}\mathbb{E}\left[\frac{e^{-y(T)}y(T)}{V(T)}\cdot \mathbf{1}_{(y \geqslant TK_0)}\right] \\
&\quad - B(T)K_0\mathbb{E}\left[\frac{e^{-y(T)}}{B(0,T;r_0)}\cdot \mathbf{1}_{(y \geqslant TK_0)}\right] \\
&= \frac{V(T)}{T}F_1 - B(0,T;r_0)K_0 F_2. \qquad (3.222)
\end{aligned}
$$

where

$$
B(0,T;r_0) = \mathbb{E}\left[\exp\left(-\int_0^T r(t)dt\right)\right] = \mathbb{E}\left[e^{-y(T)}\right]
$$

is a zero-bond price maturing at time $T$ and

$$
V(T) = \mathbb{E}\left[\exp\left(-\int_0^T r(t)dt\right)\left(-\int_0^T r(t)dt\right)\right] = \mathbb{E}\left[e^{-y(T)}y(T)\right]
$$

is a discounted price of the "underlying asset" $y(T)$. An interesting feature of Asian interest rate options is that they are discounted by using their own underlying. Obviously, $e^{-y(T)}/B(T)$ and $e^{-y(T)}y(T)/V(T)$ define two martingales, respectively, and guarantee no arbitrage over time. Hence, the characteristic function of $F_1$ can be given by

$$
\begin{aligned}
f_1(\phi) &= \mathbb{E}\left[\frac{e^{-y(T)}y(T)}{V(T)}e^{i\phi y}\right] = \mathbb{E}\left[\frac{y(T)e^{(i\phi-1)y(T)}}{V(T)}\right] \\
&= \mathbb{E}\left[\frac{y(T)}{V(T)}\exp\left((i\phi - 1)\int_0^T r(t)dt\right)\right]. \qquad (3.223)
\end{aligned}
$$

Similarly,

$$
\begin{aligned}
f_2(\phi) &= \mathbb{E}\left[\frac{e^{-y(T)}}{B(T)}e^{i\phi y(T)}\right] = \mathbb{E}\left[\frac{e^{(i\phi-1)y(T)}}{B(T)}\right] \\
&= \mathbb{E}\left[\frac{1}{B(T)}\exp\left((i\phi-1)\int_0^T r(t)dt\right)\right].
\end{aligned}
\tag{3.224}
$$

$V(T)$ and $f_1(\phi)$ can be calculated by the following manipulations:

$$
V(T) = -\frac{\partial}{\partial\lambda}\mathbb{E}\left[e^{-\lambda y(T)}\right]\big|_{\lambda=1}
\tag{3.225}
$$

and

$$
f_1(\phi) = -\frac{1}{V(T)}\frac{\partial}{\partial\lambda}\mathbb{E}\left[e^{-\lambda y(T)}\right]\big|_{\lambda=1-i\phi}.
\tag{3.226}
$$

Dependent on whether the interest rate is specified either as a mean-reverting square-root process or as a mean-reverting Ornstein-Uhlenbeck process, we can give the full formula of the expression $-\frac{\partial}{\partial\lambda}\mathbb{E}\left[e^{-\lambda y(T)}\right]$.

**Case 1**: A mean-reverting square root process (CIR, 1985b; Ju, 1997):

$$
\begin{aligned}
-\frac{\partial}{\partial\lambda}\mathbb{E}\left[e^{-\lambda y(T)}\right] =\ & -B(0,T;r_0) \\
&\times \left[\frac{2\kappa\theta\left[2\gamma e^{-\gamma T} + \kappa_1(1 - e^{-\gamma T})\right]}{4\gamma^3 e^{(\kappa-\gamma)T}}\times\right. \\
&\quad \left[\gamma e^{-\gamma T}(\kappa_1 - 1) + \kappa_1(1 - \gamma T)(1 - e^{-\gamma T}) + \gamma\right] \\
&\quad -\frac{r_0\left(1 - e^{-\gamma T}\right)}{\gamma + 0.5\kappa_2(1 - e^{-\gamma T})} \\
&\quad \left.-\frac{\lambda r_0\sigma^2\left[\gamma T e^{-\gamma T} - 0.5(1 - e^{-2\gamma T})\right]}{\gamma\left[\gamma + 0.5\kappa_2(1 - e^{-\gamma T})\right]^2}\right].
\end{aligned}
\tag{3.227}
$$

with

$$
\begin{aligned}
\gamma &= \sqrt{\kappa^2 + 2\sigma^2} \\
\kappa_1 &= \kappa + \gamma, \qquad \kappa_2 = \kappa - \gamma.
\end{aligned}
$$

**Case 2**: A mean-reverting O-U process (Vasicek, 1977):

$$-\frac{\partial}{\partial \lambda}\mathbb{E}\left[e^{-\lambda y(T)}\right] = -B(0,T;r_0)\left[\left(\frac{\sigma^2}{\kappa^3}-\frac{\theta}{\kappa}\right)(e^{-\kappa T}-1)\right.$$
$$\left.-\frac{\lambda\sigma^2}{2\kappa^3}(e^{-2\kappa T}-1)+\frac{r_0}{\kappa\lambda^2}\right]. \tag{3.228}$$

By using these two results, we can compute $f_1(\phi)$. Thus, we have

$$F_j = \frac{1}{2}+\frac{1}{\pi}\int_0^\infty \text{Re}\left(f_j(\phi)\frac{-i\phi K_0 T}{i\phi}\right)d\phi, \quad j=1,2. \tag{3.229}$$

The put option price is given by using the put-call parity:

$$Put_{AIR} = B(0,T;r_0)K_0 F_2 - \frac{V(T)}{T}F_1 \tag{3.230}$$

where

$$F_j = \frac{1}{2}-\frac{1}{\pi}\int_0^\infty \text{Re}\left(f_j(\phi)\frac{-i\phi K_0 T}{i\phi}\right)d\phi, \quad j=1,2. \tag{3.231}$$

The expressions of (3.222) and (3.230) possess a clear structure and the hedge-ratios can be derived analytically. In comparison with Ju's expression in which $F_1$ and $F_2$ are put together in a single integral form, this pricing formula can be understood more easily and interpreted more meaningfully. All of these features are of practical and theoretical importance. Some straightforward extensions can be made, for example, to interest rate models with stochastic volatility (Longstaff and Schwarz, 1992), or to multi-factor interest rate models. However, such extension would be technically rather tedious and causes some difficulties in implementation.

# 3.5 Correlation Options

## 3.5.1 Introduction

Accompanied by a radical development of derivative markets worldwide in the past decade, more and more trading activities involving different markets or different products raise an increasing demand for effective new financial instruments for the purpose of hedging and arbitrage. To meet these needs, correlation options are generated as a generic term for a class of options such as exchange options, quotient options and spread options. Usually, the payoffs of correlation options are affected by at least two underlying assets. Hence, the correlation coefficients among these underlying assets play a crucial role in the valuation of correlation options and indicate the nomenclature of such particular options. Among correlation options, spread options have been introduced in several exchanges as their official financial products while quotient options and product options are mainly provided and traded in the OTC markets. The New York Mercantile Exchange (NYMEX) launched an option on a crack (fuel) futures spread on October 7, 1994. The New York Cotton Exchange (NYCE) and the Chicago Board of Trade (CBOT) proposed options on the cotton calendar spread and on the soybean complex spread, respectively.

While correlation options are drawing more and more attention in risk management and derivatives trading, their valuation issue presents a great challenge in finance theory. Particularly, the valuation of spread options is a proxy for the complexity of this pricing issue. The earliest version of the pricing formula for spread options is a simple application of the Black-Scholes formula by assuming that the spread between two asset prices follows a geometric Brownian motion, and is then referred to as one-factor model. The limitations and problems of this extremely simplified model are obvious and have been extensively discussed by Garman (1992). A two-factor model where the underlying assets follow two distinct geometric Brownian motions, respectively, and the correlation between them is also permitted, requests calculating an integral over the cumulative normal distribution. This implies a double integral in practical implementation. Shimko (1994) developed a pricing formula for spread options incorporating stochastic convenience yield as an enhanced version of a two-factor model. Wilcox [Goldman, Sachs and Co.,1990] applied an arithmetic Brownian motion to specify the spread movement. The resulting pricing formula, however, is inconsistent with the principle of no arbitrage. Recently, Poitras (1998) modelled the underlying asset as an arithmetic Brownian motion and constructed three partial differential equations (PDE) for two underlying assets and their spread respectively to avoid the arbitrage opportunities occurring in the Wilcox model. But the drawback of specifying asset price process as an arithmetic Brownian motion still remains in his model. Hence, we are falling in a dilemma: specifying asset prices as a geometric Brownian motion leads to double integration in the pricing formula, while modelling asset prices as an arithmetic Brownian motion makes it feasible to obtain a tractable pricing formula, but it is not coherent with standard models for options. Exchange options can be considered as a special case of spread options where the strike price is set to be zero. Due to this contractual simplification, a simple pricing formula à la Black-Scholes for exchange options can be derived (Margrabe, 1978). Product options and quotient options are two other examples of correlation options and their valuations in a two-factor model present no special difficulty by applying the bivariate normal distribution function. However, it has not yet been studied how to price correlation options in an environment of stochastic volatilities and stochastic interest rates.

In this section, we attempt to apply the Fourier transformation technique to obtain alternative pricing formulae for exchange options, product options and quotient options. The favorite feature of the Fourier transformation is that it presents not only an elegant pricing formula allowing for a single integration, but also accommodates a general specification of state variables, for example, stochastic volatilities, stochastic interest rates and even jump components. By employing the martingale approach, we can construct some new types of equivalent martingale measures that ensure the absence of arbitrage in the risk-neutral valuation of quotient or product options. However, as in the Black-Scholes world, we can not give a simple tractable pricing formula for spread options incorporating stochastic volatility and stochastic interest rates.

To incorporate stochastic volatilities into correlation options, we specify two asset price processes with two independent Brownian motions with stochastic volatilities simultaneously, and however, the two asset prices are stochastically correlated. Precisely, the asset price processes take the following form

$$\frac{dS_j(t)}{S_j(t)} = r(t)dt + \sigma_{j1}\sqrt{v_1(t)}dw_1(t) + \sigma_{j2}\sqrt{v_2(t)}dw_2(t), \quad j = 1, 2.$$

$$(3.232)$$

Setting $X_1(t) = \ln[S_1(t)/S_1(0)]$ and $X_2(t) = \ln[S_2(t)/S_1(0)]$ yields

$$
\begin{aligned}
dX_j(t) &= \left[ r(t) - \frac{1}{2}\sigma_{j1}^2 v_1(t) - \frac{1}{2}\sigma_{j2}^2 v_2(t) \right] dt \\
&\quad + \sigma_{j1}\sqrt{v_1(t)}dw_1(t) + \sigma_{j2}\sqrt{v_2(t)}dw_2(t).
\end{aligned} \tag{3.233}
$$

with $X_1(0) = 0$ and $X_2(0) = 0$. For the purpose of demonstrating how to model the stochastic volatilities for exchange options, we adopt the Heston model and let the variance $v_j(t)$ follow a square root process. For an Ornstein-Uhlenbeck process we can proceed with the same steps. We have

$$
dv_j(t) = \kappa_j[\theta_j - v_j(t)]dt + \sigma_j\sqrt{v_j(t)}dz_j(t), \quad j = 1, 2. \tag{3.234}
$$

$$
dw_1(t)dw_2(t) = 0, \quad dw_1(t)dz_1(t) = \rho_1 dt, \quad dw_2(t)dz_2(t) = \rho_2 dt. \tag{3.235}
$$

The instantaneous correlation coefficient between $dS_1/S_1$ and $dS_2/S_2$ is therefore stochastic and given by

$$
\begin{aligned}
\rho(t) &= Corr\left( \frac{dS_1(t)}{S_1(t)}, \frac{dS_2(t)}{S_2(t)} \right) \\
&= \frac{\sigma_{11}\sigma_{21}v_1(t) + \sigma_{12}\sigma_{22}v_2(t)}{\sqrt{\sigma_{11}^2 v_1(t) + \sigma_{12}^2 v_2(t)}\sqrt{\sigma_{21}^2 v_1(t) + \sigma_{22}^2 v_2(t)}}.
\end{aligned} \tag{3.236}
$$

The uncertainty of $\rho(t)$ is caused by the volatilities (variances) $v_j(t)$. Since $v_j(t) \geqslant 0$, the parameters $\sigma_{ij}$ determine whether these two underlying assets are correlated positively or negatively. By setting $v_j(t)$ to be deterministic, i.e., the values of $\theta_j, \sigma_j$ and $\kappa_j$ are nil, we obtain the usual two-factor model. In this case, the processes in (3.232) are simplified to be

$$
\begin{aligned}
\frac{dS_j(t)}{S_j(t)} &= r(t)dt + \sigma_{j1}dw_1(t) + \sigma_{j2}dw_2(t) \\
&= r(t)dt + \eta_j dW_j(t), \quad j = 1, 2.
\end{aligned} \tag{3.237}
$$

where $\eta_j = \sqrt{\sigma_{j1}^2 + \sigma_{j2}^2}$ and the new Wiener processes $W_j(t)$ are composed of $w_1(t)$ and $w_2(t)$ with the different weights such that $dW_1 dW_2 = \rho dt$. Therefore, the model in (3.233) is more inclusive than an usual two-factor model.

## 3.5.2   Exchange Options

A European-style exchange option entitles its holder to exchange one asset for another and can be considered as an extended case of a standard option. To value this type of options, we assume that both assets are risky and follow a geometric Brownian motion. Thus, the strike price is no longer deterministic. In fact, this is the only point which distinguishes an exchange option from a plain vanilla option. Margrabe (1978) developed a pricing formula for exchange options in the Black-Scholes framework. Although exchange options are not traded on organized exchanges, they are implied in many financial contracts, for example, performance incentive fee, margin account and dual-currency option bonds etc. The valuation of exchange options is therefore a basis for understanding and valuing these financial contracts. The payoff of exchange options at expiration is given by

$$
C(T) = \begin{cases} S_1(T) - S_2(T) & \text{if} \quad S_1(T) > S_2(T) \\ 0 & \text{if} \quad S_1(T) > S_2(T) \end{cases} . \tag{3.238}
$$

Obviously, exchange call options on asset 1 for asset 2 are identical to exchange put options on asset 2 for asset 1. If these two assets are stochastically dependent on each other, then valuation of exchange options is linked to a joint distribution of two assets. Additionally, with the price process of one asset, say $S_2$, being reduced to be deterministic, exchange options degenerate to the corresponding standard options. According to Margrabe (1978), the pricing formula *à la* Black-Scholes can be expressed as:

$$
C = S_1 N(d) - S_2 N(d - v\sqrt{T}) \tag{3.239}
$$

with

$$
d = \frac{\ln(S_1/S_2) + \frac{1}{2}v^2 T}{v\sqrt{T}}, \qquad v = \sqrt{v_1^2 + v_2^2 - 2\rho v_1 v_2}.
$$

Here $v_i, i = 1, 2$, represents the volatility of the $i$-th asset and $\rho$ is their correlation coefficient. The purpose of this subsection is to develop a model for exchange options capturing stochastic volatilities. On the analogy of the standard option pricing formulae, we can rewrite the pricing formula for exchange options as:

$$
\begin{aligned}
C(S_1, T; S_2) &= S_1 F_1(S_1(T) \geqslant S_2(T)) - S_2 F_2(S_1(T) \geqslant S_2(T)) \\
&= S_1 F_1 \left( \ln \frac{S_1(T)}{S_2(T)} \geqslant 0 \right) - S_2 F_2 \left( \ln \frac{S_1(T)}{S_2(T)} \geqslant 0 \right) \\
&= S_1 F_1 \left( X_1(T) - X_2(T) \geqslant \ln \frac{S_2(0)}{S_1(0)} \right) \\
&\quad - S_2 F_2 \left( X_1(T) - X_2(T) \geqslant \ln \frac{S_2(0)}{S_1(0)} \right).
\end{aligned}
$$

(3.240)

It is obvious that instead of using a $T$-forward measure to get a suitable CF for $F_2$, we need to take $S_2$ as numeraire to derive the CF for $F_2$. The way of proceeding is the same as for $F_1$. Consequently, we obtain two CFs

$$
f_1(\phi) = \mathbb{E} \left[ \exp \left( - \int_0^T r(t)dt \right) \exp \left( (i\phi + 1)X_1(T) - i\phi X_2(T) \right) \right]
$$

(3.241)

and

$$
f_2(\phi) = \mathbb{E} \left[ \exp \left( - \int_0^T r(t)dt \right) \exp \left( i\phi X_1(T) - (i\phi - 1)X_2(T) \right) \right].
$$

(3.242)

The probabilities $F_1$ and $F_2$ are then

$$
F_j = \frac{1}{2} + \frac{1}{\pi} \int_0^\infty \mathrm{Re} \left( \frac{f_j(\phi)}{i\phi} \exp \left( -i\phi \ln \frac{S_2(0)}{S_1(0)} \right) \right) d\phi, \quad j = 1, 2. \quad (3.243)
$$

Under the specifications given in the above subsection, we can calculate $f_1(\phi)$ and $f_2(\phi)$ as follows:

$$
f_1(\phi)
$$

$$= \mathbb{E}\left[\exp\left(-\int_0^T r(t)dt\right)\exp\left((i\phi+1)X_1(T)-i\phi X_2(T)\right)\right]$$

$$= \mathbb{E}\left[\exp\left(-\int_0^T r(t)dt+(i\phi+1)\left(\int_0^T r(t)dt\right.\right.\right.$$

$$-\frac{1}{2}\sigma_{11}^2\int_0^T v_1(t)dt-\frac{1}{2}\sigma_{12}^2\int_0^T v_2(t)dt$$

$$+\sigma_{11}\int_0^T\sqrt{v_1(t)}dw_1(t)+\sigma_{12}\int_0^T\sqrt{v_2(t)}dw_2(t)\bigg)$$

$$-i\phi\left(\int_0^T r(t)dt-\frac{1}{2}\sigma_{21}^2\int_0^T v_1(t)dt-\frac{1}{2}\sigma_{22}^2\int_0^T v_2(t)dt+\right.$$

$$\left.\left.\sigma_{21}\int_0^T\sqrt{v_1(t)}dw_1(t)+\sigma_{22}\int_0^T\sqrt{v_2(t)}dw_2(t)\right)\right)\bigg]$$

$$= \mathbb{E}\left[\exp\left(-\frac{1}{2}[\sigma_{11}^2+i\phi(\sigma_{11}^2-\sigma_{21}^2)]V_1-\frac{1}{2}[\sigma_{12}^2+i\phi(\sigma_{12}^2-\sigma_{22}^2)]V_2\right.\right.$$

$$+[\sigma_{11}+i\phi(\sigma_{11}-\sigma_{21})]\int_0^T\sqrt{v_1(t)}dw_1(t)+$$

$$\left.\left.+[\sigma_{12}+i\phi(\sigma_{12}-\sigma_{22})]\int_0^T\sqrt{v_2(t)}dw_2(t)\right)\right]$$

$$= \mathbb{E}\left[\exp\left(-\frac{1}{2}[\sigma_{11}^2+i\phi(\sigma_{11}^2-\sigma_{21}^2)]V_1-\frac{1}{2}[\sigma_{12}^2+i\phi(\sigma_{12}^2-\sigma_{22}^2)]V_2\right.\right.$$

$$+[\sigma_{11}+i\phi(\sigma_{11}-\sigma_{21})]\times$$

$$[\rho_1\int_0^T\sqrt{v_1(t)}dz_1(t)+\sqrt{1-\rho_1^2}\int_0^T\sqrt{v_1(t)}dy_1(t)]$$

$$+[\sigma_{12}+i\phi(\sigma_{12}-\sigma_{22})]\times$$

$$\left.\left.[\rho_2\int_0^T\sqrt{v_2(t)}dz_2(t)++\sqrt{1-\rho_2^2}\int_0^T\sqrt{v_2(t)}dy_2(t)]\right)\right]$$

$$= \exp[-A_1\frac{\rho_1}{\sigma_1}(v_1(0)+\kappa_1\theta_1 T)-A_2\frac{\rho_2}{\sigma_2}(v_2(0)+\kappa_2\theta_2 T)]\times$$

$$\mathbb{E}\left[\exp\left(\frac{1}{2}\{A_1^2(1-\rho_1^2)+2A_1\frac{\rho_1\kappa_1}{\sigma_1}-B_1\}V_1+\right.\right.$$

$$\left.\left.\frac{1}{2}\{A_2^2(1-\rho_2^2)+2A_2\frac{\rho_2\kappa_2}{\sigma_2}-B_2\}V_2+A_1\frac{\rho_1}{\sigma_1}v_1(T)+A_2\frac{\rho_2}{\sigma_2}v_2(T)\right)\right]$$

$$\tag{3.244}$$

with

$$A_j=\sigma_{1j}+i\phi(\sigma_{1j}-\sigma_{2j})\qquad B_j=\sigma_{1j}^2+i\phi(\sigma_{1j}^2-\sigma_{2j}^2),\quad j=1,2.$$

and

$$V_j = \int_0^T v_j(t)dt \qquad j = 1, 2.$$

By using the usual technique of calculating expectations, we obtain the first CF for stochastic volatility following a mean-reverting square root process. Note that $f_1(\phi)$ in (3.241) and $f_2(\phi)$ in (3.242) are symmetric and, we immediately get:

$$
\begin{aligned}
&f_2(\phi) \\
={} &\exp[-A_1^* \frac{\rho_2}{\sigma_2}(v_2(0) + \theta_2 T) - A_2^* \frac{\rho_1}{\sigma_1}(v_1(0) + \theta_1 T)] \times \\
&\mathbb{E}\left[\exp\left(\frac{1}{2}\{A_1^{*2}(1 - \rho_2^2) + 2A_1^* \frac{\rho_2 \kappa_2}{\sigma_2} - B_1^*\}V_2 + A_1^* \frac{\rho_2}{\sigma_2}v_2(T)\right.\right. \\
&\left.\left.+\frac{1}{2}\{A_2^{*2}(1 - \rho_1^2) + 2A_2^* \frac{\rho_1 \kappa_1}{\sigma_1} - B_2^*\}V_1 + A_2^* \frac{\rho_1}{\sigma_1}v_1(T)\right)\right]
\end{aligned}
$$

$$(3.245)$$

with

$$A_j^* = \sigma_{2j} + i\phi(\sigma_{2j} - \sigma_{1j}) \qquad B_j^* = \sigma_{2j}^2 + i\phi(\sigma_{2j}^2 - \sigma_{1j}^2), \quad j = 1, 2.$$

With two CFs being calculated, we have the closed-form pricing formula for exchange call options. It is easy to establish a model including random jumps and stochastic volatilities which follow a mean-reverting O-U process by MPO. We omit these works here.

It is worth mentioning some additional properties of exchange options: First of all, the two characteristic functions are perfectly symmetric and independent on the specification of interest rates. This means that interest rates are not of any relevance for the values of exchange options. This property is also observable in formula (3.240). Secondly, if $S_2$ is deterministic, then the pricing formula is simplified to the standard one. Thirdly, the exchange call options on asset $S_1$ for asset $S_2$ is identical to the exchange put options on asset $S_2$ for $S_1$. Hence, by applying the put-call parity of exchange options $C(S_1; K = S_2) + S_2 = P(S_1; K = S_2) + S_1$,[56] we can obtain the corresponding pricing formula for exchange put options.

---

[56]The put-call parity of exchange options differs from the normal one for European options. One can derive this parity by directly applying definitions of exchange put and call options. Once again, interest rates play no role in this parity.

### 3.5.3 Quotient Options

Quotient options are options written on the ratio of two assets and, therefore, are also called ratio options. Assume that two underlying assets follow the processes given in (3.237), then the logarithms of their prices are binormally distributed. A straightforward calculation using the risk-neutral valuation approach yields a pricing formula for quotient options as follows

$$Cq = e^{-rT + \eta_2(\eta_2 - \rho\eta_1)T} \frac{S_1(0)}{S_2(0)} N(d_1) - e^{-rT} K N(d_2) \qquad (3.246)$$

with

$$
\begin{aligned}
d_2 &= \frac{\ln[S_1(0)/KS_2(0)] - \frac{1}{2}T(\eta_1^2 - \eta_2^2)}{\sqrt{(\eta_1^2 - 2\rho\eta_1\eta_2 + \eta_2^2)T}}, \\
d_1 &= d_2 + \sqrt{(\eta_1^2 - 2\rho\eta_1\eta_2 + \eta_2^2)T}.
\end{aligned}
$$

For simplicity, we assume the notional amount of quotient options to be one. Here we give an alternative valuation expression for quotient options, which has the ability to incorporate stochastic state variables.

$$
\begin{aligned}
Cq &= e^{-rT}\mathbb{E}\left[\left(\frac{S_1(T)}{S_2(T)} - K\right)\mathbf{1}_{\left(\frac{S_1(T)}{S_2(T)} \geqslant K\right)}\right] \\
&= e^{-rT}\mathbb{E}\left[\left(\frac{S_1(T)}{S_2(T)} - K\right)\mathbf{1}_{(X_1(T) - X_2(T) \geqslant \ln K + \ln S_2(0) - S_1(0))}\right] \\
&= e^{-rT}\frac{S_1(0)}{S_2(0)}\mathbb{E}\left[\exp(X_1(T) - X_2(T))\mathbf{1}_{(X_1(T) - X_2(T) \geqslant \ln K^*)}\right] \\
&\quad - e^{-rT}\mathbb{E}\left[K\mathbf{1}_{(X_1(T) - X_2(T) \geqslant \ln K^*)}\right] \qquad (3.247)
\end{aligned}
$$

with $K^* = KS_2(0)/S_1(0)$. Let $q(t) = \mathbb{E}[\exp(X_1(t) - X_2(t))]$, we can immediately construct a martingale

$$M(t) = \exp(X_1(t) - X_2(t))/q(t),$$

which has an expected value of one and implies a measure transformation. Therefore, we obtain the following CFs of $F_1$ and $F_2$

$$f_1(\phi) = \mathbb{E}\left[M(T)\exp(i\phi(X_1(T) - X_2(T)))\right]$$

$$= \mathbb{E}\left[\exp((1+i\phi)(X_1(T) - X_2(T))/q(T)\right] \quad (3.248)$$

$$f_2(\phi) = \mathbb{E}\left[i\phi(X_1(T) - X_2(T))\right]. \quad (3.249)$$

The pricing formula for call options takes the form of

$$Cq = e^{-rT}q(T)\frac{S_1(0)}{S_2(0)}F_1 - e^{-rT}KF_2. \quad (3.250)$$

Obviously, for the case of $K = 1$, the quotient options are reduced to exchange options whose value is equal to $S_2(0)Cq$. For the simple two-factor model given in (3.237), we can derive $f_j(\phi)$ as follows:

$$f_1(\phi) = \exp\left(-\frac{T}{2}(1+i\phi)(\eta_1^2 - \eta_2^2) + T(\eta_2^2 - \rho\eta_1\eta_2)\right.$$
$$\left. +\frac{T}{2}(1+i\phi)^2(\eta_1^2 - 2\rho\eta_1\eta_2 + \eta_2^2)\right), \quad (3.251)$$

$$f_2(\phi) = \exp\left(-\frac{T}{2}i\phi(\eta_1^2 - \eta_2^2) - \frac{T}{2}\phi^2(\eta_1^2 - 2\rho\eta_1\eta_2 + \eta_2^2)\right), \quad (3.252)$$

and

$$q(T) = \exp((\eta_2^2 - \rho\eta_1\eta_2)T). \quad (3.253)$$

We can easily find that the exponent term $(\eta_2^2 - \rho\eta_1\eta_2)T$ in $q(T)$ is exactly the exponent term appearing in the pricing formula for quotient options in a two-factor model in (3.246). The CFs and $q(T)$ incorporating stochastic volatilities are much more complicated and are given in Appendix D.

### 3.5.4   Product Options

Product options are options whose payoff at expiration depends on the product of the prices of two underlying assets. A special example of this type of options is the foreign equity option with domestic strike price or the domestic equity option with foreign strike price. In these cases, two underlying assets are the foreign (domestic) equity and the exchange rate of domestic (foreign) currency against foreign (domestic) currency.

For example, let $S_1(t)$ denote the price of a stock quoted in US-dollar, and $S_2(t)$ denote the exchange rate of DM against US-Dollar. Since the strike price $K$ of a foreign domestic option, from the point of view of a German investor, is given in DM, the terminal payoff of such an option is equal to $Max[\, S_1(T)S_2(T) - K, 0]$. Product options designed to link an asset and a foreign currency can provide international investors with the possibility to not only hedge the undesired variability of asset prices, but also protect them from bearing the exchange rate risks. The existing pricing formula for product options in a two-factor model is given by

$$Cp = e^{(r+\rho\eta_1\eta_2)T}S_1(0)S_2(0)N(d_1) - e^{-rT}KN(d_2) \qquad (3.254)$$

with

$$
\begin{aligned}
d_2 &= \frac{\ln[S_1(0)S_2(0)/K] + 2rT - \frac{1}{2}(\eta_1^2 + \eta_2^2)T}{\sqrt{(\eta_1^2 + 2\rho\eta_1\eta_2 + \eta_2^2)T}} \\
d_2 &= d_1 + \sqrt{(\eta_1^2 + 2\rho\eta_1\eta_2 + \eta_2^2)T}.
\end{aligned}
$$

Alternatively, according to the payoff function of product options, it is straightforward to have the following pricing equation:

$$
\begin{aligned}
Cp &= e^{-rT}\mathbb{E}\left[(S_1(T)S_2(T) - K)\,\mathbf{1}_{(S_1(T)S_2(T)\geqslant K)}\right] \\[2mm]
&= e^{-rT}S_1(0)S_2(0)\mathbb{E}\left[\exp(X_1(T) + X_2(T))\mathbf{1}_{(X_1(T)+X_2(T)\geqslant \ln K^*)}\right] \\[2mm]
&\quad - e^{-rT}K\mathbb{E}\left[\mathbf{1}_{(X_1(T)+X_2(T)\geqslant \ln K^*)}\right] \qquad (3.255)
\end{aligned}
$$

with $K^* = K/(S_1(0)S_2(0))$. Similarly to the above subsection, we construct a martingale

$$M(t) = \frac{\exp(X_1(T) + X_2(T))}{p(t)}$$

with $p(t) = \mathbb{E}[\exp(X_1(T) + X_2(T))]$. The two CFs are then given by

$$
\begin{aligned}
f_1(\phi) &= \mathbb{E}\left[M(T)\exp(i\phi(X_1(T) + X_2(T)))\right] \\
&= \mathbb{E}\left[\exp((1 + i\phi)(X_1(T) + X_2(T)))/p(T)\right], \qquad (3.256)
\end{aligned}
$$

$$f_2(\phi) = \mathbb{E}\left[i\phi(X_1(T) + X_2(T))\right]. \qquad (3.257)$$

Product options can be priced as follows:

$$Cp = e^{-rT}p(T)S_1(0)S_2(0)F_1 - e^{-rT}KF_2. \qquad (3.258)$$

In a two-factor model, the CFs and $p(T)$ take the following full form:

$$
\begin{aligned}
f_1(\phi) &= \exp\Big( 2i\phi rT - \eta_1\eta_2 T - \frac{T}{2}(1+i\phi)(\eta_1^2 + \eta_2^2) + \\
&\quad \frac{T}{2}(1+i\phi)^2(\eta_1^2 + 2\rho\eta_1\eta_2 + \eta_2^2) \Big),
\end{aligned}
\qquad (3.259)
$$

$$
f_2(\phi) = \exp\Big( 2i\phi rT - \frac{T}{2}i\phi(\eta_1^2 + \eta_2^2) - \frac{T}{2}\phi^2(\eta_1^2 + 2\rho\eta_1\eta_2 + \eta_2^2) \Big),
\qquad (3.260)
$$

and

$$p(T) = \exp(2rT + \eta_1\eta_2 T). \qquad (3.261)$$

As in the case of quotient options, the term $e^{-rT}p(T)$ is exactly equal to the term appearing in the pricing formula for product options in a two-factor model in (3.254). The CFs and $p(T)$ with stochastic volatilities are given in Appendix D.

# 3.6   Other Exotic Options

Exotic options are generally classified into two classes: the first one has an exotic probability pattern, i.e., path-dependent probabilities to exercise options; the other has an unusual payoff pattern, i.e., complex payoff structure at maturity. Barrier options and Asian options are two typical path-dependent options and have been dealt with in previous sections whereas digital options, basket options and chooser options belongs to the second group. Options with both features are very rare and lack necessary intuition in practical hedging and risk management. Generally speaking, options with an exotic payoff pattern can be more easily evaluated than path-dependent options. In this section, we briefly discuss how to value digital options and chooser options in our extended framework.

Digital options are also called binary options and have a discontinuous payoff. This means that option holders have either a certain amount of cash or nothing at the time of exercise, dependently on whether the terminal stock price is greater than the strike price or not. Therefore, the prices of digital call options can be expressed by

$$C_{digital} = B(0, T; r_0) \cdot Z \cdot F(S(T) > K), \qquad (3.262)$$

where $Z$ is the contractual amount of cash. Obviously, the probability $F(S(T) > K)$ corresponds to the probability $F_2$ in the pricing formula for plain vanilla options, which can be derived by MPO according to the particular processes of $S(t)$, volatility $v(t)$ and interest rate $r(t)$ as well as random jumps. However, due to the discontinuous payoff pattern, hedging with digital options is difficult, especially with near ATM-digital options. To overcome this problem, one can approximate the discontinuous payoff stepfunction by a continuous function as follows

$$C(T)_{digital} = \begin{cases} 0 & \text{if } S(T) < K - \varepsilon \\ Z\frac{S(T)-K+\varepsilon}{2\varepsilon} & \text{if } K - \varepsilon \leqslant S(T) \leqslant K + \varepsilon \\ Z & \text{if } S(T) > K + \varepsilon \end{cases}, \quad (3.263)$$

where $\varepsilon > 0$. As $\varepsilon \to 0$, the new payoff will converge to the original digital payoff. The pricing formula for (3.263) can be obtained in the usual way. Hence, the hedge ratios are the limit cases of the hedge ratios of the new pricing formula.

Chooser options give option holders an opportunity to decide at a future time $T_0 < T$ whether options are calls or puts with a predetermined strike price $K$ (identical for both call and put) in the remaining time to expiry $T - T_0$. Therefore, chooser options makes it possible for investors to hedge with ambiguous short or long positions up to time $T_0$. We have

$$C_{chooser} = B(0, T_0; r_0) \max\{C(S_{T_0}; T - T_0), P(S_{T_0}; T - T_0)\}, \quad (3.264)$$

where $C(S_{T_0}; T - T_0)$ denotes the call price at the time $T_0$ with a maturity of $T - T_0$. By using the put-call parity, we restate (3.264) as

$$C_{chooser} = B(0, T_0; r_0) \times$$

$$\max\{C(S_{T_0}; T - T_0),$$
$$C(S_{T_0}; T - T_0) - S_{T_0} + KB(0, T - T_0; r_{T_0})\}$$
$$= B(0, T_0; r_0) \times$$
$$[C(S_{T_0}; T - T_0) + \max\{KB(0, T - T_0; r_{T_0}) - S_{T_0}, 0\}]$$
$$= C(S_0; T) + P(S_0; T_0, K_0) \tag{3.265}$$

with

$$K_0 = KB(0, T - T_0; r_0).$$

This result implies that a chooser option is composed of a call option with a maturity of $T$ and a strike price of $K$, and a put option with a maturity of $T_0$ and a strike price of $K_0$. Because of the choice property, a chooser option is more expensive than a plain vanilla option. Thus, more choices are compensated by more costs. Based on the formula (3.265), we can value chooser options with stochastic volatilities, stochastic interest rates and random jumps.

These two examples demonstrate that the valuation of exotic options with unusual payoff can be generally reduced to the valuation problem for normal European options. MPO is then applicable to most of the exotic options with unusual payoffs.

# 3.7 Appendices

## 3.7.1 C: Proofs for Probabilities Involving a Maximum or a Minimum

**Proof of Proposition 1:**

Since $X(t)$ is defined to be $X(t) = \ln S(t) - \ln S_0 = x(t) - x_0$, we have $P = \Pr(m_T^X \leqslant z_1) = \Pr(m_T^X \leqslant \ln K - x_0)$. It is sufficient to prove that the probability $\Pr(m_T^X \leqslant \ln K - x_0)$ given in (3.149) satisfies the Kolmogorov's backward equation with respect to the backward variable $x_0$: (Here we express $x$ and $v$ as $x_0$ and $v_0$, respectively, to remind us that they are backward variables)

$$\frac{1}{2}v^2\frac{\partial^2 P}{\partial x_0^2} + \frac{1}{2}\sigma^2\frac{\partial^2 P}{\partial v_0^2} - \frac{1}{2}v^2\frac{\partial P}{\partial x_0} + \kappa(\theta - v)\frac{\partial P}{\partial v_0} = \frac{\partial P}{\partial \tau}$$

subject to the boundary condition

$$P = \Pr(m_T^X \leqslant 0) = 1.$$

We rewrite $P = \Pr(m_T^X \leqslant \ln K - x_0)$ as

$$P = \Pr(m_T^X \leqslant \ln K - x_0) = P_1 + e^{-z_1} P_2 \qquad (3.266)$$

with

$$P_1 = \frac{1}{2} - \frac{1}{\pi} \int_0^\infty \mathrm{Re}\left( f_2(\phi) \frac{\exp(-i\phi(\ln K - x_0))}{i\phi} \right) d\phi,$$

$$P_2 = \frac{1}{2} + \frac{1}{\pi} \int_0^\infty \mathrm{Re}\left( f_2(\phi) \frac{\exp(i\phi(\ln K - x_0))}{i\phi} \right) d\phi.$$

It is clear that $P = \Pr(m_T^X \leqslant 0) = P_1 + P_2 = 1$ and the boundary condition is then fulfilled. Since $v(t)$ follows a mean-reverting O-U process, as shown in Subsection 2.2.3, the CF $f_2(\phi)$ for the case of $\rho = 0$ can be suggested to have a solution of the form

$$f_2(\phi) = \exp\left( \frac{1}{2} D(\tau) v_0^2 + E(\tau) v_0 + F(\tau) \right).$$

It is easy obtain the derivatives of $P_1$ with respect to $x_0$ and $v_0$ as follows:[57]

$$\frac{\partial P_1}{\partial x_0} = -\frac{1}{\pi} \int_0^\infty \mathrm{Re}\left( f_2(\phi) \frac{\exp(-i\phi(\ln K - x_0))}{i\phi} i\phi \right) = \mathcal{G}(i\phi),$$

$$\frac{\partial^2 P_1}{\partial x_0^2} = \mathcal{G}(-\phi^2), \qquad \frac{\partial P_1}{\partial v_0} = \mathcal{G}(D(\tau) v_0 + E(\tau)),$$

$$\frac{\partial^2 P_1}{\partial v_0^2} = \mathcal{G}(D(\tau) + \{D(\tau) v_0 + E(\tau)\}^2),$$

$$\frac{\partial P}{\partial \tau} = \mathcal{G}\left( \frac{1}{2} D_\tau^2 v_0 + E_\tau v_0 + F_\tau \right).$$

---

[57] For convenience, an operator $\mathcal{G}$ is introduced to express

$$\mathcal{G}(z) = -\frac{1}{\pi} \int_0^\infty \mathrm{Re}\left( f_2(\phi) \frac{\exp(-i\phi(x(T) - x_0))}{i\phi} z \right).$$

Setting them into the above backward equation yields the following equation:

$$-\tfrac{1}{2}v_0^2(\phi^2 + i\phi) + \kappa(\theta - v_0)(D(\tau)v_0 + E(\tau))$$

$$+\tfrac{1}{2}\sigma^2(D(\tau) + \{D(\tau)v_0 + E(\tau)\}^2) = \tfrac{1}{2}D_\tau^2 v_0^2 + E_\tau v_0 + F_\tau.$$

After rearranging the equation with respect to $v_0^2$ and $v_0$, we arrive at three ordinary differential equations (ODEs):

$$\frac{1}{2}D_\tau = -s_1^* - \kappa D + \frac{1}{2}\sigma^2 D^2,$$

$$E_\tau = -s_2^* + \kappa\theta D - \kappa E + \sigma^2 E D,$$

$$F_\tau = \kappa\theta E + \frac{1}{2}\sigma^2 E^2 + \frac{1}{2}\sigma^2 D,$$

which are identical to the ODEs in Appendix A and determine the suggested functions $D, E$ and $F$. Hence, $P_1$ satisfies the Kolmogorov's backward equation. For the term $e^{-z_1}P_2$ we can proceed in the same way and finally obtain the same ODEs for $e^{-z_1}P_2$. Since both $P_1$ and $e^{-z_1}P_2$ fulfill the backward equation, $\Pr(m_T^X \leqslant 0)$ fulfills the same backward equation. The proof is completed.

The probability $\Pr(X(T) \geqslant \ln K - x_0, m_T^X \geqslant \ln H - y_0)$ is two-dimensional, and consequently, must satisfy the backward equation

$$\frac{1}{2}v_0^2\frac{\partial^2 P}{\partial z^2} + \frac{1}{2}\sigma^2\frac{\partial^2 P}{\partial v_0^2} - \frac{1}{2}v_0^2\frac{\partial P}{\partial z} + \kappa(\theta - v_0)\frac{\partial P}{\partial v_0} = \frac{\partial P}{\partial \tau}$$

for $z \in (x_0, y_0)$ subject to two boundary conditions

$$\Pr(X(T) \geqslant \ln K - x_0, m_T^X \geqslant 0) = 0$$

and

$$\Pr(X(T) \geqslant \ln K - x_0, m_T^X \geqslant \ln K - x_0) = \Pr(m_T^X \geqslant \ln K - x_0).$$

The proof follows the same way as done for $\Pr(m_T^X \leqslant 0)$ and is not shown in detail.

**Proof of Proposition 2:**

The Kolmogorov's backward equation is

$$\frac{1}{2}rv^2\frac{\partial^2 P}{\partial x_0^2} + \frac{1}{2}r\sigma^2\frac{\partial^2 P}{\partial r^2} + r(1-v^2)\frac{\partial P}{\partial x_0} + \kappa(\theta-r)\frac{\partial P}{\partial r} = \frac{\partial P}{\partial \tau}$$

subject to the boundary condition

$$P = \Pr(m_T^X \leqslant 0) = 1.$$

The boundary condition is obviously satisfied by $\Pr(m_T^X \leqslant 0)$ given in (3.158). Suggesting a solution for $f_2(\phi)$ as in Subsection 2.3.2 with $\rho = 0$, and carrying out the same procedure shown above, we can prove that $\Pr(m_T^X \leqslant 0)$ is actually equal to (3.158).

**Proof of Proposition 3:**

The proof of proposition 3 parallels these of propositions 1 and 2.

## 3.7.2   D: Derivation of the CFs for Correlation Options

Calculating the CFs for product options and quotient options can be generally reduced to calculating the expectation $\mathbb{E}[\exp(aX_1(T) + bX_2(T))]$ with $a$ and $b$ as arbitrary complex numbers. We expand this expectation in a more full form as follows (see also Subsection 3.5.2):

$$\begin{aligned}
&\mathbb{E}\left[\exp\left(aX_1(T) + bX_2(T)\right)\right] \\
=\ &\exp[(a+b)rT - A_1\frac{\rho_1}{\sigma_1}(v_1(0) + \kappa_1\theta_1 T) - A_2\frac{\rho_2}{\sigma_2}(v_2(0) + \kappa_2\theta_2 T)] \times \\
&\mathbb{E}\left[\exp\left(\frac{1}{2}\{A_1^2(1-\rho_1^2) + 2A_1\frac{\rho_1\kappa_1}{\sigma_1} - B_1\}\int_0^T v_1(t)dt + A_1\frac{\rho_1}{\sigma_1}v_1(T)\right.\right. \\
&\left.\left.+\frac{1}{2}\{A_2^2(1-\rho_2^2) + 2A_2\frac{\rho_2\kappa_2}{\sigma_2} - B_2\}\int_0^T v_2(t)dt + A_2\frac{\rho_2}{\sigma_2}v_2(T)\right)\right]
\end{aligned}$$

with

$$A_j = a\sigma_{1j} + b\sigma_{2j} \qquad B_j = a\sigma_{1j}^2 + b\sigma_{2j}^2, \quad j = 1, 2.$$

By applying the formula (2.60) we can obtain the closed-form solution for the expectation value. For $a = 1$ and $b = 1$, we can calculate $p(T)$ for product options and $q(T)$ for quotient options. Setting different values for $a$ and $b$ enables us to get the closed-form solutions for CFs.

**Case 1**: Quotient options

$f_1(\phi)$ has the following coefficients:

$$a = 1 + i\phi, \qquad b = -(1 + i\phi),$$

and $f_2(\phi)$ has the following coefficients:

$$a = i\phi, \qquad b = -i\phi.$$

**Case 2**: Product options

$f_1(\phi)$ has the following coefficients:

$$a = 1 + i\phi, \qquad b = 1 + i\phi,$$

and $f_2(\phi)$ has the following coefficients:

$$a = i\phi, \qquad b = i\phi.$$

# 4 Conclusions

In this book, we developed an extended, unified option pricing framework considering stochastic volatilities, stochastic interest rates and random jumps. We call this framework Modular Pricing of Options (MPO). It extends the world of Black-Scholes and collects some main ideas for option pricing. The tool to establish our MPO is Fourier analysis with which we are able to derive a number of new closed-form pricing formulae for options, both plain vanilla and exotic style, allowing for mutually independent stochastic volatilities, stochastic interest rates and random jumps, as well as correlation between stock returns and volatilities.

The Fourier analysis is rather intuitive: Instead of directly calculating the equivalent martingale probabilities in an option pricing formula, we at first derived their corresponding characteristic functions and then calculated the probabilities via Fourier inversion. In Chapter 1, we have given two principles for constructing CFs in a pricing formula for European-style options. The second one is an enhanced version of the first, permitting that asset prices are a more general function of returns.[58] In fact, the relevant probabilities in advanced option pricing models can no longer be given by normal distribution as in the Black-Scholes formula. Fortunately, we can obtain closed-form solutions for characteristic functions for a wide range of processes, as shown in Chapter 2. In order to do this, we have two methods available. The pure PDE approach used by Heston (1993), who ends up with a system of ODEs, and the more elaborated approach used by Scott (1997), who applied stochastic calculus to compute characteristic functions directly. Given the processes for stock price and other stochastic factors, we find that it is too difficult with the PDE-approach to get closed-form solutions for many CFs while the second method turns out to be much more elegant

---

[58] Usually, it is assumed that asset prices are an exponential function of returns.

and straightforward. It has the advantage that there is no need to guess a suitable form of the CFs. Instead, these transformations can be easily perceived in the process of calculating the CFs. Change of numeraire is a key to understand how to arrive at the characteristic functions under two equivalent martingale measures which guarantee no arbitrage. The Feynman-Kac formula is a powerful tool to calculate expectations, and is used repeatedly to help us derive closed-form solutions.

For the first two stochastic factors, we have discussed three cases:

1. The mean-reverting square root process which was initially used to model interest rates and squared volatilities by CIR (1985b) and Heston (1993), respectively.

2. The mean-reverting O-U process which was applied by Vasicek (1977) to obtain his well-known model for the term structure of interest rates, and by Schöbel and Zhu (1999) to specify stochastic volatility and derive a complete option pricing formula that essentially extends the works of S&S (1991) and Scott (1987).

3. The mean-reverting double square root process which was used by Longstaff (1989) to get a nonlinear model of the term structure of interest rates. In this study, I employ this process to model the dynamics of stochastic volatilities.

These three distinct processes present the main stream of financial modelling of stochastic interest rates and stochastic volatilities, and span most of the contemporary research works on these two topics. An important insight into the issues of option pricing is that options and bonds have the same pricing kernel as long as volatilities and interest rates are specified by the same process. One can develop more complicated multi-factor models by using a linear combination of the above three alternative processes. But the method of getting a pricing formula remains the same, as discussed in this book. The pricing models for correlation options in Section 3.4 are some examples. Beside interest rates and volatilities, we considered random jumps, which are classified by

1. Pure jumps which were studied for the first time by Cox and Ross (1976). In their model they used no diffusion terms. Here, pure jumps are added to option pricing models, as an additional stochastic factor.

2. Lognormal jumps which are characterized by a lognormally distributed jump size and therefore might be a good candidate to capture abnormalities in financial markets as done by Merton (1976), Bates (1996) and BCC (1997);

3. Pareto jumps which are adopted in this study from a recent paper by Duffie, Pan and Singleton (1999) and are marked by the Pareto distributed jump size.

Using Fourier transformation techniques, we have successfully established a comprehensive world to embrace these factors and processes. The concept of MPO is not only of theoretical importance, but also provides us with practical convenience. As indicated by its name, MPO can be implemented by modular programming. Additionally, since each process corresponds to a unique formula as shown in Chapter 2, different pricing problems involving the same stochastic process can share the same module in a computer program.

Next, we have dealt with exotic options. Valuation of barrier options and Asian options is particularly difficult because it has to do with path-dependent probabilities. In two special cases, we partially solved the pricing problem for barrier options and obtained closed-form solutions in our extended framework. Two questions are left open as a challenge for future research: Firstly, how can we derive a general closed-form solution for barrier options in the presence of correlation between stock returns and volatilities? (or, is there a closed-form solution in the extended framework at all?), Secondly, how can we incorporate random jumps into pricing barrier options in our framework? Zhou (1998) studied this problem in a context of default risks and could only solve it by using Monte Carlo methods. We successfully incorporated stochastic volatilities and stochastic interest rates into geometric average Asian options, but not into arithmetic average Asian options. The key here is to establish a visual process of the geometric average of stock prices, which follows a geometric Brownian motion. Random jumps are also incorporated into geometric average Asian options by using the Markovian property of Poisson processes. Additionally, we considered the valuation issue for correlation options which include spread options, exchange options, quotient options and product options as subclasses. Since two underlying assets are involved in the valuation of correlation options, we can specify these assets jointly with two Brownian motions, and each one has its own stochastic volatility. Along these lines, alternative pricing formulae for correlation options except for spread options are derived. Finally, we briefly derived the pricing formulae for binary options and chooser options by MPO, illustrating how to deal with the exotic options with unconventional payoffs.

Some further possible extensions of MPO are possible. The first one may be to value contingent claims on interest rates via Fourier analysis, for example, bond options. The effectiveness of MPO may be not so obvious as for interest rates models, as it is for options, because most of the interest rate models are of single-factor. However, MPO should be a promising way if applied to (multi-factor) affine models of the term structure and their contingent claims. Chen and Scott (1995), Duffie, Pan and Singleton (1999) as well as Schöbel and Zhu (2000) discussed the application of Fourier analysis to the valuation of interest rate sensitive derivatives. As shown in Schöbel and Zhu (2000), we can conveniently solve the convex boundary problem for the exercise region in a multi-factor model by the Fourier analysis approach. The other possible extension may be to introduce more general Levy processes in which the random intensity jump component depends on the size of the previous jump, as in Chernov, Gallant, Ghysels and Tachen (1999). In this book, we concentrate only on how to derive comprehensive pricing models, and ignore empirical aspects with regard to Fourier analysis. In fact, CFs and Fourier analysis have received considerable attentions in testing asset pricing models since it is straightforward to construct maximum-likelihood and moments estimators based on CFs. A recent work of Singleton (1999) presents a detailed treatment on this issue. However, empirical testing with characteristic functions is beyond the scope of this book.

# List for Notations and Symbols

| | |
|---|---|
| $B(0, T; r_0)$ | zero-bond price |
| $C$ | price of a call option |
| $f_j(\phi)$ | characteristic function (CF) |
| $f^*(\phi)$ | discounted characteristic function |
| $F_j$ | the exercise probability for a call option |
| $\mathcal{F}_t$ | filtration generated by $S(u), u \leqslant t$ |
| $H$ | barrier of a barrier option |
| $i$ | imaginary unit, $\sqrt{-1}$ |
| $\mathbf{1}$ | indicator function |
| $J$ | jump size |
| $K$ | exercise price of a call option |
| $M(t)$ | martingale |
| $P$ | original probability measure |
| $Q$ | equivalent martingale measure |
| $Q_j$ | equivalent martingale measure with different numeraire |
| $r(t)$ | instantaneous interest rate |
| $\mathbb{R}$ | the set of real numbers |
| $S(t)$ | stock price or equity price |
| $t$ | variable for calendar time |
| $T$ | calendar time or maturity |
| $v(t)$ | instantaneous volatility or variance |
| $x(t)$ | $\ln S(t)$ |
| $Y(t)$ | Poisson process |
| $w(t)$ | standard Brownian motion |
| $\kappa$ | reverting velocity in a mean-reverting process |

| $\theta$ | mean in a mean-reverting process |
| $\lambda$ | market price of risk or jump intensity |
| $\pi$ | constant, $3.1415926\cdots\cdots$ |
| $\rho$ | correlation coefficient |
| $\sigma$ | volatility in a mean-reverting process |
| $\sigma_J$ | standard deviation of the logarithm of jump size $J$ |
| $\mu_J$ | mean of the logarithm of jump size $J$ |
| $\tau$ | variable for maturity $T$ |
| ATM | at the money |
| ATP | at the period for Asian option |
| GA | geometric average of $S(t)$ |
| ITM | in the money |
| ITP | in the period for Asian option |
| OTM | out of the money |
| OTP | out of the period for Asian option |
| RJ | random jumps |
| SI | stochastic interest rate |
| SV | stochastic volatility |

# References

Abramowitz, M. and I. A. Stegun (1965): *Handbook of Mathematical Functions with formulae, Graphs and Mathematical Tables*, $9^{th}$ Edition. Dover Publications, New York

Ball, C. A. and A. Roma (1994): Stochastic Volatility Option Pricing, *Journal of Financial and Quantitative Analysis*, **29**, 581-607

Bakshi, G. S., C. Cao and Z. Chen (1997): Empirical Performance of Alternative Option Pricing Models, *Journal of Finance*, **52**, 2003-2049

Bakshi, G. S. and Z. Chen (1997): Equilibrium Valuation of Foreign Exchange Claims, *Journal of Finance*, **52**, 799-826

Bakshi, G. S. and D. Madan (1999): Spanning and Derivative Security Valuation, Forthcoming in *Journal of Financial Economics*

Bates, D. (1996): Jumps and Stochastic Volatility: Exchange Rate Processes Implicit in Deutsche Mark Options, *Review of Financial Studies*, **96**, 69-107

Beaglehole, D. and M. Tenney (1992): Corrections and additions to 'A Nonlinear Equilibrium Model of the Term Structure of Interest Rates', *Journal of Financial Economics*, **28**, 346-353

Beckers, S. (1980): The Constant Elasticity of Variance Model and Its Implications for Option Pricing, *Journal of Finance*, **35**, 97-112

Beckers, S. (1983): Variances of Security Price Returns Based on High, Low and Closing Prices, *Journal of Business*, **56**, 97-112

Billingsley, P. (1986): *Probability and Measure*, $2^{nd}$ Edition. Wiley Inc, New York

Björk, T. (1996): Interest Rate Theory, *in* W. J. Runggaldier (Ed.), *Financial Mathematics*, 53-122, Springer, Berlin, New York

Black, F. (1976a): Studies of Stock Price Volatility Changes, In: *Proceeding of the 1976 Meeting of the American Statistical Association*, 177-181

Black, F. (1976b): The Pricing of Commodity Contracts, *Journal of Financial Economics*, **3**, 167-179

Black, F. and M. Scholes (1973): The Valuation of Options and Corporate Liabilities, *Journal of Political Economy*, **81**, 637-654

Blattberg, R. C. and N. Gonedes (1974): A Comparison of the Stable and Student Distributions as Statistical Models for Stock Prices, *Journal of Business*, **47**, 244-280

Boyle, P. P. (1977): Options: A Monte-Carlo Approach, *Journal of Financial Economics*, **4**, 323-338

Breeden, D. (1979): An Intertemporal Asset Pricing Model with Stochastic Consumption and Investment Opportunities, *Journal of Financial Economics*, **7**, 265-296

Brown, S. J. and P. H. Dybvig (1986): The Empirical Implications of the Cox, Ingersoll and Ross Theory of the Term Structure of Interest Rates, *Journal of Finance*, **41**, 617-632

Carr, P. and D. B. Madan (1998): Option Valuation Using the Fast Fourier Transform, Working Paper, Robert H, Smith School of Business, University of Maryland

Chen, R. and L. Scott (1995): Interest Rate Options in Multifactor Cox-Ingersoll-Ross Models of the Term Structure, *Journal of Derivatives*, **3**, 53-72

Chernov, M., A. R. Gallant, E. Ghysels and G. Tauchen (1999): A New Class of Stochastic Volatility Models with Jumps: Theory and Estimation, Working Paper, The Pennsylvania State University

Chung, K. L. (1974): *A Course in Probability Theory.* $2^{nd}$ Edition, Academic Press, New York

Cox, D. R. and H. D. Miller (1972): The Theory of Stochastic Process, $3^{rd}$ Edition. Chapman and Hall Ltd

Cox, J. C. (1975): Notes on Options Pricing: Constant Elasticity of Variance Diffusions, Working Paper, Stanford University

Cox, J. C. and S. A. Ross (1976): The Valuation of Options for Alternative Stochastic Processes, *Journal of Financial Economics*, **3**, 145-166

Cox, J. C., S. A. Ross and M. Rubinstein (1979): Option Pricing: a Simplified Approach, *Journal of Financial Economics,* **7**, 229-263

Cox, J. C., J. E. Ingersoll, Jr. and S. A. Ross (1985a): An Intertemporal General Equilibrium Model of Asset Prices, *Econometrica,* **53**, 363-384

Cox, J. C., J. E. Ingersoll, Jr and S. A. Ross (1985b): A Theory of the Term Structure of Interest Rates, *Econometrica,* **53**, 385-407

Cox, J. C. and M. Rubinstein (1985): *Options Markets.* Prentice-Hall Inc, New Jersey

Coutadon, G. (1982): The Pricing of Options on Default-free Bonds, *Journal of Financial and Quantitative Analysis,* **17**, 75-100

Derman, E and I. Kani (1994): Riding on the Smile, *RISK,* **7**, 32-39

Dothan, U. (1978): On the Term Structure of Interest Rates, *Journal of Financial Economics,* **6**, 59-69

Duan, J. C. (1996): A Unified Theory of Option Pricing under Stochastic Volatility–from GRACH to Diffusion, Working Paper, Department of Finance, Hong Kong University of Science and Technology

Dupire, B. (1994): Pricing with A Smile, *RISK,* **7**, 18-20

Duffie, D. (1988): *Security Markets: Stochastic Models.* Academic Press, Boston

Duffie, D. (1996): *Dynamic Asset Pricing Theory.* $2^{nd}$ Edition. Princeton University Press, Princeton, New Jersey

Duffie, D. and R. Kan (1996): A Yield Factor Model of Interest Rates, *Mathematical Finance,* **6**, 379-406

Duffie, D. and J. Pan and K. Singleton (1999): Transform Analysis and Asset Pricing for Affine Jump-Diffusions, Working Paper, Graduate School of Business, Stanford University

Dumas, B., J. Fleming and R. Whaley (1998): Implied Volatility Functions: Empirical Tests, *Journal of Finance,* **53**, 111-127

Fama, E. F. (1965): The Behavior of Stock Market Prices, *Journal of Business,* **38**, 34-105.

Fu, M., D. Madan and T. Wang (1995): Pricing Continuous Time Asian Options: A Comparison of Analytical and Monte-Carlo Methods, Working paper, University of Maryland.

Garman, M. (1992): Spread the Load, *RISK,* **5**, 68 and 84.

Garman, M. and S. Kohlhagen (1983): Foreign Currency Options Values, *Journal of International Money and Finance*, **2**, 231-237.

Geman, H., N. E. Karouri and J-C. Rochet (1995): Changes of Numeraire, Changes of Probability and Option Pricing, *Journal of Applied Probability*, **32**, 443-458.

Geske, R. (1979): The Valuation of Compound Options, *Journal of Financial Economics*, **7**, 63-81.

Goldman, M., H. Sosin and M. Gatto (1979): Path Dependent Options: Buy at the Low, Sell at the High, *Journal of Finance*, **34**, 111-127.

Harrison, J. M. (1985): *Brownian Motion and Stochastic Flow Systems*, Wiley Press, New York

Harrison, J. M. and D. Kreps (1979): Martingales and Arbitrage in Multiperiod Security Markets, *Journal of Economic Theory*, **20**, 381-408

Heath, D., R. Jarrow and A. Morton (1992): Bond Pricing and the Term Structure of Interest Rates: A New Methodology for Contingent Claim Valuation, *Econometrica*, **60**, 77-105

Heston, S. (1993): A Closed-Form Solution for Options with Stochastic Volatility with Applications to Bond and Currency Options, *Review of Financial Studies*, **6**, 327-343

Heston, S. (1997): A Simple New Formula for Options With Stochastic Volatility, Working Paper, John M. Olin School of Business, Washington University in St. Louis

Heston, S. and S. Nandi (1997): A Closed-Form GRACH Option Model, Working Paper, Federal Reserve Bank of Atlanta

Ho, T.S. and S. B. Lee (1986): Term Structure Movements and Pricing Interest Rate Contingent Claims, *Journal of Finance*, **41**, 1011-1029

Hull, J. (1997): *Options, Futures and Other Derivatives*, $3^{rd}$ Edition. Prentice Hall Inc, New Jersey

Hull, J. and A. White (1987): The Pricing of Options On Assets With Stochastic Volatilities, *Journal of Finance*, **42**, 281-300.

Hull, J. and A. White (1990): Pricing Interest Rate Derivative Securities, *Review of Financial Studies*, **3**, 573-592

Hull, J. and A. White (1993): One-factor Interest Rate Models and the Valuation of Interest Rate Derivative Securities, *Journal of Financial and Quantitative Analysis*, **28**, 235-254

Ingersoll, Jr. J. E. (1987): *Theory of Financial Decision Making,* Rowman & Littelfield Publishers,Inc., Maryland

Johnson, H., S. Kotz and N. Balakrishnan (1994): *Continuous Univariate Distribution,* Vol. 1., John Wiley & Sons Inc., New York

Johnson, H. and D. Shanno (1987): Option Pricing When the Variance Is Changing, *Journal of Financial and Quantitative Analysis,* **22**, 143-151

Jorion, P. (1988): On Jump Processes in the Foreign Exchange and Stock Markets, *Review of Financial Studies,* **1**, 427-446

Ju, N. J. (1997): Fourier Transformation, Martingale, and the Pricing of Average Rate Derivatives, Working Paper, Haas School of Business, University of California, Berkeley

Karlin, S. and H. Taylor (1975): *A First Course in Stochastic Process,* $2^{nd}$ Edition. Academic Press, San Diego

Karlin, S. and H. Taylor (1975): *A Second Course in Stochastic Process,* $2^{nd}$ Edition. Academic Press, San Diego

Levy, E. (1992): Pricing European Average-rate Currency Options, *Journal of International Money and Finance,* **11**, 474-491

Levy, E. and S. Turnbull (1992): Average Intelligence, *RISK,* **5**, 53-59

Longstaff, F.A. (1989): A Nonlinear General Equilibrium Model of the Term Structure of Interest Rates, *Journal of Financial Economics,* **23**, 195-224

Longstaff, F.A. (1992): Multiple Equilibria and Term Structure Models, *Journal of Financial Economics,* **32**, 333-344.

Longstaff, F.A. (1995): Hedging Interest Rate Risk With Options On Average Interest Rates, *Journal of fixed Income,* **4**, 37-45

Longstaff, F.A and E. S. Schwartz (1992): Interest Rate Volatility and the term Structure: A Two Factor General Equilibrium Model, *Journal of Finance,* **47**, 1259-1282

Longstaff, F.A and E. S. Schwartz (1995): A Simple Approach to Valuing Risky Fixed and Floating Rate Debt, *Journal of Finance,* **50**, 789-819

MacBeth, J. and L. Merville (1979): An Empirical Examination of the Black-Scholes Call Option Pricing Model, *Journal of Finance,* **34**, 369-382

Malliaris, A.G. and W. A. Brock (1991): *Stochastic Methods in Economics and Finance*, $6^{th}$ Edition. North-Holland, New York

Mandelbrot, B. (1963): The Variation of Certain Speculative Prices, *Journal of Business,* **36**, 394-419

Margrabe, W. (1978): The Value of An Option to Exchange One Asset for Another, *Journal of Finance,* **33**, 177-186

Merton, R.C. (1971): Optimum Consumption and Portfolio Rules in A Continuous-time Model, *Journal of Economic Theory,* **3**, 3731-413

Merton, R.C. (1973a): Theory of Rational Option Pricing, *Bell Journal of Economic and Management Science,* **4**, 141-183

Merton, R.C. (1973b): An Intertemporal Capital Asset Pricing Model, *Econometrica,* **41**, 867-888

Merton, R.C. (1976): Option Pricing When Underlying Stock Returns are discontinuous, *Journal of Financial Economics,* **3**, 125-144

Merton, R. C. (1990): *Continuous-time Finance,* Basil Blackwell, Oxford

Musiela, M. and M. Rutkowski (1997): *Martingale Methods in Financial Modelling,* Springer-Verlag Berlin Heidelberg

Nandi, S. (1998): How important is the correlation between returns and volatility in a stochastic volatility model? Empirical Evidence from Pricing and Hedging in the S&P 500 Index Options Market, *Journal of Banking and Finance,* **22**, 589-610

Nagel, H. (1999): Zur Optionsbewertung bei Stochastischer Volatilität am Beispiel der DTB: Eine Theoretische und Empirische Analyse, Dissertation, University of Tübingen

Nelson, D. B. and D. P. Foster (1994): Asymptotic Filtering Theory for Univariate ARCH Models, *Econometrica,* **62**, 1-41

Poitras, G. (1998): Spread Options, Exchange Options, and Arithmetic Brownian Motion, *The Journal of Futures Markets,* **18**, 487-517

Poterba, J.M. and L. H. Summers (1988): Mean-reversion in Stock Prices: Evidences and Implications, *Journal of Financial Economics,* **22**, 27-60

Protter, P. (1995): *Stochastic Integration and Differential Equations,* $3^{rd}$ Edition. Springer, Berlin New York

Øksendal, B. (1995): *Stochastic Differential Equations, 4$^{th}$* Edition. Springer, Berlin, New York

Revuz, D. and M. Yor (1991): *Continuous Martingales and Brownian Motion, 2$^{nd}$* Edition. Springer-Verlag, Berlin New York

Rabinovitch, R. (1989): Pricing Stock and Bond Options when the Default-Free Rate is Stochastic, *Journal of Financial and Quantitative Analysis, 24, 447-457*

Rich, D. R. (1994): The Mathematical Foundations of Barrier Option-Pricing Theory, *Advances in Futures and Options Research*, Vol 7, pages 267-311. JAI Press Inc

Rubinstein, M. (1985): Nonparametric Tests of Alternative Options Pricing Models Using All Reported Trades and Quotes on the 30 Most Active CBOE Options from August 23, 1976 through August 31,1978, *Journal of Finance,* **40**, 455-480

Rubinstein, M. (1994): Implied Binomial Trees, *Journal of Finance,* **49**, 771-818

Rubinstein, M. and E. Reiner (1991): Breaking down the Barriers, *RISK,* **4**(8), 28-35

Schmalensee, R. and R. Trippi (1978): Common Stock Volatility expectations Implied by Option Premia, *Journal of Finance,* **33**, 129-147

Schöbel, R. (1995): *Kapitalmarkt und zeitkontinuierliche Bewertung,* Physica-Verlag, Heidelberg

Schöbel, R. and J. W. Zhu (1999): Stochastic Volatility with an Ornstein-Uhlenbeck Process: an Extention, *European Finance Review 3,* 23-46

Schöbel, R. and J. W. Zhu (2000): A Fourier Analysis Approach to the Valuation of Interest Rate Derivatives, Working Paper, University of Tübingen

Scott, L. O. (1987): Option Pricing When the Variance Changes Randomly: Theory, Estimation and an Application, *Journal of Financial Quantitative Analysis,* **22**, 419-438

Scott, L. O. (1997): Pricing Stock Options in a Jump-diffusion Model with Stochastic Volatility and Interest Rates, *Mathematical Finance,* **7**, 413-426

Shimko, D. C. (1994): Options on Futures Spreads: Hedging, Speculation, and Valuation, *The Journal of Futures Markets,* **14**, 183-213

Singleton, K (1999): Estimation of Affine Diffusion Models Based on the Empirical Characteristic Function, Working Paper, Stanford University

Stuard, A. and O. J. Keith (1991): *Kendall's Advanced Theory of Statistics, Vol. 1.* 5$^{th}$ Edition. Edward Arnord, London

Turnbull, S. and L. McD. Wakeman (1991): A Quick Algorithm for Pricing European Average Options, *Journal of Financial Quantitative Analysis,* **26**, 377-389

Vasicek, O. (1977): An Equilibrium Characterization of the Term Structure, *Journal of Financial Economics,* **5**, 177-188

Vorst, A C F. (1990): Analytical Boundaries and Approximations of the Prices and Hedge Ratios of Average Exchange Rate Options, Working Paper, Erasmus University Rotterdam

Wiggins, J. B. (1987): Option Values under Stochastic Volatility: Theory and Empirical Estimates, *Journal of Financial Economy,* **19**, 351-372

Wilcox, D. (1990): Energy Futures and Options: Spread Options in Energy Markets, Working Paper, Goldman Sachs & Co., New York

Zhang, P. G. (1997): *Exotic Options: A Guide to Second Generation Options,* World Scientific Publishing Co., Singapore

Zhou, C. S. (1998): Jump Risk, Default Rates, and Credit Spreads, Working paper, The Anderson Graduate School of Management, University of California, Riverside

# Lecture Notes in Economics and Mathematical Systems

For information about Vols. 1–305
please contact your bookseller or Springer-Verlag

Vol. 449: F. Fang, M. Sanglier (Eds.), Complexity and Self-Organization in Social and Economic Systems. IX, 317 pages, 1997.

Vol. 450: P. M. Pardalos, D. W. Hearn, W. W. Hager, (Eds.), Network Optimization. VIII, 485 pages, 1997.

Vol. 451: M. Salge, Rational Bubbles. Theoretical Basis, Economic Relevance, and Empirical Evidence with a Special Emphasis on the German Stock Market.IX, 265 pages. 1997.

Vol. 452: P. Gritzmann, R. Horst, E. Sachs, R. Tichatschke (Eds.), Recent Advances in Optimization. VIII, 379 pages. 1997.

Vol. 453: A. S. Tangian, J. Gruber (Eds.), Constructing Scalar-Valued Objective Functions. VIII, 298 pages. 1997.

Vol. 454: H.-M. Krolzig, Markov-Switching Vector Auto-regressions. XIV, 358 pages. 1997.

Vol. 455: R. Caballero, F. Ruiz, R. E. Steuer (Eds.), Advances in Multiple Objective and Goal Programming. VIII, 391 pages. 1997.

Vol. 456: R. Conte, R. Hegselmann, P. Terna (Eds.), Simulating Social Phenomena. VIII, 536 pages. 1997.

Vol. 457: C. Hsu, Volume and the Nonlinear Dynamics of Stock Returns. VIII, 133 pages. 1998.

Vol. 458: K. Marti, P. Kall (Eds.), Stochastic Programming Methods and Technical Applications. X, 437 pages. 1998.

Vol. 459: H. K. Ryu, D. J. Slottje, Measuring Trends in U.S. Income Inequality. XI, 195 pages. 1998.

Vol. 460: B. Fleischmann, J. A. E. E. van Nunen, M. G. Speranza, P. Stähly, Advances in Distribution Logistic. XI, 535 pages. 1998.

Vol. 461: U. Schmidt, Axiomatic Utility Theory under Risk. XV, 201 pages. 1998.

Vol. 462: L. von Auer, Dynamic Preferences, Choice Mechanisms, and Welfare. XII, 226 pages. 1998.

Vol. 463: G. Abraham-Frois (Ed.), Non-Linear Dynamics and Endogenous Cycles. VI, 204 pages. 1998.

Vol. 464: A. Aulin, The Impact of Science on Economic Growth and its Cycles. IX, 204 pages. 1998.

Vol. 465: T. J. Stewart, R. C. van den Honert (Eds.), Trends in Multicriteria Decision Making. X, 448 pages. 1998.

Vol. 466: A. Sadrieh, The Alternating Double Auction Market. VII, 350 pages. 1998.

Vol. 467: H. Hennig-Schmidt, Bargaining in a Video Experiment. Determinants of Boundedly Rational Behavior. XII, 221 pages. 1999.

Vol. 468: A. Ziegler, A Game Theory Analysis of Options. XIV, 145 pages. 1999.

Vol. 469: M. P. Vogel, Environmental Kuznets Curves. XIII, 197 pages. 1999.

Vol. 470: M. Ammann, Pricing Derivative Credit Risk. XII, 228 pages. 1999.

Vol. 471: N. H. M. Wilson (Ed.), Computer-Aided Transit Scheduling. XI, 444 pages. 1999.

Vol. 472: J.-R. Tyran, Money Illusion and Strategic Complementarity as Causes of Monetary Non-Neutrality. X, 228 pages. 1999.

Vol. 473: S. Helber, Performance Analysis of Flow Lines with Non-Linear Flow of Material. IX, 280 pages. 1999.

Vol. 474: U. Schwalbe, The Core of Economies with Asymmetric Information. IX, 141 pages. 1999.

Vol. 475: L. Kaas, Dynamic Macroeconomics with Imperfect Competition. XI, 155 pages. 1999.

Vol. 476: R. Demel, Fiscal Policy, Public Debt and the Term Structure of Interest Rates. X, 279 pages. 1999.

Vol. 477: M. Théra, R. Tichatschke (Eds.), Ill-posed Variational Problems and Regularization Techniques. VIII, 274 pages. 1999.

Vol. 478: S. Hartmann, Project Scheduling under Limited Resources. XII, 221 pages. 1999.

Vol. 479: L. v. Thadden, Money, Inflation, and Capital Formation. IX, 192 pages. 1999.

Vol. 480: M. Grazia Speranza, P. Stähly (Eds.), New Trends in Distribution Logistics. X, 336 pages. 1999.

Vol. 481: V. H. Nguyen, J. J. Strodiot, P. Tossings (Eds.). Optimation. IX, 498 pages. 2000.

Vol. 482: W. B. Zhang, A Theory of International Trade. XI, 192 pages. 2000.

Vol. 483: M. Königstein, Equity, Efficiency and Evolutionary Stability in Bargaining Games with Joint Production. XII, 197 pages. 2000.

Vol. 484: D. D. Gatti, M. Gallegati, A. Kirman, Interaction and Market Structure. VI, 298 pages. 2000.

Vol. 485: A. Garnaev, Search Games and Other Applications of Game Theory. VIII, 145 pages. 2000.

Vol. 486: M. Neugart, Nonlinear Labor Market Dynamics. X, 175 pages. 2000.

Vol. 487: Y. Y. Haimes, R. E. Steuer (Eds.), Research and Practice in Multiple Criteria Decision Making. XVII, 553 pages. 2000.

Vol. 488: B. Schmolck, Ommitted Variable Tests and Dynamic Specification. X, 144 pages. 2000.

Vol. 489: T. Steger, Transitional Dynamics and Economic Growth in Developing Countries. VIII, 151 pages. 2000.

Vol. 490: S. Minner, Strategic Safety Stocks in Supply Chains. XI, 214 pages. 2000.

Vol. 491: M. Ehrgott, Multicriteria Optimization. VIII, 242 pages. 2000.

Vol. 492: T. Phan Huy, Constraint Propagation in Flexible Manufacturing. IX, 258 pages. 2000.

Vol. 493: J. Zhu, Modular Pricing of Options. X, 170 pages. 2000.